# From Zeno to Arbitrage

# From Zeno to Arbitrage

*Essays on Quantity,*
*Coherence, and Induction*

Brian Skyrms

OXFORD
UNIVERSITY PRESS

UNIVERSITY PRESS

Great Clarendon Street, Oxford, OX2 6DP,
United Kingdom

Oxford University Press is a department of the University of Oxford.
It furthers the University's objective of excellence in research, scholarship,
and education by publishing worldwide. Oxford is a registered trade mark of
Oxford University Press in the UK and in certain other countries

First Edition published in 2012

Impression: 1

British Library Cataloguing in Publication Data
Data available

Library of Congress Cataloging in Publication Data
Data available

ISBN  978–0–19–965280–8 (hbk.)
       978–0–19–965281–5 (pbk.)

Printed in Great Britain by
MPG Books Group, Bodmin and King's Lynn

# Contents

# Preface

The chapters in the book center on the concept of probability. What is the framework within which probability comfortably lives? What are the coherence principles that must be satisfied for degrees of belief to be probabilities, and how do these principles generalize to probability change? What is the relation between coherent degrees of belief, beliefs about chances, and inductive inference? What constraints does coherence put on inductive skepticism?

Probability, in all its manifestations, is a quantity. It is not therefore out of the way that Part I deals with fundamental issues concerning the nature of quantity. These go back to Zeno of Elea and extend to modern theories of infinitesimals. I do not have in mind so much the well-known paradoxes of motion, but instead a basic paradox in the foundations of the theory of quantity—Zeno's *paradox of measure*. The very short version of a long story is that the kernel of Zeno's paradox survives in proofs of the existence of non-measurable sets. These raise interesting, if underappreciated, philosophical issues when the quantity in question is probability rather than the geometrical quantities that Zeno had in mind.

We have degrees of belief about frequencies; knowledge of frequencies informs our degrees of belief. These concepts dance together. The mathematics of frequency is clear, and hardly open to dispute. The mathematics of coherent degrees of belief is still controversial, even if well-trodden, ground. It is even more controversial to hold that belief change is somehow constrained by considerations of coherence. Part II is about how this is so. It can be summed up by the theory of arbitrage, and is done so in Chapter 10 of Part II.

The interaction between frequency and coherence is discussed in Part III. *Coherent belief and belief change, frequency*, and indeed *chance* are all tied together in inductive inference. De Finetti's theorem is the touchstone. If your beliefs are such that only frequency matters (exchangeability), then you believe in induction. You believe that chance equals limiting relative frequency, close enough as makes no odds. You believe that induction will lead you to learn the limiting relative frequency. There are generalizations of this theorem. The key concept is that of symmetry of degrees of belief. In this framework, questions of inductive skepticism can be addressed in a precise way. It turns out to be remarkably difficult to be a *complete* inductive skeptic.

# Acknowledgements

The chapters collected here appeared over a period of 26 years, and are reprinted with the kind permission of the original publishers:

"Zeno's Paradox of Measure" (1983) in R. Cohen et al. (eds.), *Philosophy, Physics and Psychoanalysis*. Dordrecht: D. Reidel, pp. 233–54.

"Tractarian Nominalism" (1981) *Philosophical Studies* 40: 199–206.

"Logical Atoms and Combinatorial Possibility" (1993) *Journal of Philosophy* 90: 219–32.

"Strict Coherence, Sigma Coherence, and the Metaphysics of Quantity" (1995) *Philosophical Studies* 77: 39–55.

"Higher-Order Degrees of Belief" (1980) in D. H. Mellor (ed.), *Prospects for Pragmatism: Essays in Honor of F. P. Ramsey*. Cambridge: Cambridge University Press, pp. 109–37.

"A Mistake in Dynamic Coherence Arguments?" (1993) *Philosophy of Science* 60: 320–8.

"Dynamic Coherence and Probability Kinematics" (1987) *Philosophy of Science* 54: 1–20.

"Updating, Supposing, and MAXENT" (1987) *Theory and Decision* 22: 225–46.

"The Structure of Radical Probabilism" (1996) *Erkenntnis* 45: 285–97.

"Diachronic Coherence and Radical Probabilism" (2006) *Philosophy of Science* (Special Issue for PSA 2004) 73: 959–68.

"Carnapian Inductive Logic for Markov Chains" (1991) *Erkenntnis* 35: 439–60.

"Carnapian Inductive Logic and Bayesian Statistics" (1996) *Statistics, Probability and Game Theory* 30: 321–36.

"Bayesian Projectibility" (1994) in D. Stalker (ed.), *Grue: Essays on the New Riddle of Induction*. LaSalle, IL: Open Court, pp. 241–62.

They are unaltered except for some typographical corrections, and the omission of some digressions from "Higher-Order Degrees of Belief."

Thanks to Peter Momtchiloff, my editor at Oxford, for suggesting this project and seeing it into print.

# PART I

# Zeno and the Metaphysics of Quantity

# Introduction

The main focus in Part I is on quantity. Chapter 2, "Tractarian Nominalism," is an exception; it deals with a world of facts. But it sets up a companion piece, "Logical Atoms and Combinatorial Possibility" (Chapter 3), in which the conceptualization of quantities moves to center stage. Questions about the proper framework for quantities go back to Zeno of Elea, and extend to modern theories of atomless mereology and of infinitesimals.

The first chapter in Part I, "Zeno's Paradox of Measure," was written for Adolf Grünbaum, my undergraduate and graduate teacher. It addresses issues that have been of long-standing interest to him, from his Ph.D. thesis "The Philosophy of Continuity" to his book, *Modern Science and Zeno's Paradoxes*. Zeno's paradox of measure is less well known than his other paradoxes, but it stands at the center of them. The paradoxes of motion can all be seen as blocking various escape routes from the basic paradox of measure. Although the paradox, as a paradox, has been resolved by the modern theory of measure and integral, the basic logic of Zeno's argument reappears in various forms in modern proofs of the existence of non-measurable sets. In a different setting, these considerations arise in contemporary discussions of subjective probability. Modern theories of infinitesimals, or alternatively of propositions without possible worlds, can be seen as alternative resolutions of the basic argument.

Chapter 2, "Tractarian Nominalism," appears to be on a completely different subject: Wittgenstein's dictum that the world is the totality of facts. It was written for Wilfrid Sellars, whose graduate seminar introduced me to the *Tractatus* and fired my interest in it. I think that it is a reasonable reading of the leading idea of the *Tractatus*, although it is certainly possible to disagree. A colleague once said, "If you look at it that way, it's just model theory." That's not so bad; all this metaphysics is just an alternative way of saying perfectly ordinary and reasonable things. The emphasis on facts deflates the importance both of ontology and of ideology. A given fact can be parsed in different ways. If we parse facts into objects and relations, we can consider recombinations of these as possibilities. This approach to possibility is developed by David Armstrong in *A Combinatorial Theory of Possibility*, where he was kind enough to reprint this essay.

Combinatorial possibility is fairly straightforward if there are logical atoms, but what if there aren't? Armstrong raises the question in his book. *What Would Logical Atomism Look Like without Logical Atoms?* It makes perfect sense, and can be analyzed using measure algebras. The world is still the totality of facts. Possible worlds are homomorphisms. Logical atoms can be put back in as ideal elements. Different combinatorial theories of possibility can arise depending on how one handles the details. There is a relevant contemporary literature discussing atomless quantities: see, for instance, Arntzenius (2011).

Chapter 4, "Strict Coherence, Sigma Coherence, and the Metaphysics of Quantity" takes up the questions with which the Zeno chapter ended. It is a natural extension of that chapter, but for philosophers interested in probability it might be a more natural entry point for Part I. Probability is a quantity. Do all events have a probability? Are there real possibilities that have zero probability? Do we have countable additivity? The standard theory of probability, due to Kolmogorov, takes the mathematics of probability to be the standard mathematics of normalized measure and adopts the answers that this theory delivers. But leading figures in modern probability theory, including Kolmogorov himself, de Finetti, and Savage, have argued in one way or another that this theory is philosophically wrong. Infinitesimals and finite additivity return in a new light. Sigma-coherence (immunity from a Dutch Book with a countable number of bets) and strict coherence initially appear to pull in different directions, but they turn out to be compatible in the setting of measure algebras.

## Bibliography

Armstrong, David (1989) *A Combinatorial Theory of Possibility*. New York: Cambridge University Press.

Arntzenius, Frank (2011) "Gunk, Topology and Measure." In *Logic, Mathematics, Philosophy: Vintage Enthusiasms*. New York: Springer, pp. 327–43.

Grünbaum, Adolf (1951) "The Philosophy of Continuity," Ph.D. thesis. Yale University.

—— (1968) *Modern Science and Zeno's Paradoxes*. London: Allen & Unwin.

Stinchcombe, Maxwell (1997) "Countably Additive Subjective Probabilities," *Review of Economic Studies* 64: 125–46.

# 1

# Zeno's Paradox of Measure

## 1. Introduction

Zeno of Elea is perhaps best known for his four paradoxes of motion: The
Dichotomy, Achilles and the Tortoise, The Arrow, and The Stadium.
These are, however, supporting pieces in a grand argument against plurality whose keystone is Zeno's paradox of measure.[1] Adolf Grünbaum has,
on several occasions,[2] called attention to the importance of this paradox,
and explained how the standard measure-theoretic resolution of it became
possible only after Cantor's theory of infinite sets.

The argument in question has emerged from Zeno's fragments only
after considerable scholarly reconstruction.[3] It is a *reductio ad absurdum* of
the thesis that an extended thing (for simplicity we can think of a unit line
segment) can be thought of as made up of an infinite number of parts. The
argument goes roughly as follows:

(I) If the parts had finite magnitude, then the whole would have
infinite magnitude.

(II) If the parts had no magnitude, then the whole would have no
magnitude.

It is set up by a prior argument to the effect that if the thing in question is
divisible ad infinitum, then it can be partitioned into an infinite number of
parts.

In the first part of this chapter, I will take a closer look at the logic of
Zeno's argument, and of the ways in which various schools attempted to
escape its embarrassments. In the second part, I will argue that despite the

---

[1] This view of the paradoxes is vigorously advocated by Owen (1957–1958).
[2] e.g. Grünbaum (1952, 1963, 1968).
[3] See Luria (1933), Fränkel (1942), Owen (1957–1958), Furley (1967, 1969), Vlastos
(1971).

profound achievements of Cantor and Lebesgue, the fundamental spirit of Zeno's paradox is still capable of mischief.

## 2. Zeno to Epicurus

### 2.1 Zeno on Infinite Divisibility

Zeno argues that if the line segment is divisible ad infinitum, it can be partitioned into an infinite number of parts. His construction is as follows:

1: Partition the line into two segments by bisecting it.
n: Refine the partition gotten at stage (n − 1) by bisecting each member of it.
ω: Take the common refinement of all the partitions gotten at finite stages of the process.

The number of parts at stage ω must be greater than any finite number.

This construction uses something slightly stronger than the stated assumption—it requires not only that each part can be divided but also that it can be divided into two equal parts. The bisection of a line segment with ruler and compass is an elementary construction, which was familiar at the time. It was perhaps an important part of the motivation for holding that the line segment is divisible ad infinitum. For the stated conclusion bisection is not essential, but it can assume importance if one wants to argue by symmetry that each member of the resulting partition has equal length.

Zeno's construction makes the daring leap from potential to actual infinity. Given that one can for any finite *n* move from the (*n* − *1*)th stage in the construction to the nth stage, Zeno proposes an additional move from the totality of the finite stages to an infinite stage. Aristotle resists this move, charging Zeno with misunderstanding the nature of infinity, but from a modern point of view it is perfectly legitimate.

It is worth looking at this construction from a modern point of view to see what it yields. Let us regard the unit line as a set of points, one for each real number in the closed interval [0, 1]. The bisection of this line partitions it into two point sets: [0, 1/2]; [1/2, 1]. (Likewise at each stage of refinement of the partition we throw the midpoints in the right-hand set. This decision as to where the midpoints go is arbitrary, but some decision must be made if we are to have a genuine partition.) A sequence of sets, the first a member of the first partition . . . the nth a member of the nth partition, such that for each *n* the (*n* + 1)th set is a subset of the nth set, will be called a *chain*. Zeno's construction comes essentially to this: each intersection of such a chain counts as a part of the line on level $\omega$. The collection of such '$\omega$-parts' is held to be an infinite partition of the unit line.

This construction gets us something. What does it get? Do we get all the points on the unit line? Do we get a partition? First, let us notice that *each point on the unit line is a member of some $\omega$-part*. For any point consider the set containing for each finite $n$, the member of the $n$th level partition of which that point is a member. This set is a chain, and the given point is in its intersection. Next we see that *each $\omega$-part contains no more than one point*. Between any two real points, there is some finite distance. Therefore, there is some finite stage n in the construction, such that at that stage the points fall into different elements of the partition. Thus they fall into different $\omega$-parts since for them to fall into the same $\omega$-part they would have to both be members of all elements of the chain of which that $\omega$-part is the intersection. The foregoing two propositions show that the $\omega$-parts do indeed form a partition of the unit line; i.e. they are a collection of disjoint sets whose union is the set of points on the line. Are the $\omega$-parts gotten by this construction then exactly the sets containing one point? Not quite. All such sets are $\omega$-parts, but some $\omega$-parts are empty. For example, the intersection of the chain: [0, 1], [0, 1/2), [1/4, 1/2), [3/8, 1/2), [7/16, 1/2) . . . is empty. Any point distinct from the midpoint eventually gets squeezed out, and the point 1/2 is not itself in any member of the chain. So the $\omega$-parts, at least in that version of the construction that I have pursued, consist of the empty set together with the unit set of each point on the real line.

I can't resist quoting here part of a passage from *De generatione et corruptione* where Aristotle is recounting a version of Zeno's argument as the argument which persuaded Democritus of the necessity of indivisible magnitudes:

Suppose then, that it is divided; now, what will be left? Magnitude? No, that cannot be, since there will then be something left not divided, whereas it was everywhere divisible. But if there is to be no body or magnitude [left] and yet [this] division is to take place, then either the whole would be made of points, and then [parts] of which it is composed will have no size, or [that which is left] will be nothing at all. (A2, 316a 24–30, quoted in Furley (1967: 84). Parenthetical insertions are Furley's.)

It is tempting to ask—but only in the spirit of speculation—how much of the foregoing analysis of Zeno's construction would have been possible for a first-rate mathematician contemporary with Aristotle, provided he accepted that the points on a unit line segment can be associated with the numbers, rational and irrational, from zero to one inclusive, and provided he accepted (perhaps only for the sake of argument) the conception of actual infinity implicit in the construction. I think that the answer is "All of it!" The facts used in the reasoning are all elementary: e.g. there is a finite distance between any two distinct points. In particular, nothing special about the structure of the reals is used. If the construction were applied to the rational line, it would still generate an infinite partition; we would simply come up with the empty set more often. There is one slightly sticky issue regarding the foregoing construction, and that regards the seemingly trivial issue of where to throw the midpoint. One might argue that the line is not really divided into two equal parts if the midpoint is thrown on one side or the other. However, if the midpoint is put on both sides there is no partition. Such questions were, in fact, discussed. This one is raised for a slightly different purpose in the pseudo-Aristotelian treatise, "Concerning Indivisible Lines."[4] The objection could be met by modifying the construction. We could, at each stage, divide the line segment into three parts: the midpoint and two intervals. At the cost of some complication, Zeno's argument could still be carried through. Returning to the discussion in "On Generation and Corruption":

But suppose that, as the body is being divided, a minute section – a piece of sawdust, as it were – is extracted, and that in this sense a body 'comes away' from the magnitude, evading the division. Even then the same argument applies. (316a34–316b3)

Suppose that the line segment is composed of an infinite number of parts. Zeno claims that this leads to absurdity in the following way:

(I) Either the parts all have zero magnitude or they all have positive magnitude.
(II) If they have zero magnitude, the line segment will have zero magnitude, since the magnitude of the whole is the sum of the magnitudes of its parts.
(III) If they have positive magnitude, then the line segment will have infinite magnitude, for the same reason.

---

[4] See also Aristotle's long discussion in the *Physics*, Bk. VIII, Ch. 8, 263a 4–264a 6, where Aristotle wrestles with the question of the midpoint and related questions having to do with open and closed intervals, and their relation to change.

(I) is never explicitly stated, but it is certainly an implicit supposition of the argument. In the first place, it assumes that the parts in question are the sorts of things that have magnitude; that questions of magnitude meaningfully apply. Call this the assumption of *Measurability*. It is challenged by Aristotle. There is something more being assumed. There would be no paradox if an infinite number of the parts had zero magnitude and a finite number had appropriate positive magnitudes. This possibility is ruled out. On what basis? One might argue that if the infinite partition of the line segment is generated by bisection, as discussed in the last section, then each part should have equal magnitude because of the equality in magnitude of all members of the finite partitions at each stage of the process which generates the infinite partition. Call this the assumption of *Invariance*. The assumptions of Measurability and Invariance legitimize (I) in a plausible way, and do a bit more as well. Invariance will enter again later in the reasoning.

(II) and (III) share the assumption that the principle that the magnitude of the whole is the sum of the magnitudes of its parts continues to hold good when we have a partition of the whole into an infinite number of parts. This requires for its intelligibility that some general sense be given to the notion of the sum of an infinite number of magnitudes. We have no such definition from Zeno. We could, of course, supply one adequate to his purposes. Let $S$ be an infinite set of magnitudes, and let $S^\star$ be the set of finite sums of magnitudes in $S$. A real number is an *upper bound* for $S^\star$ if and only if it is greater than or equal to every member of $S^\star$. Let the sum of $S$ be defined as the least upper bound of $S^\star$ if a real least upper bound exists, and as infinity otherwise. I will call this the principle of *Ultra-Additivity*. Zeno probably simply thought that any reasonable principle relating the magnitude of the whole to that of an infinite partition of it would have to satisfy (II) and (III). Nevertheless, it may be useful to have an explicit formation of such a principle at hand while considering the argument.

On the principle of Ultra-Additivity, (II) is perfectly correct. From a modern viewpoint, we would say so much the worse for the principle. This does not appear to be a line that was taken in ancient times. Neither the school of Plato, nor that of Aristotle, nor the Atomists appear to have challenged (II).

At first glance, (III) may appear to be a mathematical blunder. Does Zeno really believe that any infinite sum of finite magnitudes is infinite?

His own paradoxes of the Dichotomy, and of Achilles and the Tortoise provide a counterexample, a fact that did not escape Aristotle.[5] However, if Zeno is here presupposing that he has in hand an *invariant* partition by means of the previously discussed construction, there is no blunder. As we noted, such an argument may already be required for (I). If so, it costs no more to use it twice.

There is a more delicate question to be raised about (III). What if the magnitudes involved were infinitesimal? Then (III) could fail. Infinitesimals are ruled out by the *Axiom of Archimedes* (probably originated by Eudoxus). This axiom entails that for any quantity, *e*, no matter how small, and any integer, *m*, no matter how large, there is an integer *n* such that *n* times *e* is greater than *m*. If the magnitudes under consideration are Archimedean, then the relevant $S^\star$ will have no upper bounds, and (III) will be justified.

The question of who, if anyone, at this time held a theory of infinitesimal magnitudes is a matter of controversy. It is of some interest that Cajori takes one of Zeno's fragments to be an ironic dismissal of the theory of infinitesimal magnitudes: "Simplicius reports Zeno as saying: 'That which when added to another does not make it greater, and being taken away from another does not make it less, is nothing'. According to this, the denial of the existence of the infinitesimal goes back to Zeno" (Cajori, 1919: 51). However, it should be noted that Cajori's interpretation of this problematic fragment is not one favored by most classicists.[6] However this

---

[5] "The infinite by way of addition is in a manner the same as the infinite by way of division. Within a finite magnitude the infinite by way of addition is realized in an inverse way (to that by way of division); for, as we see the magnitude being divided ad infinitum, so, in the same way the sum of successive fractions when added to one another (continually) will be found to tend towards a determinate limit. For if, in a finite magnitude, you take a determinate fraction of it, and then add to that fraction in the same ratio, and so on [i.e., so that each part has to the preceding part the same ratio as the part first taken has to the whole], but not each time including (in the part taken) one and the same amount of the original whole, you will not traverse (i.e., exhaust) the finite magnitude. But if you increase the ratio so that it always includes one and the same magnitude, whatever it is, you will traverse it, because any finite magnitude can be exhausted by taking away from it continually any definite magnitude however small" (Aristotle, *Physics*, Bk. III, 6, 206b, tr. Heath in Heath, 1949: 106).

[6] Let me put Zeno's statement in context of the fragment that contains it, using Furley's translation: "[Simplicius first summarizes this step in the following words—'If a thing has no magnitude or bulk (παχος) or mass, it would not exist.' Then he gives the reasoning in full]. For if it were added to something else that does exist, it would make it no greater; for if it were of no magnitude, and were added, it would not contribute anything to that magnitude. So it would follow that what was added was nothing. If when it is taken away, the other thing is to

may be, it remains that (III) requires the assumption of the Archimedean axiom.

Zeno has shown that the supposition of all the following leads to paradox: the line segment (or more generally any body with positive magnitude) can be partitioned into an infinite number of parts such that: (I) the concept of Magnitude applies to the parts (Measurability); (II) the parts have equal magnitude (Invariance); (III) there are no infinitesimal magnitudes (Archimedean Axiom); and (IV) the magnitude of the whole is the sum of the magnitudes of the parts in the sense given (Ultra-Additivity). The argument as we have reconstructed it contains no fallacy. A consistent theory of non-trivial magnitudes must give up some part of the foregoing. That Zeno had raised a genuine problem seems to have been well enough understood by his contemporaries. Different solutions were explored by different schools.

## 2.2 Aristotle's Answer to Zeno

Aristotle blocks the paradox of measure at two places. As we have already noted, he denies that infinite divisibility allows the construction of an infinite partition. Aristotle will follow the construction to any finite level $n$, but not to level $\omega$. Thus: "A thing is infinite only potentially, i.e. the

---

be no smaller, and is to be no bigger when it is added, it is clear that what was added or taken away was nothing" (Furley, 1967: 64). It may help to juxtapose this passage with one from *De generatione et corruptione* where Aristotle is explaining an argument which supposedly led Democritus to a doctrine of indivisible bodies: "Similarly, if it is made out of points, it will not be a quantity. For when they were in contact and there was one magnitude and they were together, they did not increase the magnitude of the whole; for when it was divided into two or more, the whole was no larger or smaller than formerly. So if they are all put together, they will not make a magnitude" (Furley, 1967: 84). Furley interprets this passage as arguing "that if a given line is divided in two, the sum of its two parts remains the same as the length of the original whole; yet there are now two points, at the inner end of each of the two half lines, where formerly there was only one; hence the extra point made no difference to the length— and so any number of points will make no difference to the length" (Furley, 1967: 85). That is, the argument is that the length of the (closed) line segment [0, 1/2] is exactly 1/2, as is the magnitude of [1/2, 1]. But the magnitude of [0, 1] is exactly 1, so the point 1/2 which is included in both [0, 1/2] and [1/2, 1] must be exactly zero. Whether or not this is its main purpose, such an argument could certainly be directed at someone who held that the midpoint (and points in general) have infinitesimal magnitude. One cannot help but wonder whether it is being so used in the pseudo-Aristotelian polemic "Concerning Indivisible Lines," 970a 21: "Further, the addition of the line will not (on the theory) make the whole line any longer than the original line to which the addition was made: For Simples will not, when added together, produce an increased total magnitude" (see also 970b 23–5 and 972a 12–14).

dividing of it can continue indefinitely . . . " (Aristotle, "On Generation and Corruption," 318a 21. See also Aristotle's discussion in 317 a 1–16 where he claims that the argument rests on a confused assumption that "point is 'immediately next' to point." It appears, however, that it is Aristotle himself who is confused here. As we have seen, the argument requires no such assumption, and it is nowhere to be found in Aristotle's lucid statement of the argument in 316at–316b 14.) Again, in the *Physics*, Bk. III, Ch. 6, we have:

Now, as we have seen, magnitude is not actually infinite. But by division it is infinite. (There is no difficulty in refuting the theory of indivisible lines.) The alternative then remains that the infinite has a potential existence.

But the phrase 'potential existence' is ambiguous. When we speak of the potential existence of a statue we mean that there will be an actual statue. It is not so with the infinite. There will not be an actual infinite (206a 16–20).

Now, as Fränkel (1942) and Owen (1957–1958) point out, Zeno has available a devastating *argumentum ad hominem* for anyone who, like Aristotle, will grant each finite $n$ but will resist the move to level $w$ on the grounds that it presupposes the completed actual infinity of all the $n$ stages. That is: "How does Achilles catch the Tortoise?" "How can I move from here to there?" Achilles does not catch the Tortoise at any finite stage of the process that Zeno describes; likewise with respect to the Dichotomy. Let us make the connection very explicit. Let me walk a unit distance. First, I walk half the distance, then half the remaining distance, etc. At each stage consider that the set of points containing my (center of mass) location, the endpoint of the interval, and all the points in between these sets form the chain: [0, 1], [1/2, 1], [3/4, 1] . . . I do not arrive at the endpoint at any finite stage of the process, but only at the $w$th stage where the set in question contains only one member—the endpoint.

Could the possibility of this line of argument have escaped Aristotle? He comes perilously close to conceding its validity later in the same discussion in the *Physics* (206b3–10):

In a way the infinite by addition is the same as the infinite by way of division. In a finite magnitude, the infinite by addition comes about in a way inverse to that of the other. For in proportion as we see division going on, in the same proportion we see addition being made to what is already marked off. For if we take a determinate part of a finite magnitude and add another part determined by the same ratio (not taking the same amount of the original whole) and so on, we shall not traverse the given magnitude.

But we *do* traverse a given magnitude. Motion is real enough for Aristotle. Zeno appears to have demonstrated, from Aristotelian premises, the existence of actual completed infinity. (Indeed the method of argument used in the dichotomy can be adapted to show how wiggling one's finger instantiates all sorts of countable ordinals.) Aristotle appears to grant the point in Bk. VI, Ch. 2 of the *Physics*: "Hence it is that Zeno's argument makes a false assumption when it asserts that you cannot traverse an infinite number of things one by one, in a finite time ... and the contact with the infinities is made *by means of moments not finite but infinite in number*" (ibid., 233a 13–31, emphasis mine), only to retract it in a curious discussion in Bk. VIII, Ch. 8 263a4–263b 9.

After a discussion of what happens to the midpoint when a line segment is bisected, he returns to the question of potential vs. actual infinity:

Therefore to question whether it is possible to pass through an infinite number of units either of time or of distance we must reply that in a sense it is and in a sense it is not. If the units are actual, it is not possible: If they are potential it is possible. For in the course of a continuous motion the traveler has traversed an infinite number of units in an accidental sense but not in an unqualified sense: For though it is an accidental characteristic of the distance to be an infinite number of half-distances, this is not its real and essential character. (ibid., 263b4–9)

Aristotle has a second related reply to the paradox: he denies *Measurability*. Points are not to be thought of as parts of lines at all, and thus are not sorts of things that have magnitude. The things that qualify as genuine parts of a line segment are non-degenerate subsegments. This is argued in Book VI of the *Physics* on the basis of Aristotle's theory of continuity as a kind of contiguity: "nothing that is continuous can be composed of indivisibles: e.g. a line cannot be composed of points, the line being continuous and the point indivisible" (ibid., 231a 24–5).

(Aristotle holds that "things are continuous if their extremities are one." Presumably an example would be the closed intervals [0, 1/2] and [1/2, 1] which are continuous and make up the interval [0, 1].[7] Aristotle does not seem to have the concept of an open interval.)

---

[7] "A thing that is in succession and touches is 'contiguous.' The 'continuous' is a subdivision of the contiguous: Things are called continuous when the touching limits of each become one and the same and are, as the word implies, contained in each other: continuity is impossible if these extremities are two. This definition makes it plain that continuity belongs to things that naturally in virtue of their mutual contact form a unity. And in whatever way

Aristotle has another reason for holding that points are not measurable parts of the line, and that is that aside from the objections stated here, he appears to hold that Zeno's argument is valid. In "On Generation and Corruption" (317a 1–9), where he explains what the fallacy of the argument is, he points only to the argument that the line can be thought of as composed of points.

Whatever Aristotle's reasons for holding that points are not legitimate parts of lines or bodies, the idea has been attractive for a number of thinkers, e.g. Whitehead. Points can, in a sense, be eliminated in favor of intervals, of course. We can take intervals as basic, and taking our cue from Zeno's construction, let chains of intervals stand for the points respectively that are the unit sets of their intersections. Points then re-emerge as logical reconstructions. (For a general account of this sort of approach, see Tarski, 1956.) Such points would naturally be assigned as the limit of the lengths of the members of the chain, i.e. length zero. So while this approach retains a faint Aristotelian flavor, it partakes of strongly non-Aristotelian elements as well.

Aristotle's answer to Zeno's paradox of measure shows the temperament of the empirical scientist rather than that of the mathematician. His response involves a theory of some subtlety, but that theory is mathematically conservative if not reactionary. With regard to both infinity and measurability his instinct was to restrict the subject to a narrow and safe domain rather than to explore uncharted waters.

### Indivisible Magnitudes

There are at least two schools that postulated some kind of indivisible magnitudes. Aristotle, in "On Generation and Corruption," cites what is essentially Zeno's argument as a motivation for the adoption of indivisible magnitudes by the Atomists. A doctrine of indivisible magnitudes was also held in the Platonic academy. Aristotle ascribes it to Plato himself:

Further, from what principle will the presence of points in the line be derived? Plato even used to object to this class of things as being a geometrical fiction. He gave the name of the principle of the line – and this he often posited – to the indivisible lines. (*Metaphysics*, 992a 19–21)

---

that which holds them together is one, so too will the whole be one, e.g. by a rivet or glue or contact or organic union" (*Physics*, Book V, Ch. 3, 227a 6–16).

It is commonly ascribed to his student Xenocrates, and the pseudo-Aristotelian polemic "Concerning Indivisible Lines" is thought to be directed at this doctrine. Details of either theory are hard to come by. The evidence available is sparse and mostly circumstantial.

One wonders, in each case, whether the indivisible magnitudes are meant to be infinitesimal or finite. Each alternative would block Zeno's argument, but they would block it in different ways. Finite indivisible magnitudes would block the construction of the partition of a thing of finite magnitude into an infinite number of equal parts. Infinitesimal indivisible magnitudes are consistent with the existence of an infinite partition, but allow for the possibility that an infinite number of positive magnitudes add up to a finite magnitude. Some commentators attribute a doctrine of infinitesimals to both schools (not to mention the Pythagoreans and Anaxagoras) but the evidence seems far from conclusive.

The Archimedean manuscript "On Method," discovered by Heiberg in 1906, shows that Archimedes used infinitesimals in a method of discovery, although he did not consider that infinitesimal methods provided a strict proof. Archimedes attributed the discovery of the volume of the pyramid and of the cone to Democritus, but says that he did not prove it rigorously. Boyer (1968: 88–9) remarks: "This creates a puzzle, for if Democritus added anything to the Egyptian knowledge here, it must have been some sort of demonstration, albeit inadequate." Boyer suggests that this may point to a theory of infinitesimals. In the light of this speculation the following fragment of Democritus becomes even more tantalizing:

If a cone is cut along a plane parallel to its base, what must we think of the surfaces of the two segments – that they are all equal or unequal? If they are unequal, they will make the cone uneven, with many step-like indentations and roughnesses: If they are equal, then the segments will be equal and the cone will turn out to have the same properties as the cylinder, being composed of equal and not of unequal circles which is quite absurd. (from Plutarch, *De communibus notitiis*, tr. Furley in Furley (1967: 100))

But whatever the truth of the matter is regarding Democritus, it appears clear that his follower Epicurus did not believe in infinitesimal magnitudes. His letter to Herodotus contains a passage which is inconsistent with that doctrine:

For when someone says that there are infinite parts in something, however small they may be, it is impossible to see how this can still be finite in size; for obviously the infinite parts must be of *some* size, and whatever size they may happen to be, the size (of the total) would be infinite. (tr. Furley in Furley (1967: 14))

It is, of course possible that Epicurus modified the doctrine of Democritus, but in that case we might expect to find a more explicit discussion of the whole issue. The main evidence regarding Xenocrates' theory is the treatise, which was presumably written to refute it: "Concerning Indivisible Lines." Unfortunately the evidence is not univocal. Owen reads the treatise as directed against finite indivisible magnitudes:

It is not certain whether the proponents of this theory [of indivisible lines] thought that every measurable distance contained a finite or an infinite number of such distances. An argument for thinking the former is that this is assumed in the fourth-century polemic *On Indivisible Lines*. An argument for thinking the contrary is that the theory was held at a time when the difficulties of incommensurable lines were fully realized. It was a commonplace that the side and diagonal of a square cannot both be finite multiples of any unit of length whatsoever. (Owen (1957–1958: 150))

On the other hand, Boyer does not hesitate to interpret the treatise as directed against a theory of infinitesimals:

The thesis of the treatise ["On Indivisible Lines"] is that the doctrine of indivisibles espoused by Xenocrates . . . is untenable. The indivisible, or fixed infinitesimal of length or area or volume, has fascinated men of many ages; Xenocrates thought that this notion would resolve the paradoxes, such as those of Zeno, that plagued mathematical and philosophical thought. (Boyer (1968: 108))

Indeed, the treatise is such a scattershot affair that it is hard to detect the target. Perhaps there was more than one target. Otherwise the author was hopelessly confused. In the beginning of the treatise, the author lists the arguments that the proponents of indivisible lines use to support their doctrine. The fourth argument is only consistent with the indivisible magnitudes being finite rather than infinitesimal:

Again, Zeno's argument proves that there must be simple magnitudes. For the body, which is moving along a line, must reach the halfway point before it reaches the end. And since there is always a halfway point in any 'stretch' which is not simple, motion – unless there be simple magnitudes – involves that the moving body touches successively one-by-one an infinite number of points in a finite time which is impossible. ("Concerning Indivisible Lines," 968a 18–21)

But later in the treatise, we have already noted the passage that appears to be inconsistent with the indivisible lines being of finite magnitude:

Further, the addition of the line will not (on the theory) make the whole line any longer than the original line to which the addition was made: for simples will not, when added together, produce an increased total magnitude. (Ibid., 970a 21–3. See also 970b 23–5, 972a 12–14; Aristotle, *Physics*, 220a 15–20; 263 a4–9; "On Generation and Corruption," 316a 24–34)

Perhaps it is best just to say that both sorts of theory were in the air, without trying to be too positive about who held which theory.

Neither of these theories leaves Zeno bereft of argument. The theory of infinitesimals was not put on a firm foundation until the work of Abraham Robinson in this century. It would not be much of a problem to embarrass whatever preliminary ideas there were about them at the time. Indeed, if the theory in question did claim that the addition of a single infinitesimal magnitude would not make the line segment any longer, then Zeno had already made the reply: "If when it is taken away, the other thing is to be no smaller, and is to be no bigger when it is added, it is clear that what was added or taken away was nothing." Owen suggests that Zeno's paradox of the Stadium is also directed against infinitesimal magnitudes. His interpretation is only possible, however, if the theory of infinitesimals in question has the simple parts of the line discretely ordered. Any respectable theory of infinitesimals would have the simple parts of infinitesimal magnitude densely ordered. But since we are not in possession of the theory of infinitesimals in question (if there was one in question) we do not know how respectable it was.

However that may be, both the Arrow and the Stadium raise difficulties for an account of motion on a theory of finite indivisible magnitudes. The flying arrow moves but does not move at any instant. Motion becomes "first here, then there." Average velocity may make sense but instantaneous velocity does not. The Stadium shows us how considerations of relative motion almost force us into infinite divisibility. Even before considering relative motion there is this problem: If something is traveling a space unit for every two time units, where is it after one time unit? Conversely, if it is traveling two space units per time unit, how much time has elapsed after it travels one space unit? (Aristotle advances such arguments in the *Physics*, Bk. VI, Ch. 2, 232b 20ff.) A theory of finite indivisible magnitudes might reject such questions, or failing that, might try to get by with a theory that only allowed rest and motion of one speed, i.e. that of one time unit per space unit. Zeno's paradox of the Stadium shows that this strategy does not escape the problem. By considering one series of bodies at rest, and two having unit speed but opposite direction, the embarrassing questions can be asked again in terms of relative motion.

Aristotle did not hesitate to use the Arrow against indivisible magnitudes. He argues that on the rival theory "the motion will consist not of motions but of starts, and will take place by a thing's having completed a motion without being in motion . . . So it would be possible for a thing to have completed a walk without ever walking . . . " (*Physics*, Bk. VI, Ch. 1, 232a 9–11). Epicurus took the point. Furley reports the following comment of Themistius:

> But our clever friend Epicurus is not ashamed to use a remedy more severe than the disease – and this in spite of Aristotle's demonstration of the viciousness of the argument. The moving object, he says, *moves* over the whole distance, but of each of the indivisible units of which the whole is composed it does not move but has *moved*. (tr. Furley in Furley (1967: 113))

With regard to degree of motion, Epicurus again accedes to Aristotle. He actually maintains that all atoms do move through the void with the same speed (though not the same direction—see Furley (1967: 121ff.)). That the Stadium shows that little or nothing is gained by this desperate move appears to have escaped Epicurus as it did Aristotle.

### 2.3 Conclusion of Section 2

We have seen that Zeno's paradox of measure rests on the following premises:

(I) *Partition*: the line segment can be partitioned into an infinite number of parts such that:

(II) *Measurability*: the concept of magnitude applies to the parts.

(III) *Invariance*: the parts all have equal positive magnitude, or zero magnitude.

(IV) *Archimedean Axiom*: there are no infinitesimal magnitudes.

(V) *Ultra-Additivity*: the magnitude of the whole is the sum of the magnitudes of the parts in the sense given.

Ancient attempts to answer Zeno focused largely on (I) and (II). Doctrines of finite indivisible magnitudes (certainly Epicurus and probably Democritus and Leucippus) rejected (I). Aristotle rejected (I) and (II). It is possible that a doctrine of infinitesimal indivisible magnitudes was also current (possibly held by Xenocrates, possibly by Democritus) which rejected (IV). (III) could have also been challenged by a holder of a doctrine of infinitesimal magnitudes. (V), Ultra-Additivity, appears to have been accepted without question by every party to the dispute. It is ironic that it is just here that the standard modern theory of measure finds the fallacy.

# 3. Post Cantor

## 3.1 Measure According to Peano and Jordan, Borel, and Lebesgue

It is no accident that Zeno was first taken seriously in the modern era by mathematicians (see Tannery, 1885) at a time when problems in the theory of integration were leading to the development of measure theory. The concept of measurability was introduced (putting aside Aristotle's response to Zeno) by Peano in 1883 and generalized by Jordan in 1892 (for details see Hawkins, 1970). In discussing areas in the plane, Peano considers (I) the class of polygons that contain the region in question and (II) the class of polygons that are contained in the given region. The area of the region should be less than or equal to the areas of the polygons in the first class and greater than or equal to the areas of the polygons in the second class. If these conditions determine a unique number [i.e. if the greatest lower bound of the areas of polygons in class (I) equals the least upper bound of polygons in class (II)], then that is the area of the region. If not "then the concept of area would not apply in this case" (from Peano, 1883; quoted in Hawkins, 1970: 87).

Thus, on the line, an interval [a, b] is assigned its length, b − a, as measure.[8] This includes points that as degenerate intervals [a, a] are assigned measure zero. These measures are fundamental, and the concept of measure is extended to other point sets as follows. Consider finite sets of intervals that cover the set of points in question in that it is contained in their union. Associate with each such covering set the sum of the lengths of intervals in it. The greatest lower bound of these numbers is called the *outer content* of the set. Working from the other side, consider finite sets of non-overlapping (pairwise disjoint) intervals whose union is contained in the set in question. Associate with each such set the sum of the lengths of its members. The least upper bound of these numbers is called the *inner content* of the set. If the outer and inner content of a point set are equal,

---

[8] Open intervals (*a*, *b*) and half-open ones are also assigned measure *b* − *a*. The endpoint makes things no bigger when added and no smaller when taken away.

then the set is measurable in the sense of Peano and Jordan and that number is its measure. If not, then the set is not measurable—the concept of measure simply does not apply.

Jordan showed that measure, so defined, is finitely *additive*. That is, if each of a finite collection of mutually disjoint sets is measurable, then their union is also and its measure is the sum of theirs. The appropriate principle of additivity is not assumed in the definition, but rather proved from the definition; and it is a rather modest kind of additivity. The stronger principle of countable additivity fails for Peano–Jordan measure. The union of a denumerable collection of measurable sets may not itself be measurable. For instance, the set of rational points in [0, 1] is not Peano–Jordan measurable. Its outer content is 1, while its inner content is 0. Yet, as Cantor had shown, it is the union of a denumerable collection of unit sets.

The basic ideas of Peano–Jordan measure could have been introduced in Aristotle's time. They depend only on finite sums of intervals. The restriction to finite additivity allows a rich theory of measurable sets. Not every set of points becomes measurable, but the assignment of measure zero to unit sets of points causes no difficulties. Finite sets of points must have measure zero, but the Greek geometers knew well enough that the line was not exhausted by any finite set of points.

Borel took a rather different approach to measure and measurability in 1898. Borel constructs the Borel measurable sets out of the intervals by finite and denumerable set theoretic operations, and defines their measure by postulating a stronger form of additivity: i.e. countable additivity. A collection of sets is called a *sigma-algebra* if it is closed under countable union and intersection, and complementation. The Borel-measurable sets on the line segment can be defined as the smallest sigma-algebra of point sets containing the open intervals. Intervals have their length as their measure. Measure is taken to be countably additive (or sigma additive). That is, a countable union of mutually disjoint intervals has as its measure the infinite sum of the lengths of the intervals. Sigma additivity can be thought of as the restriction of the fancied principle of ultra-additivity of Part I to denumerable collections. Any denumerable set of points, e.g. the rationals in [0, 1], has Borel measure zero since it is a countable union of singletons each of which has measure zero. Since [0, 1] has measure 1, the set of irrational points in [0, 1] has measure 1. As Grünbaum has emphasized, this causes no problems because this set had been shown by

Cantor to be uncountable. For this reason, Borel's theory of measure was only conceivable after Cantor's fundamental investigations of infinite cardinality.

This is not to suggest that only countable point sets have measure zero. Consider the famous Cantor ternary set. It can be constructed by starting with [0, 1] and then removing the middle third open interval (1/3, 2/3). Thus we have at stage 1 of the construction the points in [0, 1/3] and [2/3, 1]. To move from stage $n$ of the construction to stage $n + 1$ we delete the middle open thirds of the closed intervals of stage $n$. The intersection of the sets at finite stages of the construction is Cantor's ternary set. It has Borel measure zero since we started with a set of measure 1 from which we have subtracted a set of points, which by countable additivity has measure one. Alternatively, it has measure zero in the sense of Peano and Jordan, since each stage $n$ in the process of construction provides a finite covering with measure (2/3) $n$, the outer content of the Cantor set is zero. Nevertheless the Cantor set is non-denumerable. The interval [0, 1] can be mapped 1-to-1 into the Cantor set. Remember Zeno's construction by infinite bisection of the line in section 2 of this chapter. For each point on the line, at each bisection it was either on the left or the right. The intersection of each chain, in Zeno's construction, contained at most one point. So each point on the line corresponds to a unique infinite sequence of 'left' and 'right'. Applying such a sequence to the stages in the construction of the Cantor set, we select the indicated left or right third, which remains, so we have corresponding to each point in the original interval a unique chain of closed intervals. The intersection of such a chain must be non-empty by the Heine–Borel theorem. The chains are constructed in such a way that no point can be in the intersection of two such chains. So each point on the original line corresponds to a unique point in the Cantor set.

Borel's bold move to countable additivity was not received without some qualms in the contemporary mathematical community. In a report on the theory of sets published in 1900, Schoenflies was critical of this as well as other aspects of Borel's theory of measure. With regard to countable additivity, he writes "the question of whether a property is extendable from finite to infinite sums cannot be settled by positing it but requires further investigation" (quoted in Hawkins, 1970: 107).

Lebesgue successfully carried out further investigations in 1902. Lebesgue generalized the notions of inner and outer content of Peano and

Jordan in such a way that the countable additivity of measure could be demonstrated; Lebesgue's definition of outer measure considers denumerable coverings. For each countable covering consider the limiting sum of the lengths of its constituent (open) intervals. The greatest lower bound of these numbers is the outer *measure* of the set in question. (Notice that the Lebesgue outer measure of the set of rationals in [0, 1] is 0.) For the inner measure of a bounded set, S, consider the closed intervals [a, b] which contain it. For each take its length, b − a, minus the outer measure of the set of points in it which are not in S. We can define the *inner measure* of S as the least upper bound of these numbers. (Of course, these numbers are all really the same. Any closed interval containing S will give the same result.)

Lebesgue was able to prove on the basis of these definitions that the Lebesgue-measurable sets include both the Borel-measurable sets and the sets measurable in the sense of Peano and Jordan; that Lebesgue measure agrees with each of these measures on the sets for which those measures were defined, and Lebesgue measure is countably additive. Furthermore, he showed that Lebesgue measure has the intuitively correct property of *translation invariance*. For a set S, and a real number a, let the set S + a contain just the points x + a for every x in S. The Lebesgue measure of any measurable set S equals the measure of S + a for any real number a.

Lebesgue's theory showed how the virtues of earlier theories could be combined and extended to provide an intuitive treatment for a very rich domain of measurable sets. In fact, at the time, it was not immediately apparent whether there were any bounded sets which were not measurable in the sense of Lebesgue.

### 3.2 *The Vitali Paradox*

In 1905 Vitali produced the first example of a non-Lebesgue-measurable set. The argument is in many ways strikingly similar to that used in Zeno's paradox of measure. Since Lebesgue measure is only countably additive, rather than ultra-additive, one following the path of Zeno would have to seek a countable partition of the unit line segment into parts that by some symmetry consideration should have the same magnitude. With such a partition in hand, he could argue that if the members of the partition have zero measure, then the unit interval must have zero measure; if they have equal positive measure, the unit interval must have infinite measure. Both alternatives contradict the fact that the unit interval has Lebesgue measure one, so the members of the partition are not Lebesgue measurable.

Vitali found such a partition. To simplify matters slightly, we will construct the partition of the half-open interval [0, 1). We can visualize this as wrapped around to form a unit circle. The relevant symmetry property of Lebesgue measure was mentioned in the preceding section. It is *translation-invariance*. Translation invariance implies translation invariance modulo 1, which in terms of our visualization means that if any Lebesgue-measurable set of points is displaced a fixed distance around the circle, the resulting set will have the same Lebesgue measure. Consider the equivalence relation: $x - y$ is rational. This partitions [0, 1) into equivalence classes. Choose one member from each of these classes to form the choice set C. For each rational, r, in [0, 1) let $C_r$ be the set gotten by adding (modulo 1) r to each member of C (i.e. by displacing C the distance r around the circle). The $C_r$s form a denumerable partition of [0, 1). Any one can be gotten by translation from any other. Since Lebesgue measure is translation-invariant, if they are Lebesgue measurable, they have the same measure. If so, the measure of [0, 1) must be either 0 or infinity. So the $C_r$s are not Lebesgue measurable. Such non-measurable sets are ubiquitous. It can be shown that every Lebesgue-measurable set with non-zero measure contains a non-measurable set. Zeno would have been delighted.

Vitali's construction requires stronger mathematical methods than Zeno's. The crucial step involves the axiom of choice. This proves to be essential in the construction of a non-measurable set (Solovay, 1970).

The only facts about Lebesgue measure used in Vitali's argument other than translation invariance are that it is *countably additive* and *real valued* (the latter being used for the Archimedean property of the real numbers). Thus, the argument establishes a more general result: any translation-invariant, countably additive, real-valued measure defined on all the subsets of [0, 1)[9] must give [0, 1) either infinite measure or measure zero.

Must we, with Aristotle, concede that intervals (areas, volumes) of positive magnitude are made up of parts to which the concept of magnitude does not apply? Or can we plausibly weaken the foregoing set of three conditions, which generate the Vitali paradox?

---

[9] Or indeed on any sigma algebra containing the $C_r$s.

### 3.3 Finite Additivity and Non-Archimedean Measure

Lebesgue measure escaped Zeno's paradox by virtue of a weaker form of additivity. This suggests that a weakening of countable additivity to finite additivity might allow us to define a finitely additive measure on a richer domain of sets. Of course, such a possibility would only be of interest if some of the virtues of Lebesgue measure could be retained; e.g. we would like each interval to have its length as its measure.

In fact, we can have this and more. There is a finitely additive, real-valued translation invariant measure defined on *all* subsets of [0, 1],[10] which agrees with Lebesgue measure on all the Lebesgue-measurable sets.[11]

Returning to Vitali's example, it is clear that such a measure must give the sets $C_r$ measure zero, for if it gave them positive measure, finite additivity and translation invariance would contradict the measure of [0, 1) being one. The $C_r$s can thus be accommodated by a finitely additive measure in the way in which the singletons were accommodated by Lebesgue measure; they have measure zero but the additivity properties of the measure are not strong enough for that to cause problems.

Some philosophers may, despite all of this, feel nagging Zenonian intuitions to the effect that a whole of positive magnitude simply should not be made up parts of measure zero. This is the intuition that measure should be *regular*; that only the null set should receive measure zero. We have seen that not even a *finitely* additive translation invariant measure can accommodate this intuition if it is real valued. But what if the values that the measure takes on lie in a domain that is non-Archimedean? Couldn't we get away with giving both the singletons and the $C_r$s infinitesimal measure in some way in which everything works out nicely?

Such speculations may be very old, but it has only been possible to give them substance since Abraham Robinson's creation of non-standard analysis (Robinson, 1966). Leibniz thought of infinitesimals as ideal elements, which nevertheless obey the same laws as the numbers. But which laws? The answer cannot be "All" in too strong a sense; otherwise we would not be able to distinguish a theory that admits infinitesimals from one which doesn't. This question had to wait for the development of

---

[10]  And indeed on all bounded subsets of the reals.
[11]  Banach (1923) and Banach and Tarski (1924).

model theory for its proper answer. Robinson showed how a non-standard model of analysis could incorporate infinitesimals, which consequently must obey the *first-order* laws that govern the real numbers.

The crucial logical property of first-order languages that Robinson's construction uses is compactness: if a set of sentences is such that every finite subset of it has a model, then the whole set in question has a model. Compactness of first-order languages depends on their limited logical resources: the logical constants being limited to truth functions, identity, and first-order quantifiers and their sentences being of only finite length. It does not depend on the languages being denumerable. Thus we could (and will) imagine first-order languages with names for every real number, which are nevertheless compact. Compactness fails for second-order logic given the 'natural' interpretation of second-order quantifiers having as their domain the power set of the domain of the first-order quantifiers. However, if we allow Henkin's general models in which higher-order quantifiers are allowed to have as their domain subsets of their natural domain, higher-order quantification theory is also compact.

Here, then, is how we get a non-standard model of analysis which contains infinitesimal elements: Consider a rich first-order language which for every real number, $r$, contains a name $o_r$; a relational symbol for every relation on the reals; and an operation symbol for every operation on the reals. Let the theory ANALYSIS consist of all the true sentences of this language, and consider the theory, which is the union of ANALYSIS with the set of all sentences of the form $o_r < y$ for each real $r$. Each finite subset of this theory has a model in the reals, so by compactness this theory does too. This is a non-standard model of the reals. The function which maps each real, $r$, onto $O_r^*$, the denotation in the non-standard model of its name, is an isomorphism. Each non-standard model contains an isomorphic copy of the reals. Working within the non-standard model, we will simply call these the standard reals. The denotation of the less-than relation totally orders the non-standard reals since the axioms of total order are first order. According to that order, the element that the model assigns as the denotation of y is an infinite element; it is greater than any of the standard reals. There is a first-order sentence that says that every number has a reciprocal and one that says that if x is greater than y, then the reciprocal of x is less than the reciprocal of y. Since the model makes these sentences true, there must be an element of the model that is the reciprocal of the infinite element and less than any positive standard real. This is an infinitesimal element. A great deal of knowledge about the structure of the infinitesimals follows from the fact that they obey all first-order generalizations about the reals.

The question as to how such infinitesimals can be incorporated into non-standard measure theory is a bit more complicated, involving non-standard (general) models for a higher-order language of analysis. (For details, see Bernstein and Wattenberg, 1969.) They show that one can construct a measure defined for all subsets of the unit interval, which takes its values in a non-standard model of the reals, which is *finitely additive, translation invariant up to an infinitesimal* which is *infinitesimally close to Lebesgue measure on the Lebesgue-measurable sets*, and which is regular (i.e. only the null set gets measure zero). The Vitali sets of the last section, and the sets containing exactly one point, will then both have infinitesimal measure.

It can be shown that in non-standard models of analysis every non-standard real is infinitesimally close to a unique standard real. Call the second the standard part of the first. Then if we have a non-standard measure of the kind described here, and derive a real-valued measure by considering only the standard parts of the values assigned by the non-standard measure, we get the sort of measure discussed at the beginning of this section: a real-valued, finitely additive, translation invariant measure defined on all subsets of [0, 1] which agrees with Lebesgue measure on the Lebesgue-measurable sets. What we gain by allowing our measure to take values in a richer range—the non-standard reals—is *regularity*.

### 3.4  The Hausdorff Paradox

We seem to have finally seen how to get rid of non-measurability. Banach showed that at the cost of weakening additivity to finite additivity on the non-Lebesgue-measurable sets, we can make every bounded set of points on the real line measurable. This does not quite lay Zeno to rest, for he was ultimately concerned with magnitudes of volumes in three-dimensional space. We have been confining ourselves to one dimension for the sake of simplicity. To complete the story, we should show that Banach's result could be extended to three-dimensional space. It is not so. A construction due to Hausdorff (1914) and further generalized by Banach and Tarski (1924) shows that one cannot in three and higher dimensional Euclidean spaces have a finitely-additive measure, which assigns the unit cube measure 1, assigns congruent point sets equal measure, and assigns a measure to all subsets of the unit cube.

Here the appropriate invariance property is congruence-invariance. Points here are to be thought of as triples of real numbers. The *Euclidean distance* between two points, (x, y, z) and (x', y', z'), is given by the Pythagorean formula:

$$[(x - x')^2 + (y - y')^2 + (z - z')^2]^{1/2}$$

Two sets of points in Euclidean three-dimensional space are congruent just in case there is a 1-to-1 function mapping the one onto the other which preserves Euclidean distance (i.e., the distance between any two points in the first set is equal to the distance between their images in the second set). Congruence invariance in one dimension is just translation invariance. The theory of Lebesgue measure for n-dimensional Euclidean space, developed analogously to the theory for one dimension, has the consequence that Lebesgue measure is congruence-invariant on the Lebesgue-measurable sets. Banach actually showed that a finitely additive congruence-invariant extension of Lebesgue measure to all bounded sets is possible in both one- and two-dimensional Euclidean space. It is only in Euclidean spaces of three and higher dimensions where the theorem fails.

In an extended note to *Grundzüge der Mengenlehre* (1914) headed "Unsolvability of the Measure Problem," Hausdorff sets out to show that it is impossible to assign to all point sets on the surface of a sphere a finitely additive, congruence-invariant measure which assigns the whole surface a positive measure. To this end, he proves the following theorem:

> The spherical surface, K, can be decomposed into disjoint sets: A, B, C, Q, where Q is countable; A, B, C are congruent to each other; the union of B and C is congruent with each of the sets A, B, C.

Since Hausdorff is here considering real-valued measure, congruence invariance together with a finite measure for the surface entails that each countable point set has measure zero. (For one can by appropriate choice of rotations generate an infinite number of disjoint congruent point sets to any given denumerable point set. If the given set has positive measure, the surface of the sphere by finite additivity could not have finite measure.) Thus, under the stated assumptions, the measure of the surface, $m(K)$, would equal $m(A) + m(B) + m(C)$. Since A, B, and C are congruent with each other, $m(A) = 1/3\ m(K)$. Since A is congruent with B U C, $m(A) = 1/2\ m(K)$.

Hausdorff's theorem again depends on the axiom of choice (as does Banach's positive result for 1 and 2 dimensions). Hausdorff works with a group of rotations about two appropriately chosen[12] axes; the group generated by 1/2 rotation about the first axis, $\phi$, and 1/3 rotation about the second, $\psi$. Hausdorff shows how this group of rotations can be decomposed into three disjoint sets: G = A U B U C, such that A · $\phi$ = B U C; A · $\psi$ = B; A · $\psi^2$ = C.[13] Let Q be the countable set of fixed points of members of G. The set of points on the surface less this denumerable set, S − Q, is the disjoint union of the orbits of the group G. The axiom of choice comes into the picture to assure the existence of a choice set, M, containing exactly one member from each orbit. S − Q consists of the union of the point sets that M is carried into by members of G. Let the *point* set A be the set of points that M is carried into by the rotations in the *set of rotations* A, likewise for B and C. Then A, B, C and Q are the requisite point sets for Hausdorff's theorem.

Hausdorff concludes: "A determination of measure for all bounded sets, which satisfies conditions . . . [congruence-invariance, unit cube has measure1, finite additivity] is therefore impossible in three and higher dimensional Euclidean space, since otherwise it would also be possible on the sphere (where one would assign to a set on the sphere the volume of the corresponding conical body as its measure)."

The paradoxical results of Hausdorff and Vitali are analyzed and generalized in a celebrated paper of Banach and Tarski (1924). There they introduce the notion of equivalence of sets of points by finite (and alternatively by denumerable) decomposition. Two sets of points (in a metric space) are equivalent by finite decomposition iff there exist finite partitions $[p_1, \ldots p_n]$, $[q_1, \ldots q_n]$ of them respectively, whose respective members are congruent ($p_1$ congruent with $q_1$ & . . . & $p_n$ congruent with $q_n$); analogously for equivalence by denumerable decomposition. Then generalizing Hausdorff's argument: "In a Euclidean space of n≥3 dimensions, two arbitrary sets, bounded and containing interior points (e.g. two

---

[12] The axes are chosen so that distinct members of the group represent distinct rotations. Hausdorff proves that this is possible.

[13] *A, B, C* are constructed by recursion on the length of elements in G. 1 is in *A*; $\phi$, $\psi$ in *B*; $\psi^2$ in *C*. Continue as follows:

| | x in A | x in B | x in C |
|---|---|---|---|
| x ends in $\psi$, $\psi^2$ | x $\phi$ in B | x $\Phi$ in A | x $\Phi$ in A |
| x ends in $\phi$ | x $\psi$ in B and x $\psi^2$ in C | x $\psi$ in C and x $\psi^2$ in A | x $\psi$ in A and x $\psi^2$ in B |

spheres of different radius) are equivalent through finite decomposition" (Banach and Tarski, 1924: 244). In the form in which they develop it, Hausdorff's paradox is perhaps better known as the Banach–Tarski paradox. The analogous theorem holds for the surface of the sphere but fails for Euclidean spaces of 1 and 2 dimensions. For these spaces, however, we have a generalization of the Vitali paradox. For Euclidean spaces of dimension 1 and higher "two arbitrary sets (bounded or not) containing interior points are equivalent by denumerable decomposition" (ibid.).

These rather surprising facts about *congruence* are at the heart of the restrictions on measurability that we have been discussing for the last three sections. They might be taken as calling into question the status of congruence-invariance as a desideratum for measure. Our intuitions in this regard are based on consideration of far simpler point sets than the ones involved in the Vitali and Hausdorff paradoxes. Before even raising questions of measure, we see that our intuitions regarding congruence of simple bodies in three-dimensional Euclidean space cannot be projected to arbitrary point sets.

One can extend Lebesgue measure to a finitely additive, *non-congruence invariant* measure on all the bounded subsets of Euclidean three-dimensional space. So measurability of all bounded sets can be achieved, but at an unexpected cost. One might wonder, however, whether if one pays the price of giving up congruence-invariance, one can avoid weakening countable additivity to finite additivity. The Vitali paradox and its generalizations, after all, used congruence invariance essentially. Things, however, are not quite so simple. Non-measurability has roots that go deeper than the metric structure of the underlying space.

## 3.5 Non-measurable Sets without Congruence Invariance

Let us recall, for a moment, Zeno's two principles from section 2. Suppose that a whole can be partitioned into an infinite number of parts. Then Zeno thought:

(I) If the parts had positive (real) magnitude, then the whole would have infinite magnitude.

(II) If the parts had zero magnitude, then the whole would have zero magnitude.

Let us by 'magnitude' understand a *countably additive* measure. Then (II) is correct for an infinite partition into a denumerable number of parts, but fails for partitions into a non-denumerably infinite number of parts. On the other hand, (I) can fail for a denumerable partition unless some extra assumptions about the magnitudes of the parts are present (e.g. that they must all be the same by some invariance argument). A fact that we have not taken explicit notice of yet is that (I) holds without restriction if the infinite partition is non-denumerable. *If a set has finite measure, it can contain at most a denumerable infinity of disjoint sets of positive measure.* Consider any partition of the set in question. Consider the set of members of this partition with measure greater than or equal to 1/2. It must be finite. Otherwise by finite additivity of measure, the measure of S could not be finite. Likewise for the set of members of the partition with measure greater than or equal to $1/2^n$ and less than or equal to $1/2^{n-1}$, for each natural number n. Each member of the partition with non-zero measure is in one of these finite collections of sets. The number of such collections is denumerable, so the number of members of the original partition with positive measure is denumerable. Non-denumerable partitions make (I) true and (II) false; denumerable partitions make (II) true [assuming countable additivity of the measure] and (I) false.

These facts make it possible to show, under the assumption of Cantor's continuum hypothesis, that there is no non-trivial countably additive measure on [0, 1] which gives all the unit point sets measure zero. The result is due to Banach and Kuratowski (1929) and was strengthened and generalized by Ulam (1930). No assumption of translation invariance is used; there is no appeal to metric considerations. Only the cardinality of the set in question plays a role. A set is of power aleph$_1$ iff it can be put into one-to-one correspondence with the ordinal numbers less than the first uncountable ordinal. The stated theorem is proved for arbitrary sets of power aleph$_1$. Cantor's continuum hypothesis enters to assure that [0, 1] is such a set.

I give the proof so that the reader can appreciate the Zenonian counterpoint: *Suppose that a countably additive (real-valued) measure is defined on a set, Z, of cardinality aleph$_1$, such that every one-element subset receives measure zero. Then the measure of Z must be either infinite or zero.* Since Z is, by hypothesis, of power aleph$_1$, there is a well-ordering such that each element of Z is preceded by only countably many elements, i.e. for each y in Z, the set {x: x < y} is countable. For each y, let $f_y(x)$ be a one-to-one mapping of this set into the positive integers. We can then consider $f(x, y)$ as a mapping from pairs (x, y) of elements of Z such that x < y, to integers.

Now, for each x in Z and each positive integer, n, let there be {y: x < y and f(x, y) = n}. We can picture these sets as arranged in an infinite matrix with denumerably many rows and uncountably (aleph$_1$) many columns:

$$A_1^1, A_2^1, \ldots A_n^1, \ldots A_\alpha^1, \ldots$$

$$A_1^2, A_2^2, \ldots A_n^2, \ldots A_\alpha^2, \ldots$$

$$\cdots \cdots \cdots \cdots \cdots \cdots \cdots \cdots$$

$$A_1^n, A_2^n, \ldots A_n^n, \ldots A_\alpha^n, \ldots$$

$$\cdots \cdots \cdots \cdots \cdots \cdots \cdots \cdots$$

The sets have been constructed so that: (a) the sets in any row are disjoint. (b) The union of the sets in any column is equal to the whole set Z minus a countable set. [(a) follows from the 1-to-1 nature of $f$ considered as a function of x. For (b), any y greater than the x of the column belongs to the set in the column for which n = f(x, y). The union of the sets in the column then differs from Z by the set of elements less than or equal to x, which, by hypothesis, is countable.]

If, in any row, there is a non-denumerable number of sets of positive measure, then by the correct form of Zeno's (I), Z cannot have finite measure. If, on the other hand, in every row only a denumerable number of sets have non-zero measure, then only a denumerable number of sets in the whole matrix have non-zero measure since there are only a denumerable number of rows. Then there must be some column that contains all sets of measure zero, since there are a non-denumerable number of columns. The set of elements in Z not contained in the union of the sets in that column must also have measure zero by the correct form of Zeno's (II) since it is the union of a denumerable number of singletons, each of which, by hypothesis, has measure zero.[14]

At this stage of the game, the elimination of non-measurable sets may appear a rather quixotic goal. Lebesgue measure has extended measurability to a far richer domain than Zeno and Aristotle imagined possible. It meshes with an elegant and powerful theory of integration adequate to the needs of the physical sciences. Perhaps Lebesgue measure should

[14] The proof, essentially as I have given it, is in Ulam (1930). He then strengthens it by showing that it holds for any set, Z, such that there is no weakly inaccessible cardinal less than or equal in power to Z.

be taken as the theory of measure for physical space, and the existence of non-measurable sets should be viewed as just a mildly surprising consequence of the theory rather than as a real difficulty. This is, I believe, the dominant view among mathematicians and mathematical physicists. The real bite of non-measurability comes not in physics or metaphysics, but in epistemology.

### 3.6  Measures of Degree of Belief

Let us turn our attention to probability measures that are meant to represent rational degrees of belief. In this area, questions of measurability take on a new pungency. It is one thing to say that some widely scattered set of points in Euclidean three-dimensional space does not have a natural volume associated with it; another to say that there must be propositions to which there cannot be a degree of belief.

Some of the assumptions used in demonstrating non-measurability also appear in a new light. Translation and congruence invariance appear now not as falsifiable claims about the structure of measure on physical space, but rather as the result of the exercise of someone's epistemological freedom. I wonder which point on a wheel of fortune will be the lowest point when it comes to rest. I come to have degrees of belief that are invariant under translation about the circumference. Can it be denied that it is reasonable and proper for me to do so? Again, shouldn't we be able to have rational degrees of belief defined over the subsets of some set of power $aleph_1$, whether or not $c = aleph_1$? Furthermore, the Zenonian intuition that only the empty set (here the null proposition) should receive measure zero is supported by a kind of betting argument. Shimony (1955) showed that regularity of probability measure is entailed by *strict coherence*: One should reject systems of bets such that one could in no possible circumstance achieve a net gain although one could suffer a net loss.

It is for reasons such as the foregoing that interest in finitely additive and non-Archimedean measure has largely been generated by the theory of personal probability. De Finetti has consistently rejected countable additivity as a postulate for the theory of personal probability. For a recent spirited defense of finite additivity, see de Finetti (1972 and 1974). Considerations of strict coherence, and of having conditional probabilities well defined in a natural way, can be used to motivate the move to non-Archimedean valued probabilities. For example, see Bernstein and Wattenberg (1969).

Let me back up, and put these questions in their proper setting. Suppose that we have a set, $U$, whose elements represent mutually exclusive and jointly exhaustive states of affairs. If we think of such states of affairs as individuated in a maximally specific way, we might call the constituents of $U$ 'possible worlds' (but this raises questions which cannot be discussed here). The subsets of this set can be thought of as statements or 'propositions' if propositions are only individuated up to necessary equivalence relative to the original set of possibilities. A set of such 'propositions' closed under negation, conjunction, and disjunction is a Boolean algebra of propositions (under countable conjunction, disjunction, and negation, a Boolean sigma algebra). A (finitely additive) measure defined on such a Boolean algebra of propositions, which takes values in [0, 1], and which gives a tautology measure 1 and a contradiction measure 0 is a *probability measure*. (I leave open the questions as to whether the algebra need also be a sigma algebra, whether the measure need also be countably additive, and whether [0, 1] is to be taken as a set of standard reals or whether a non-standard model of the reals can also be utilized, these being material to the issues in question.) The question of measurability then is whether the set of all subsets of $U$ can be taken as the appropriate sigma algebra of propositions, or whether we are forced to restrict our probability assignments to some smaller Boolean algebra.[15]

Suppose that degrees of belief are represented (obviously with some idealization) by a numerical-valued function from a Boolean algebra of propositions. There are well-known pragmatic virtues associated with that function being a probability measure. If it is not, and degrees of belief are used in the standard way in determining the fairness of bets, then the agent in question leaves himself open to a Dutch Book: a finite system of bets each of which he considers fair or favorable, such that the net result is a loss no matter what happens. A belief function that leaves one open to a Dutch Book is said to be incoherent. Coherent belief evaluation functions must be (finitely additive) probability measures. De Finetti argues that there is no comparable coherence argument for countable additivity; and that the imposition of countable additivity as a postulate

---

[15] One way to do this would be first to assign a finitely additive probability measure to the sentences of a first-order language, and then extend it to a countably additive probability measure on the sigma algebra generated by the sets of models which satisfy sentences of the language (see Fenstad, 1980).

has the undesirable consequences of (1) creating unmeasurable sets and (2) precluding probability assignments which are perfectly acceptable from a personalistic point of view, e.g. a uniform distribution on a denumerable set of possibilities. Consequently, he develops his theory of personal probability only under the assumption of finite additivity. Savage (1954) does likewise.

The question of the relation of additivity to coherence is not, however, quite so simple. Consider de Finetti's example of the uniform distribution on a denumerable set of possibilities (e.g. what ticket will win in a denumerable lottery). Finite additivity allows the uniform distribution, which gives each ticket exactly zero chance of winning, while maintaining probability one that some ticket wins. I would love to have the chance of betting against someone having such a probability assignment. For each ticket, I will bet him $100 against nothing that it wins; he will consider each of these bets fair. After the lottery, I collect my $100. If he declines fair bets on the grounds that not betting is just as good, I can do as well offering favorable bets. I will bet $101 against $1/2 that the first ticket wins; $101 against $1/2n that the nth ticket wins. After the lottery, I am assured a net winning of at least $100. The second example reveals clearly what the first may not; that in each case I am assuming sigma-additivity of the *payoff values* in totaling up my net gain in the infinite system of bets. In fact, if we make these two assumptions: that a denumerable set of bets is permissible and that the *payoff-values* are sigma-additive, then one can show that the correlative notion of coherence implies countable additivity of the probability measure. The first notice of this fact of which I am aware is in Spielman (1977).

Let a *betting system* be a function from possible states of affairs to payoff values. A *bet* on a proposition $p$, is a betting system which has a gain, $a$, associated with every state of affairs in $p$, and a loss, $b$, associated with every state of affairs in the negation of $p$. The *aggregate* of two betting systems, $B_1 \# B_2$, is the betting system that has at each possible state of affairs $w$, the sum of the payoffs associated with $B_1$ and $B_2$:

$$B_1 \# B_2(w) = B_1(w) + B_2(w)$$

Probability is to perform the practical function of placing a value, *expected value*, on bets and betting arrangements when the agent is uncertain as to the state of the world. It would be an attractive property for such evaluations to have that they are *extensional* in the sense that the valuation depend only on the betting system (the function from possible states of affairs to payoff values), and not on how it is described. Otherwise the agent would regard two different prices fair for the same arrangement, and could be systematically exploited by someone who repeatedly bought an arrangement from him cheap and resold it to him dear. Similar considerations support the contention that valuation under uncertainty, *expected value*, should be additive over aggregation:

$$EV\,(B_1 \,\#\, B_2) = EV(B_1) + EV(B_2)$$

For the agent would presumably sell a betting arrangement with expected value of X for X or more, and buy it for X or less. If payoff value is additive, expected value had better be! Now if $p$ and $q$ are mutually exclusive propositions; $B_1$ and $B_2$ are bets on $p$ and $q$ respectively at the same stakes, then $B_1 \,\#\, B_2$ is a bet on their disjunction $p \lor q$. In particular, let $B_1$ be the bet that gains a dollar if $p$ loses, nothing otherwise; $B_2$ be the bet that gains a dollar if $q$ loses, nothing otherwise; $B_3$ be the bet that gains a dollar if $p \lor q$ loses, nothing otherwise. Then $B_1 \,\#\, B_2 = B_3$, so by extensionality $EV(B_1 \,\#\, B_2) = EV(B_3)$ and by additivity of expected value over aggregation, $EV(B_1) + EV(B_2) = EV(B_3)$. Since these expected values equal by definition the respective probabilities of $p$, $q$, and p $\lor$ q, we have finite additivity, pr (p) + pr (q) = pr (p $\lor$ q). Now the point of going through all this is to call attention to the fact that if payoff value is countably additive, then we can consider denumerable aggregates of bets, whose payoffs at each possible state of affairs, $w$, is the denumerable sum of the payoffs of its constituents:

$$\#_i B_i = \Sigma_i B_i(w\}$$

and run the analogous argument for countable additivity.

All the considerations that came into play regarding non-measurable sets in previous sections are now again on the table: finite and countable additivity, invariance, regularity, Archimedean and non-Archimedean values for the measure; domains of various cardinality on which the measure is to be defined. This is not the place to attempt to sort them out. Perhaps enough has been said to show that the truly deep issues first raised by Zeno still deserve to engage our interest.

# Bibliography

Archimedes [n.d.] *The Works of Archimedes*. Tr. T. L. Heath. (With a supplement, *The Method of Archimedes*.) New York: Dover.

Aristotle (1941) *The Basic Works of Aristotle*, ed. Richard McKeon, New York: Random House. (Unless otherwise noted, all of the translations of Aristotle's works referred to in this chapter are to be found in this edition, which is a selection of translations originally published in the *Works*, translated under the editorship of W. D. Ross. 12 vols. London: Oxford University Press, 1908–31.)

Banach, S. (1923) "Sur le problème de la mesure," *Fundamenta Mathematicae* 4: 30–1.

Banach, S. and Kuratowski, C. (1929) "Sur une généralisation du problème de la mesure," *Fundamenta Mathematicae* 5(14): 127ff.

Banach, S. and Tarski, A. (1924) "Sur la décomposition des ensembles de points en parties respectivement congruentes," *Fundamenta Mathematicae* 6: 244–77.

Bernstein, A. and Wattenberg, F. (1969) "Non-Standard Measure Theory." In W. A. J. Luxemberg (ed.), *Applications of Model Theory Algebra, Analysis and Probability*, pp. 171–85. New York: Holt Rinehart & Winston.

Boyer, C. B. (1968) *A History of Mathematics*. New York: Wiley.

Cajori, F. (1915) "The History of Zeno's Arguments on Motion," *American Mathematical Monthly* 22: 1–6, 77–82, 109–15, 143–9, 179–86, 215–20, 253–8, 292–7.

—— (1919) *A History of Mathematics*. 2nd ed. New York: Macmillan.

de Finetti, B. (1972) *Probability, Induction and Statistics*. New York: Wiley.

—— (1974) *Theory of Probability*. Tr. A. Machi. 2 vols. New York: Wiley.

Fenstad, J. E. (1980) "The Structure of Probabilities Defined on First-Order Languages." In *Studies in Inductive Logic and Probability II*, ed. Jeffrey, pp. 251–62. Berkeley: University of California Press.

Fränkel, H. (1942) "Zeno of Elea's Attacks on Plurality," *American Journal of Philology* 63: 1–25, 193–206. Revised version in Furley and Allen (1970–5), vol. 2, 102–42.

Fritz, K. von (1945) "The Discovery of Incommensurability by Hippasus of Metapontum," *Annals of Mathematics* 46: 242–64.

Furley, D. J. (1967) "Indivisible Magnitudes." In *Two Studies in the Greek Atomists*, ed. D. J. Furley. Princeton: Princeton University Press.

—— (1969) "Aristotle and the Atomists on Infinity." In *Naturphilosophie bei Aristoteles und Theophrast*, pp. 85–96. Heidelberg: Lothar Stiehm.

Furley, D. J. and Allen, R. E. (1970–5) *Studies in Presocratic Philosophy*. 2 vols. London: Routledge & Kegan Paul.

Grünbaum, A. (1952) "A Consistent Conception of the Extended Linear Continuum as an Aggregate of Unextended Elements," *Philosophy of Science* 19: 290–5.

—— (1963) *Philosophical Problems of Space and Time*, ch. 6. New York: Knopf.

—— (1968) *Modern Science and Zeno's Paradoxes*. London: Allen & Unwin.

Hausdorff, F. (1914) *Grundzüge der Mengenlehre*. Leipzig: Veit.

Hawkins, T. (1970) *Lebesgue's Theory of Integration*. New York: Chelsea.

Heath, T. L. (1949) *Mathematics in Aristotle*. London: Oxford University Press.

Lee, H. D. P. (1936) *Zeno of Elea*. Cambridge: Cambridge University Press.

Luria, S. (1933) "Die Infinitesimallehre der antiken Atomisten," *Quellen und Studien zur Geschichte der Mathematik* 2: 106–95.

Mau, J. (1954) *Zum Problem des Infinitesimalen bei den antiken Atomisten*. Berlin: Akademie.

Owen, G. E. L. (1957–8) "Zeno and the Mathematicians," *Proceedings of the Aristotelian Society* 58: 199–222. Reprinted in Furley and Allen (1970–5).

pseudo-Aristotle (1913) "Concerning Indivisible Lines." Tr. H. H. Joachim. In *The Works of Aristotle*, vol. 6, ed. W. D. Ross. Oxford: Clarendon Press.

Robinson, A. (1966) *Non-Standard Analysis*. Amsterdam: North Holland.

Savage, L. J. (1954) *The Foundations of Statistics*. New York: Wiley.

Shimony, A. (1955) "Coherence and the Axioms of Confirmation," *Journal of Symbolic Logic* 20: 1–28.

Solovay, R. M. (1970) "A Model of Set Theory in which Every Set of Reals Is Lebesgue-Measurable," *Annals of Mathematics* 92: 1–56.

Spielman, S. (1977) "Physical Probability and Bayesian Statistics," *Synthese* 36: 235–69.

Tannery, P. (1885) "Le concept scientifique du continu: Zenon d'Elée et Georg Cantor," *Revue philosophique* 20(2): 385–10.

Tarski, A. (1956) "Foundations of the Geometry of Solids." In *Logic, Semantics, Metamathematics*, tr. and ed. J. H. Woodger. Oxford: Clarendon Press.

Ulam, S. (1930) "Zur Masstheorie in der allgemeinen Mengenlehre," *Fundamenta Mathematicae* 16: 140–50.

Vitali, G. (1905) *Sul problema della misura dei gruppi di punti di una retta*. Bologna: Gamberini e Parneggiani.

Vlastos, G. (1971) "A Zenonian Argument against Plurality." In *Essays in Ancient Greek Philosophy*, ed. J. P. Anton with G. L. Kustas, pp. 119–44. Albany, NY: SUNY Press.

# 2

# Tractarian Nominalism
## (for Wilfrid Sellars)

In the *Tractatus* Wittgenstein sketches a metaphysical position which displays nominalistic sympathies although it is certainly not nominalistic in the terms either of Ockham, or of Quine and Goodman.[1] In this chapter, I would like to explore a version of this position, and to say in what ways it is nominalistic and in what ways it is not. My aim is not, however, faithful exegesis of the *Tractatus*. The view, which I call Tractarian Nominalism, will have no part of Wittgenstein's interpretation of quantifiers, his fixed-domain treatment of possible worlds, or his quasi-intuitionist attitude towards infinity. Rather, I would like to give what I take to be the central idea of the *Tractatus* free play in less cramped quarters. The resulting metaphysics does, I believe, represent a viable ontological position. It has an advantage over traditional nominalism in the way in which it is connected to questions of epistemology. And it has an important consequence for the philosophy of logic.

## 1. Tractarian Nominalism

Wittgenstein's truly daring idea was that the ontology of the subject (nominalism) and the ontology of the predicate (Platonism) were both equally wrong and one-sided; and that they should give way to the ontology of the assertion. We may conceive of the world not as a world of individuals or as a world of properties and relations, but as a world of

---

The dedication is not to be taken as implying that Sellars is a Tractarian Nominalist; this note is not to be taken as implying that he is not

[1] Of "Steps toward a constructive nominalism" and "A world of individuals" but compare Quine's views in "Whither physical objects?"

facts—with individuals and relations being equally abstractions from the facts. John would be an abstraction from all facts-about-John; Red an abstraction from being-red-facts; etc.

Of course *in the metalanguage of the Tractatus*, facts became the objects named, and their properties and relations (being-a-fact-about-John; being-a-being-red-fact) assume the office of the first-order objects and relations with which we started. If stated with no restrictions as to language, the metaphysics of the *Tractatus* is incoherent.[2] Wittgenstein chose to interpret his theory in the most grandiose way, and then bite the bullet by agreeing that the language of the *Tractatus* is nonsense. His show of facing up to the consequences by 'throwing away the ladder' is, however, hardly more than a bit of theater. It would be more satisfactory to take the modest position that what is being attempted is not a theory of all language but rather a theory of the functioning of the object language used to describe the world. Let us take this tack, and table the question of what is going on in our metalanguage.

The world, then, can be thought of as a collection of facts. Facts are primitive entities. Nevertheless we can say something about their nature in terms of the way in which we classify them. An atomic fact can be completely characterized by a relational-classification (e.g. is-a-loves-fact) and its coordinate object-classifications (e.g. with John standing in the first place of the loving relation and Mary in the second). We may then, in the vulgar way, think of an atomic fact as associated with a representation consisting of an $n + 1$-tuple: an *n*-ary relation followed by n objects. But the representation need not be unique. <Loves, John, Mary> and <is-Loved-by, Mary, John> are representations of the same fact.

I see no just reason to maintain that n has to be finite. A relation associated with a fact might be a relation with an infinite number of terms. In such a case, 'n-tuple' in the foregoing should be interpreted as: 'family indexed by the ordinal n'. This raises the immediate prospect of a grand all-embracing fact.

If it is a fact that John loves Mary and it is a fact that Jane desires George, and if we are allowed to infer from the two two-place relations of love and desire, a four-place relation Rxyzw which holds for xyzw just in case x loves y and z desires w, then there is the fact that this relation is exemplified

---

[2] The most immediate incoherence being simply the consequence that facts are and are not objects.

by <John, Mary, Jane, George>. The most liberal attitude for closure conditions for relations will lead to the all-encompassing world-fact.

Conversely, *if* we allow a property of being-the-child-of-Adam, or being-the-Parent-of-Cain, then the fact-that-Cain-is-the-child-of-Adam, i.e. that Adam-is-the-Parent-of-Cain, has not only the two representations:

<child-of, Cain, Adam>   <parent of, Adam, Cain>

but also:

<child-of-Adam, Cain>   <parent-of-Cain, Adam>

So the world could be characterized by a set of monadic representations of facts.

Which level should we take as fundamental? Does it make any difference? First, an epistemological point. The fact representations that we take as fundamental are coordinate with the objects and relations that we take as fundamental. The way we break things up depends on what objects and relations we take as being most generally useful in characterizing the world. This determination is made by science, not logic. (E.g. at a crude level of science greenness may be a fundamental property but grueness is not.) Science judges which are the fundamental objects and relations of the world. This is a pragmatic evaluation.

This determination affects the way we think about possibilities. Possible worlds are collections of compossible facts. We think about possible facts and possible worlds in two quite different ways. For possible worlds whose objects and relations are subsets of this world our possibilities are essentially combinatorial. We rearrange some or all of our relationships between some or all of the objects to get our possibilities. It is possible for the mat to be on the cat. (Of course not all combinations count as possible—the mat cannot be larger than itself—but I think that it is still fair to say that the reasoning involved here is basically combinatorial.)[3]

The combinatorial economy, which makes the fundamental predicates valuable for the scientist, is reflected in our conception of possibility.

Wittgenstein believes that this is the only conception of possibility that we can have, and indeed that all possible worlds must contain exactly the same objects. I regard this restriction as inessential to Tractarian Nominalism,

---

[3] I will not attempt here any account of how combinatorial possibility is so restricted.

and indeed, as rather unfortunate. There might be more, or other, objects than there are. There might be other forces in nature, other physical properties and relations. To cash these intuitions we must think of possibilities analogically. There might be other things that play the role of our objects; other things that play the role of our relations.

For the Tractarian Nominalist, these two stages in the construction of possibilia are logically quite different. He takes both objects and relations quite seriously, and puts them on a par. Neither is reduced to the other. So in the combinatorial phase of the construction of possibilia, isomorphic possible worlds are regarded as distinct! There are genuinely different individuals standing in the same relations. At this stage of the game the Tractarian Nominalist is what David Kaplan calls a 'haecciatist.'

In the analogical phase, however, the game is quite different. Suppose that in addition to some objects and relations from our world, there are some 'new' objects $a$, $b$, $c$ and some 'new' relations $R_1$, $R_2$, $R_3$. The only significance of these new blocks lies in their arrangement vis-à-vis each other and vis-à-vis the elements of the real world. A possible world made of 'other' new objects $d$, $e$, $f$ and 'other' new relations $R_5$, $R_6$, $R_7$ arranged in the same way would not be a different world, but the same one. So at this stage, haecciatism fails, and a kind of Ramsey sentence (on the level of the models) approach to the 'new' elements prevails.

## 2. What is Nominalistic about Tractarian Nominalism?

In what sense is Tractarian Nominalism nominalism at all? It is certainly not nominalism in the sense of Goodman ['A world of individuals'] or Quine ['On what there is'], since it finds quantification over properties and relations of individuals just as acceptable as quantification over individuals, and cashes both in terms of facts.

But its properties and relations are all properties and relations of individuals and its facts are all first-order facts: facts 'about' individuals. There are no higher-order facts: facts consisting of relations between relations and objects or relations between relations and relations. In particular, there are no causal relations between relations and individuals.

But can it be quite right to say that there are no higher-order facts? If Socrates is wise then wisdom has the second-order property of being instantiated, and indeed the second-order property of being-instantiated-by-Socrates.

We can say that the-fact-that-wisdom-is-instantiated-by-Socrates is not really a second-order fact but merely a redescription of the first-order fact that Socrates is wise. There is no first-order atomic fact that can be described as the fact that wisdom is instantiated, but that wisdom is instantiated is determined by the first-order atomic facts. What the Tractarian Nominalist means to deny then is that there are any *autonomous* higher-order propositions. *What he means to deny is that there are two distinct possible worlds which share all the same first-order facts.*[4] He will countenance only such higher-order truths as are supervenient in this way on the first-order facts.

Thus Tractarian Nominalism contrasts with the sort of free-swinging Tractarian Platonism that countenances all sorts of higher-order facts, which are not so supervenient. (For example: someone who holds that we can perceive properties and relations, and that such perceptions need not reduce to relations between objects.)

Tractarian Nominalism is motivated by the view of science or epistemology that suggests that either we don't, or cannot, have evidence for such autonomous higher-order facts. Here I think that Tractarian Nominalism makes contact with the epistemological wellsprings of nominalist thought; while Quine–Goodman nominalism can only appeal to philosophical conscience or taste.

## 3. Tractarian–Nominalistic Logic

To what sort of logic should a Tractarian Nominalist subscribe? It has already been emphasized that he can make sense of all the sentences of second-order qualification theory. It should be apparent that second-order quantification theory with the usual quantifier rules is *sound* for him. A generous treatment of properties and relations leads to the conclusion that it is also *complete*!

Suppose that we treat the properties and relations in the world as closed under truth-functions and projection (e.g. if x is a parent of y is a relation, x is a parent is a property; if is happy is a property and is tall is a property, is happy and tall is a property, etc.). (However we feel about such generosity

---

[4] This model theoretic sense of reducibility sets off the Tractarian nominalist from Bergman's 'Elementarist,' who holds quite a different thesis.

we should note that it creates no new truths, since the truths that we can state by reference to this enlarged class of predicates and relations we have already by supervenience.)[5]

Then Tractarian possible worlds with respect to second-order logic correspond to Henkin's *general models* of second-order logic, rather than to what logicians have called the *'natural'* models. The 'natural' models are only natural if we are nominalists in a rather different sense from the one being developed here. In the 'natural' models the property quantifiers are interpreted as ranging over all subsets of the objects of the world (and the relations quantifiers over all subsets of the appropriate Cartesian product of the individual domain). In other words, properties and relations are taken as parasitic on objects. What properties and relations exist in a model depends on what objects do. In Tractarian Nominalism, however, we regard the relational quantifiers as ranging over real physical relations whose existence is every bit as contingent as that of physical objects— and consequently the relations which exist in a world may only corres- pond to some subset of the 'natural' domain, and it is basically this fact which makes second-order logic complete for the Tractarian Nominalist.

Since the Tractarian Nominalist recognizes only such higher-order propositions as are supervenient on first-order models, we cannot extend the argument to higher-order logic. The natural logic for a Tractarian Nominalist is second-order quantification.

## 4. Conclusion

It is clear by now that the metaphysics that I have been referring to by the provocative oxymoron 'Tractarian Nominalism' is neither wholly Tractarian nor wholly nominalistic, although it is in sympathy with strands of both lines of thought. It is perhaps closer to Russell's view in the second edition of *Principia Mathematica* than to the *Tractatus*.[6] (Russell, however, has no thesis of supervenience.) For it, I claim these virtues: First, it shifts our focus of attention from the metaphysics of the subject (or the individual variable) to

---

[5] Note, in this connection, that there is no real need for negative facts, disjunctive facts, etc. in the semantics of Tractarian nominalism since the propositions they are intended to service are supervenient on the first-order atomic facts. This points up the difference between Tractarian Nominalism as here presented, and the positions of Russell, Armstrong, and Bergmann.

[6] Compare Russell, Putnam, and Armstrong.

the metaphysics of the whole assertion, which is really 'where the action is.' That Matilda does the waltz, that Matilda waltzes, that Matilda dances waltzingly, that the waltz is danced by Matilda, etc. should not be thought of as radically metaphysically different; they all come to much the same thing. The Tractarian Nominalist can say that we have here different ways of specifying the same fact, even though the conception of the waltz has found accommodation in quite different parts of speech. Second, I claim that the traditional epistemological motivations for nominalism can be better taken as motivations for Tractarian Nominalism. This is almost a corollary to the first point, since our epistemological concern is primarily with knowledge of truths rather than with acquaintance with the denotata of subject terms or individual variables. Third, I claim that the view helps us to think in a level-headed way about possibilities and possible worlds. In particular, it helps us distinguish stages in the construction of possibilia and it helps us to see at which stage haecciatism is appropriate and at which stage it is not. Fourth, Tractarian Nominalism gives a metaphysical foundation for second-order logic. This comes from treating properties and relations as contingent existents on a par with individuals. Both are ontologically parasitic on, and epistemologically prior to, facts. Both are investigated by empirical science. The criteria of individuation of physical properties in a science at any time may not always be crystal clear, but neither are the criteria of individuation for physical objects.

(It is easier to distinguish the property of being-an-electron from the property of being-a-proton, than to distinguish the electrons from each other!) Given a generous attitude toward closure of properties and relations under truth functions and projections, Tractarian Nominalism supplies a natural reading on which standard second-order logic is not only sound, but also complete. I think that Tractarian Nominalism is a live metaphysical option, and an attractive one.[7]

## Bibliography

Armstrong, D. M. (1978) *Universals and Scientific Realism*, 2 vols. Cambridge: Cambridge University Press.

---

[7] I would like to thank David Armstrong, Alan Code, Ed Gettier, Leslie Tharp, and Kent Wilson for helpful comments on an earlier version of this chapter.

Bergmann, G. (1957) "Elementarism," *Philosophy and Phenomenological Research* 18: 107–14. Reprinted in *Meaning and Existence*, pp. 115–23. Madison, WI: University of Wisconsin Press, 1968.

Goodman, N. (1956) "A World of Individuals." In *The Problem of Universals*. Notre Dame, IN: Notre Dame University Press.

Goodman, N. and Quine, W. V. O. (1947) "Steps Toward a Constructive Nominalism," *Journal of Symbolic Logic* 12: 97–122.

Henkin, L. (1956) "Completeness in the Theory of Types," *Journal of Symbolic Logic* 15: 89–91.

Kaplan, D. (1975) "How to Russell a Frege-Church," [*sic*], *Journal of Philosophy* 72: 716–29.

Putnam, H. (1970) "On Properties." In *Essays in Honor of Carl G. Hempel*, ed. Rescher et al. Dordrecht: D. Reidel. Reprinted in H. Putnam, *Mathematics, Matter and Method*. Cambridge: Cambridge University Press, 1975.

Quine, W. V. O. (1961) "On What There Is." In *From a Logical Point of View*, pp. 1–19. 2nd rev. ed., New York and Evanston: Harper.

——(1976) "Whither Physical Objects?" *Boston Studies in the Philosophy of Science*, 39: 497–504. Dordrecht: D. Reidel.

Russell, B. and Whitehead, A. N. (1927) *Principia Mathematica*. Second ed. Cambridge: Cambridge University Press, especially the preface to the second edition and Appendix C.

# 3

# Logical Atoms and Combinatorial Possibility

> When I speak of 'simples', I ought to explain that I am speaking of something not experienced as such, but known only inferentially as the limit of analysis. It is quite possible that, by greater logical skill, the need for assuming them may be avoided.
>
> Bertrand Russell

One remarkable aspect of the philosophy of logical atomism advocated by Bertrand Russell and Ludwig Wittgenstein is the lack of any careful argument for the existence of logical atoms. Was logical atomism atomistic simply because that was the way in which Russell and Wittgenstein knew how to give a semantics for logic? Russell[1] almost says as much, when pressed in the discussion at the end of the second lecture on logical atomism:

Mr. Carr:[2]   You think there are simple facts that are not complex. Are complexes all compounded of simples? Are not the simples that go into complexes themselves complex?

Mr. Russell:   No facts are simple. As to your second question, that is, of course, a question that might be argued—whether when a thing is complex it is necessary that it should in analysis have constituents that are simple. I think that it is perfectly possible to suppose that complex things are capable of

---

I am indebted to David Armstrong for raising the fundamental question discussed in this essay. For further discussion, see his (1989: ch. 5). I would also like to thank Ernest Adams, John Bell, George Berger, Bill Demopoulos, Wayne Henry, Bill Harper, Joe Lambert, Peter Simons, and Peter Woodruff for valuable discussions. This paper generalizes the (atomic) framework sketched in my (1981).

[2] This is Herbert Wildon Carr—Leibniz scholar, Russell's friend, and organizer of these lectures.

analysis ad infinitum, and that you never reach the simple. I do not think that it is true, but it is a thing that one might argue, certainly. I do myself think that complexes—I do not like to talk of complexes—are composed of simples, but I admit that is a difficult argument, and it might be that analysis could go on forever.

*Mr. Carr:*   You do not mean that in calling the thing complex, you have asserted that there really are simples?

*Mr. Russell:*   No, I do not think that that is necessarily implied.

By 1924, Russell seems even less inclined to make that difficult argument, as indicated by the epigraph to this chapter. That passage from "Logical Atomism" also seems to be quite an explicit denial of an interpretation[3] that takes Russell as believing that he had found the ultimate simples in the world of sense data. Nevertheless, he goes on in the same paragraph to affirm his belief in the existence of simples: "Nevertheless it seems obvious to me (as it did to Leibniz) that what is complex must be composed of simples, though the number of constituents may be infinite." The reference to Leibniz is not casual, for Russell's study of Leibniz is an important source of his logical atomism. The principal thesis of Russell's *A Critical Exposition of the Philosophy of Leibniz*,[4] as he puts it in his preface to the second edition, is that "Leibniz's philosophy was almost entirely derived from his logic." Russell's philosophy of logical atomism was an attempt to derive a more adequate metaphysics from a modern logic that appreciated the crucial role of relations and quantification. It is therefore of some interest to look at Leibniz's argument for the existence of logical atoms, which Russell discusses in *A Critical Exposition of the Philosophy of Leibniz* (105–7). Russell cites Leibniz's letter to de Volder:

A thing which can be divided into several (already actually existing) is an aggregate of several, and . . . is not one except mentally, and has no reality except what is borrowed from its constituents. Hence I inferred that there must be in things indivisible unities, because otherwise there would be in things no true unity, and no reality not borrowed. Which is absurd. For where there is no true unity there is no true multiplicity. And where there is no reality not borrowed, there will never

---

[3] This is the interpretation of Russell advanced by Pears (1985). Pears' essay is one of the few extended discussions on reasons for belief in logical atoms in the critical literature on logical atomism.

[4] (1937).

be any reality, since this must in the end belong to some subject . . . (ibid., 242; cf. also 241–3)

Russell does not seem especially impressed with this argument. He speaks of its "drift," and in his discussion brings in dynamical considerations to prevent Leibniz from appearing foolish. At any rate, he could not have subscribed to it in 1918, for in that case his answer to Carr's last question would have had to be "yes." And in 1959, in his own account of his philosophical development, he denies that atomism was ever an essential part of logical atomism and cites the interchange with Carr in support of this view.[5] For Russell, atomism provided an attractive and natural framework for the semantics of modern logic, but it was not thought of as a metaphysical necessity and he does not advance an argument for its correctness. Wittgenstein does give a cryptic argument in the *Tractatus Logico-Philosophicus*:[6]

> 2.02 The object is simple.
> 2.021 Objects form the substance of the world. Therefore they cannot be compound.
> 2.0211 If the world had no substance, then whether a proposition had sense would depend on whether another proposition was true.

The argument remains problematic even in the light of Russell's explanation of it in his preface to the *Tractatus*. Russell explains that Wittgenstein, like himself, believes that the meaning of a name is its denotation. But, unlike Russell, he does not replace most putative names by quantified variables, but rather goes the other way by construing quantified statements as conjunctions and disjunctions. Quantified variables are to be replaced by names. The names may name a complex or a simple. Now, Russell explains:

His ground for maintaining that there are simples is that every complex presupposes a fact. . . . . The assertion that there is a certain complex reduces to the assertion that its constituents are related in a certain way, which is the assertion of a fact: thus if we give a name to the complex the name only has meaning in virtue of the truth of a certain proposition, namely the proposition asserting the relatedness of the constituents of the complex. (ibid., 12)

Wittgenstein takes it as a *reductio ad absurdum* that whether a proposition has sense would depend on whether another proposition is true, and

---

[5] (1959: 221).    [6] (1922); see also 3.23, 3.24, 4.22, 4.221, 4.2211.

concludes that simples must exist, and indeed must exist necessarily, and that propositions about complexes must be analyzable in principle in terms of propositions about simples.

The argument is still far from clear. Is it to be supposed that a proposition involving a complex lacks a sense if the complex does not exist? If so, then the absurdity is to be had even if there are simples. If not, where is the argument? From an exegetical standpoint, the problem is compounded by 3.24, where Wittgenstein opts for the second answer: "The proposition in which there is mention of a complex, if this does not exist, becomes not nonsense but simply false." This appears to contradict 2.0211, at least on Russell's reading of it.[7] Consistency could be restored by claiming that the semantics of the propositions in which there is mention of a complex works one way under the atomistic hypothesis and another way under its negation; but without independent justification, this would amount to begging the question. Other difficulties with Wittgenstein's argument will emerge in the course of the discussion, but first I need to develop a firmer conception of what a logically atomless metaphysics might be.

## 1. Atoms Cast Out

Let me construct a model atomistic universe. The model will be special,[8] but it will be used to illustrate some fairly general techniques. The atomic individuals will be space–time points. For the sake of simplicity, space–time will be finite and have only one dimension; I take our space–time points to lie on the unit interval. Thus, every real number in the closed interval [0, 1] can be thought of as a name of an atomic individual. I shall want to include chunks of space–time—in this case intervals—among the complex objects, and I shall also want to include more complex "scattered individuals." So for the individuals, let us take the open intervals and close under the Boolean operations of complement and countable union (or fusion) and intersection (or common part). The resulting Boolean algebra is the Borel algebra generated by the open intervals. If I discard the null

---

[7] For a careful critical discussion of Wittgenstein on this point, see Fogelin (1976: 12–15). Other readings of 3.24 may be possible, however.

[8] The example is not so special as one might think. Two metric spaces are said to be Borel-equivalent just in case there is a one-to-one mapping from one onto the other which takes Borel sets into Borel sets and whose inverse takes Borel sets into Borel sets. Every complete separable metric space is Borel-equivalent to the unit interval, [0, 1].

element of this algebra, I am left with the system of the Borel individuals of this universe. The atomic individuals are Borel individuals, as are the closed, open, and half-open intervals, and a rich hierarchy of complex individuals. An element of a Boolean algebra is said to be an atom of the algebra if the only things included in it are itself and the null element. So the atomic individuals—the points—are atoms of the Borel algebra. A Boolean algebra is said to be atomic if every element except the null element contains an atom. The Borel algebra here is atomic.

Each atomic individual will be characterized by the value of the descriptive quantitative variables at it. For simplicity, I consider a single quantity that could be thought of as shade of gray, taking values again ranging from 0 to 1. There are atomic properties (shade of gray = .3) but also complex properties (shade of gray in (.2, .6); in [0, .2] or [.6, 1]; . . .). I construct an atomic Boolean algebra of properties in just the same way as I did the Boolean algebra of individuals. The atoms of this Borel algebra of properties are the atomic properties specifying a sharp value for the descriptive quantity. Facts can be plotted on the unit square, with the x-axis corresponding to individual and the y-axis corresponding to property. A point in this space represents an atomic fact in the sense of Russell and Wittgenstein—that is, the ascription of an atomic relation (in this case a property) to an atomic individual. Since the properties have been derived from quantities, atomic facts will not be independent, and in this sense the Tractarian picture already begins to break down.[9] But given the importance of quantitative variables for the physical description of the world, these complications need to be faced, as Wittgenstein himself realized in "Some Remarks on Logical Form."[10] Nevertheless, a combinatorial theory of possibility with a strong Tractarian flavor is still feasible. The world—being the totality of facts—corresponds to a function from the unit interval into the unit interval. Any such function can be thought of as a possible world.

This atomistic picture is a miniature example of a standard way of describing physical reality. But one might argue that it makes more discriminations than one should attribute to reality. We should have a conception of reality rich enough to accommodate discriminations of any finite degree of precision, but my model goes further than this in discriminating—for instance—

---

[9] And so we do not have the free generators of algebraic logic.    [10] (1929).

between the closed interval [1/4, 1/2] and the half-open interval [1/4, 1/2).
What happens if one bisects the interval [1/4, 3/4]?

Does the midpoint fall away "like a little bit of sawdust"?[11] There is a
tradition that thinks that these questions should have no answer, and that
we should not discriminate between closed, open, and half-open intervals,
and that points should not be thought of as parts of the line. It goes back to
Aristotle and includes—as Russell well knew—his friend Alfred North
Whitehead.[12] It is perhaps Whitehead whom he had in mind when he said,
"It is quite possible that, by greater logical skill, the need of assuming them
could be avoided."[13]

How should we take the atoms out of the standard Borel algebra
picture of the unit interval? Let me follow the intuition that [1/4, 1/2]
and [1/4, 1/2) should be identified because their putative difference is
smaller than any finite discrimination—that is, has length zero. Length is
generalized to the Borel sets as Lebesgue measure. [I could let the complexes include all the Lebesgue measurable sets at the cost of some simplicity of exposition, with no essential difference.] So my general procedure
will be to identify Borel sets that differ by a set of measure zero and let the
resulting entities inherit the Boolean structure from the Borel algebra.
Mathematically, this consists of forming the quotient algebra of the Borel
$\sigma$-algebra modulo the $\sigma$-ideal of sets of measure zero.[14] Two Borel sets are
said to be equivalent if their symmetric difference is a set of measure zero.
Finite or countable unions and intersections of equivalent sets are equivalent. The classes of equivalent sets form the desired quotient algebra. It is
*atomless*. The atoms of the Borel algebra have all gotten identified with the
null set. The elements of this quotient algebra minus the null element can
be thought of as representing the complex parts of the unit interval, in a
way congenial to the intuitions of Aristotle and Whitehead.

Returning to my model universe, we see that it could fail to have logical
atoms in three ways. One might have atomic individuals and nonatomic

[11] See Aristotle "On Generation and Corruption," 316a 34ff.
[12] See his (1919). Russell is aware of Whitehead's basic stance already in 1914; see his (1914).
[13] Russell in his (1936) attempts to implement Whitehead's program for the logical construction of instants.
[14] This example is not so special as one might think. Any separable atomless Boolean measure algebra with measure of the universal element equal to one (i.e., a probability measure) is isomorphic to this quotient algebra with Lebesgue measure. This theorem is due to C. Caratheodory, and is proved in Royden (1963: 321).

properties; atomic properties and nonatomic individuals; or both properties and individuals nonatomic. This illustrates a variety of ways in which Wittgenstein's argument for logical atomism can fail. It fails in the first case because the lack of atomicity is in the algebra of properties rather than the algebra of individuals. It fails in the second case because all individuals are complex but nevertheless have necessary existence. It is not true here that "every complex presupposes a fact." To complete the discussion, I could add contingent individuals to the picture. In a world where one space–time region is very dark and the rest of space–time is very light, I could speak of "the dark spot." The existence of the dark spot is contingent; it presupposes a fact.[15] I can now add another physical variable, "temperature." Then 'The dark spot is hot' would express a proposition. If this proposition is simply false in worlds in which the dark spot does not exist—as Wittgenstein suggests in 3.24—then his argument appears to fail even though the existence of the complex involved is contingent.

## 2. Atoms Recaptured

My specimen atomless Boolean algebra—the Borel sets of the unit interval modulo the sets of Lebesgue measure zero—does not contain point sets, but it can, so to speak, approximate them arbitrarily closely. Thus, we can think of the intervals $\{0, 1\}$, $\{0, 3/4\}$, $\{1/4, 1\}$, $\{1/4, 3/4\}$, $\{3/8, 5/8\}$, $\{7/16, 9/16\}$ as giving increasingly good approximations to the nonexistent point, $1/2$. More abstractly, we can define an approximation set without any reference to a nonexistent entity being approximated, as a set, F, of elements of our Boolean algebra with the following properties:

(1) If $x \in F$ and y in F, then $x \wedge y \in F$.
(2) If $x \in F$ and $x \leq y$, then $y \in F$.
(3) F does not contain the null element.

The third condition is a consistency condition; the second says that, if an element is an approximation, then any element it is contained in is an (perhaps less good) approximation; the first says that, if two elements are approximations, then their common part is an approximation. (If two elements are both members of the same approximation set, then they

---

[15] I leave a precise specification of the example up to the reader.

must have a common part in view of conditions one and three.) Conditions one and two can be combined as follows:

(4)  $x \in F$ and $y \in F$ if and only if $x \wedge y \in F$

An approximation set is maximal if it is not a subset of another approximation set, or, equivalently, if for every element x of the Boolean algebra, either x or its complement is a member of the approximation set. (In algebraic terms, maximal approximation sets are ultrafilters.)

Consider the atomic Boolean algebra consisting of the Borel sets on the unit interval. Here, for each point, the set of Borel sets having that point as a member is a maximal approximation set. This suggests that when we have an atomless Boolean algebra, we may be able to use approximation sets to construct atoms for it. This was, indeed, the leading idea of Whitehead's program to develop geometry by logical construction from an atomless foundation and it is the basis of the "method of extensive abstraction" in his *An Inquiry Concerning the Principles of Natural Knowledge*. That book, however, left many mathematical and logical questions to be answered, and the projected volume of *Principia Mathematica*, which was to have given a rigorous development of geometry from Whitehead's point of view, was never written. The fundamental theorems in this area were not established until the work of M. H. Stone[16] and that of L. H. Loomis and R. Sikorski.[17]

For any Boolean algebra, *B*, we can consider the set, meta*B*, of all *B*'s maximal approximation sets. The set of all subsets of meta*B* is an atomic Boolean algebra taking set union, intersection, and complement as the Boolean operations. Moreover, it contains a replica of the original Boolean algebra as a subalgebra. To see this, let h map members of *B* to subsets of meta*B*. Thus:

(5)  If $x \in B$, then $h(x) = \{F$ in meta$B \mid x \in F\}$.

That is to say that $h(x)$ is the set of all maximal approximation sets that have x as a member. It follows from the definitions of *h* and of maximal approximation sets that *h* preserves the Boolean operations. For example, to see that:

(6)  $h(x \wedge y) = h(x) \cap h(y)$

notice that by the definition of *h*:

[16] (1936).     [17] Loomis (1947); Sikorski (1948).

(7)  F $\in$ $h$(x $\wedge$ y) if and only if (x $\wedge$ y) $\in$ F

and since F is an approximation set, by (4):

(8)  (x $\wedge$ y) $\in$ F if and only if x $\in$ F and y $\in$ F

and by the definition of h again:

(9)  x $\in$ F and y $\in$ F if and only if F $\in$ $h$(x) and F $\in$ $h$(y)

The fact that complement is preserved follows in similar fashion from the definition of $h$ and the fact that the approximation sets in question are maximal.[18] Thus, h is a homomorphism from the Boolean algebra, B, into the field of all subsets of metaB. Call the field of all sets into which h maps an element of B, imageB. A little more argument shows that $h$ is an isomorphism.[19] Thus, imageB is the isomorphic image of B. This is Stone's famous result that every Boolean algebra is isomorphic to a field of sets. For my purposes, it shows how every Boolean algebra can be embedded, in a natural way, in an atomic Boolean algebra.[20]

A Boolean $\sigma$-algebra has more structure than a Boolean algebra, and for this reason the analogue of the Stone representation theorem can fail. That is, a Boolean $\sigma$-algebra may fail to be isomorphic to a $\sigma$-field of sets. The appropriate representation theorem for Boolean $\sigma$-algebras was found independently by Loomis and Sikorski.[21] For every Boolean $\sigma$-algebra, $B$, there are a $\sigma$-field, $S$, of sets, and a $\sigma$-ideal, $I$, of $S$ such that $B$ is

---

[18]  For a maximal approximation set, F, for each element of B, either it or its complement (but not both) is in F. Thus: y $\in$ F if and only if $\neg$ y $\notin$ F, which, together with the definition of $h$, gives the result that $h$ preserves complement.

[19]  The key step is to show that $h$ maps only the null element of B onto the null set. Suppose x is an element of B other than the null element. Then the class, $\{y \in B \,|\, y \geq x\}$, is an approximation set and, by a standard argument, can be extended to a maximal approximation set, F. Then $h$(x) cannot be the empty set because by the definition of $h$, F is a member of $h$(x).

[20]  It should be noted that the proof of this theorem makes essential use of the axiom of choice. Thus, in an intuitionistic setting, a more radical version of an atomless metaphysics might be maintained wherein embeddibility in an atomistic metaphysics is not provable. In this chapter, however, I shall assume classical metatheory.

[21]  Loomis embeds in a larger space than Sikorski. The natural thing to try first would be to make a space of $\sigma$-ultrafilters. But in our example of an atomless Boolean algebra, there are no $\sigma$-ultrafilters. We need less stringent requirements for the sets of the original Boolean algebra, which are to be the points in the space of the representation. Loomis takes them to be the "selection sets" of the original Boolean algebra: sets that for every element of the original Boolean algebra contain either it or its complement. Sikorski, however, works in the Stone space of the original Boolean algebra.

isomorphic to the quotient algebra $S/I$. This shows how every Boolean σ-algebra can be regarded as gotten by the quotient construction illustrated in section 1, from an algebra that can be embedded in atomic Boolean σ-algebra. In particular, an atomless Boolean σ-algebra can be gotten from an atomic Boolean σ-algebra by taking a subalgebra and using the quotient construction.

## 3. Combinatorial Possibility

One of the attractive features of logical atomism is that it makes the combinatorial semantics—the combinatorial theory of possibility—so straightforward. Possibility just consists of rearrangement of atomic individuals, properties, and relations that have been abstracted from atomic facts. If we dispense with the restriction to a fixed domain, we get essentially the quasicombinatorial set-theoretic semantics that is taught in standard logic courses. If one discounts the bad argument in the *Tractatus*, one is left with the conclusion that the real reason why logical atomism was atomistic was simply that Russell and Wittgenstein did not see the way to give a combinatorial semantics for a model of reality that was not atomistic. How can one give such a combinatorial theory of possibility?

Let me consider first the atomistic model of the unit square, with all the points included. Here a possible world is a *function*, $f$, from the unit interval on the x-axis to the unit interval on the y-axis. For every spatial position, x, there is an atomic fact that the shade at x has the value $f(x)$. The world is, in an obvious way, the totality of facts, and a possible world corresponds, in an obvious way, to a totality of compossible facts. From the point of view of strict logical atomism, any function, no matter how wild, qualifies as a possible world. (It need not be continuous, or even measurable.) Here we form possibilities by varying the quantities at each space–time point, like sliding beads on the wires of an abacus. If any function counts as a possible world, a modified principle of independence survives. The choice of a quantity value at one space–time point is independent of the choice of a value at another space–time point.

Such a point function, $f$, mapping x points to y points, induces a set function, $h$, mapping elements of the Boolean algebra of all subsets of the y-axis to elements of the Boolean algebra of elements of the x-axis. Thus:

(10)    $$h(Y) = f^{-1}(Y)$$

$h$ is a function from the Boolean algebra of properties to the Boolean algebra of individuals that preserves Boolean structure:

(11)    $$\begin{aligned} h(Y \cap Z) &= h(Y) \cap h(Z) \\ h(Y \cup Z) &= h(Y) \cup h(Z) \\ h(-Y) &= -h(Y) \end{aligned}$$

That is to say that this is a homomorphism. (It also preserves infinitary Boolean structure, which is to say that it is an $m$-homomorphism for arbitrary cardinal $m$. Thus, it preserves all mereological structure.) If we are interested in well-behaved worlds, given by a Borel measurable function from [0, 1] to [0, 1], then that function induces in the same way a $\sigma$-homomorphism from the Borel algebra of [0, 1] onto itself.

In the context of our atomistic example, the inducing world-function, $f$, is recoverable from the homomorphism, $h$, by considering the unit sets of points—the atoms of the Boolean algebra—on the y-axis. For any point, y, on the y-axis, $h(\{y\})$ is the set of points on the x-axis that $f$ maps to y. For two distinct points, y and y', $h(\{y\})$ and $h(\{y'\})$ must be disjoint because $h$ is a homomorphism. Thus, by considering $h(\{y\})$ for each y, we can reconstruct the point function, $f$, which induces it. The world function, and the homomorphism that it induces, carry the same information.

When we have only atomless Boolean algebras of properties and/or individuals, it makes no sense to talk of points and point functions, but it makes perfect sense to talk of homomorphisms from the Boolean algebra of properties to that of individuals. *This gives us a combinatorial notion of possible worlds, which can be applied even in atomless cases.*

An alternative approach to possibility where we do not have appropriate atomic Boolean algebras might be to put the atoms back in—in the way suggested by the representation theorems discussed in section 2—and then to construe possible worlds set theoretically as the logical atomists did. We might call this a *metacombinatorial* theory of possibility, since we first create an atomic Boolean algebra on the metalevel and then apply the combinatorial theory of possibility to it.

It is of some interest for the theory of possibility to determine the extent to which the two approaches agree or disagree. This is a large question, but one example will serve to show that even in the most favorable cases, the metacombinatorial theory generates a different set of possible worlds than the combinatorial theory. Consider again the unit square. I shall leave the properties atomic but take the algebra of individuals as atomless. Thus, the y-axis is equipped with the Borel $\sigma$-algebra including points but the x-axis is equipped with the Borel $\sigma$-algebra modulo the $\sigma$-ideal of sets of Lebesgue measure zero. A mapping from the y-axis Boolean algebra, By, to the x-axis Boolean algebra, Bx, is a $\sigma$-homomorphism if it is not only a homomorphism, but also preserves countable Boolean joins and meets (unions and intersections; fusions and common parts). [This structure is important for the theory of measure and integration.] A real function, $f$, from [0, 1] to [0, 1] will be said here to induce a $\sigma$-homomorphism, $h$, if for every Borel set $Y$:

(12) $$h(Y) = [f^{-1}(Y)]$$

The square brackets around '$f^{-1}(Y)$' here indicate an element in the quotient algebra, Bx, with which the inverse image of Y is associated. The function, $f$, is Borel measurable if the inverse image under it of every Borel set is a Borel set. In this setting, I shall take $\sigma$-homomorphisms as combinatorial possible worlds and real functions as meta-combinatorial possible worlds. The relationships are as follows:[22]

(A) Each Borel measurable function from [0, 1] to [0, 1] induces a $\sigma$-homomorphism.

(B) Each $\sigma$-homomorphism is induced by a Borel-measurable function.[23]

(C) Two Borel-measurable functions induce the same $\sigma$-homomorphism if and only if they differ on a set of Lebesgue measure zero.

Even if we confine it to measurable functions, the metacombinatorial theory here generates more possible worlds than does the combinatorial theory. For example, the metacombinatorial theory distinguishes between the possible world where $f(x) = 1/2$ for all $x$, and the Dirichlet world where $f(x) = 3/4$ for all rational x and ½ for all irrational x. But these two functions differ only on a set of Lebesgue measure zero, and so by (C) they

---

[22] For details, see Sikorski (1964).

[23] This will be true whenever the property and individual Boolean algebras can be gotten as quotient algebras of the Borel $\sigma$-algebra of a complete separable metric space modulo a $\sigma$-ideal of that space.

are the same possible world in the sense of $\sigma$-homomorphism. (On the other hand, in the completely general case where we impose no regularity conditions, it is possible to have $\sigma$-homomorphisms that are not induced by any point mapping.)[24] The two approaches to possibility are definitely not equivalent.

## 4. Facts and Propositions

Even if there are no logical atoms, we have seen how one can implement a natural theory of combinatorial possibility at the level of possible worlds. *Possible worlds consist of homomorphisms.*

What are the facts in this model and what is the relation of the world to its facts?

Returning to my example, let me say that a possible fact consists of a pair $<X, Y>$ where X is an element of the Boolean algebra of individuals and Y is an element of the Boolean algebra of properties.

The interpretation will be that the space–time region X contains only shades in the quality region Y. If we have a collection of all the facts, F, the world homomorphism can be recovered thus:

$$(13) \qquad h(Y) = \in_i \{ X_i | <X_i, Y> \in F \}$$

Conversely, the world homomorphism determines the facts. For $X, Y$ in the appropriate Borel algebras:

$$(14) \qquad <X, Y> \in F \text{ iff } X \leq h(Y)$$

For all intents and purposes, *the world is the totality of facts.*

For every possible fact $<X, Y>$ there is the corresponding basic proposition. Basic propositions are not, in general, independent. We might close the propositions under finite, countable, or even arbitrary uncountable truth functions. The facts determine the truth values of the basic propositions directly. For them, truth is correspondence with the facts. The truth values of the other propositions are then determined by their truth functions. There is no need to add an additional class of general propositions. Universal propositions are already contained in the class of

---

[24]   See Sikorski (1964: sect. 32).

basic propositions. Let V be the greatest element in the algebra of individuals [i.e., the whole of space–time] and Y be any property. Then <V, Y> is the fact that 'All is Y.' It comes from the world homomorphism mapping Y onto V. Existential propositions are gotten when we close under truth functions. Thus, 'There is some Y' is gotten as the negation of 'All is non-Y.' (Non-Y is in the Boolean algebra of properties if Y is.) Thus, we have quantification without the residual atomism of individual variables.

So far, the points at issue have been illustrated with respect to monadic predication. The picture is much the same for relational predication. Consider two-place relations between space–time regions. In the atomic case, we can visualize pairs of spatial points forming the unit square, with a 'relational' real-valued function taking values in the unit interval lying above the unit square. Without the presumption of atomicity, we can think of a homomorphism from the algebra of relations taking values in the algebra that is the product of the algebra of individuals with itself. Then, if R is a relation and X and X' are individual space–time regions, the relational predication, "RXX' ", is true if the world homomorphism maps R onto a region whose projection onto the first coordinate of the product algebra includes X and whose projection onto the second coordinate of the product algebra includes X'. 'All bears R to All' is true if the homomorphism maps R onto a region of the product algebra whose projection onto each coordinate is the maximal element, V. 'All bears R to some' is true if the homomorphism maps R onto a region whose projection onto the first coordinate is the maximal element and whose projection onto the second coordinate is not the null element.

# 5. Conclusion

Russell did not really have any arguments to offer for the existence of logical atoms, other than that their postulation allowed a simple and elegant version of analytical metaphysics with an associated combinatorial semantics. His considered judgment appears to have been that atomism was not an essential part of the philosophy of logical atomism, its name notwithstanding. And he seems to have been open to the possibility that mathematical tools for a non-atomistic version of logical atomism might be developed in the future. Wittgenstein did have a sort of argument against logical atoms in the *Tractatus*, but it does not stand up well under scrutiny.

Mathematical tools for the analysis of the issue of atomism were subsequently developed by Caratheodory,[25] Tarski,[26] Stone, Loomis, Sikorski, and others. For the concerns of metaphysics, I note four main points. (1) A metaphysics without logical atoms makes perfect sense, either because atomism fails for individuals, or because atomism fails for properties, or both. Atomless Boolean algebras can be constructed as quotient algebras. (2) Logical atomism can always be maintained by inflating one's metaphysics, provided one's metatheory is classical. How this can be done is shown by the representation theorems of Stone for Boolean algebras and of Loomis–Sikorski for Boolean σ-algebras. (3) A combinatorial theory of possibility can be implemented even if atomism fails, by taking possible worlds to be homomorphisms or σ-homomorphisms. This reduces to the standard combinatorial theory in the case of atomism. (4) A combinatorial theory of possibility based on an atomless model and a metacombinatorial theory based on inflating an atomless model to an atomic one as in (2), and then applying the combinatorial theory, give related but different results.

## Bibliography

Aristotle (1941) "On Generation and Corruption." In Richard McKeon, (ed.), *The Basic Works of Aristotle*. New York: Random House.

Armstrong, David (1989) *A Combinatorial Theory of Possibility*. New York: Cambridge University Press.

Caratheodory, C. (1963) *Algebraic Theory of Measure and Integration*. Tr. F. E. J. Linton. New York: Chelsea.

Fogelin, R. J. (1976) *Wittgenstein*. New York: Routledge & Kegan Paul.

Loomis, L. H. (1947) "On the Representation of σ-complete Boolean Algebras," *Bulletin of the American Mathematical Society* 53: 757–60.

Pears, David (1985) (ed.) *The Philosophy of Logical Atomism*. La Salle, IL: Open Court.

Royden, H. L. (1963) *Real Analysis*. 2nd ed. New York: Macmillan.

Russell, Bertrand (1936) "On Order in Time," *Proceedings of the Cambridge Philosophical Society* 32: 216–28.

[25] (1963).
[26] "Foundations of the Geometry of Solids," and "On the Foundations of Boolean Algebra," in his (1956a, b: 24–9, 230–341).

——(1937) *A Critical Exposition of the Philosophy of Leibniz*. 2nd ed. London: Allen & Unwin.

——(1956) "The Philosophy of Logical Atomism." In R. C. Marsh (ed.), *Logic and Knowledge*, pp. 178–281. London: Allen & Unwin.

——(1959) *My Philosophical Development*. London: Allen & Unwin.

Sikorski, R. (1948) "On the Representations of Boolean Algebras as Fields of Sets," *Fundamenta Mathematica* 35: 247–56.

——(1964) *Boolean Algebras*. 2nd ed. Berlin: Springer.

Skyrms, Brian (1981) "Tractarian Nominalism," *Philosophical Studies* 40: 199–206.

Stone, M. H. (1936) "The Theory of Representations for Boolean Algebras," *Transactions of the American Mathematical Society* 40: 37–111.

Tarski, A. (1956a) "On the Foundations of Boolean Algebra." In J. H. Woodger (ed.), *Logic, Semantics and Metamathematics*. New York: Oxford.

——(1956b) "Foundations of the Geometry of Solids." In J. H. Woodger (ed.), *Logic, Semantics and Metamathematics*. New York: Oxford.

Whitehead, Alfred North (1914) *Our Knowledge of the External World as a Field for Scientific Method in Philosophy*. La Salle, IL: Open Court.

——(1919) *An Inquiry Concerning the Principles of Natural Knowledge*. New York: Cambridge University Press.

Wittgenstein, Ludwig (1922) *Tractatus Logico-Philosophicus*. Tr. C. K. Ogden, preface Bertrand Russell. New York: Routledge & Kegan Paul.

——(1929) "Some Remarks on Logical Form," *Proceedings of the Aristotelian Society* 9: 162–71.

# 4

# Strict Coherence, Sigma Coherence, and the Metaphysics of Quantity

## 1. Introduction

In 1955 Abner Shimony introduced a strong notion of coherence, which has become known as strict coherence. It is a variation on a theme by Ramsey and de Finetti: that of testing the coherence of your system of beliefs by seeing how much damage can be done by a cunning bettor with a finite number of bets, each of which you take to be fair. The bettor makes a Dutch Book against you if his bets taken together guarantee that you must suffer a loss; that is to say that no matter what the outcomes of the events upon which bets are placed you suffer a net loss. Let us say that a bettor makes a weak Dutch Book against you if you can suffer a loss but cannot enjoy a gain: that is to say that there are possible outcomes of the events on which bets are made such that you suffer a net loss and no such outcomes which yield a net gain. If no Dutch Book can be made against you, your beliefs are coherent; if—in addition—no weak Dutch Book can be made against you, your beliefs are strictly coherent.

Betting quotients are coherent if and only if they are finitely-additive probabilities. They satisfy the stronger requirement of strict coherence if and only if they are finitely-additive probabilities that assign a positive probability to every possible event (Kemeny, 1955). Coherence is a pragmatic consistency condition. Strict coherence adds to this a requirement of open-mindedness. The strictly coherent agent does not assign probability zero to anything unless it must be judged impossible by

I would like to thank Louis Narens for comments on an earlier version of this chapter.

virtue of the underlying Boolean logic. Strict coherence is epistemologically attractive and was easily implementable in the context of finite
Carnapian inductive logic in which it was introduced. But it has not
played a central role in standard Bayesian theory because of mathematical
difficulties in implementing it in infinite probability spaces. This chapter
will discuss two ways in which strict coherence can be recaptured in
important infinite cases.

There is another natural way in which the notion of coherence can be
strengthened. That is to allow the cunning bettor a countably infinite
number of bets with which to make the Dutch Book (with the net payoff
of an infinite number of bets being defined as usual as the limit of the
sequence of partial sums). We will call the corresponding notion of
coherence sigma-coherence. Real-valued betting quotients are sigma-
coherent if and only if they are sigma-additive (countably additive) probabilities (Adams, 1962). That is to say that the probability of a countable
number of pairwise disjoint events is the infinite sum—the limit of the
sequence of finite partial sums—of those events.

Sigma-additivity is part of the standard modem theory of measure and
integration and has been part of standard treatments of probability since
Kolmogorov's 1933 treatment of probability as a branch of measure
theory. However, some important thinkers—including de Finetti and
Savage—take the position that the imposition of sigma coherence begs
important questions and that sigma-additivity is not in general philosophically justified. And sigma-additivity leads to non-measurable sets, which
themselves merit serious philosophical attention.

What follows is a relatively non-technical introduction to the subject,
developing the interplay between epistemological and metaphysical concerns by means of simple examples.

## 2. Paradoxes of the Infinite

Suppose that a wheel of fortune that you take to be fair is to be spun. The
theory of personal probability should be capable of modeling your beliefs
in such a case. We can take the wheel as having unit circumference so that
the precise outcome of a spin is a point in the unit interval [0, 1), and
outcome events—or outcome propositions—are sets of such points. That
you take the wheel to be fair means that your degrees of belief should be

appropriately translation invariant; that is to say that your probability for the outcome to be in some set of points should be the same as your probability for the outcome to be in a second set of points where the second set is gotten from the first by sliding the points in the original set around the circumference of the wheel by some fixed distance.

Let us suppose to begin with that you have a pre-Pythagorean theory unit interval. For you the points are the rational points and the events are sets of rational points. Now, by a form of argument due originally to Zeno of Elea (see Skyrms, 1983a), you can have neither strictly coherent nor sigma coherent degrees of belief. First, suppose that your beliefs are strictly coherent. By strict coherence each point on the circumference must have some positive probability and by translation invariance those probabilities must all be the same. Then, since there are an infinite number of points, there must be some finite number of points such that the sum of their probabilities exceeds one—violating coherence. Strict coherence is beyond reach.

Next, suppose that your beliefs are sigma coherent. Points cannot have positive probability by the argument of the last paragraph. So each point has probability zero. Then, since the rationals are countable and the whole space is the union of the (unit sets of) points, the whole space must have probability zero by sigma additivity—violating coherence. Sigma coherence is also unattainable.

Pythagoreans already know a flaw in the presuppositions of the foregoing argument. There are more points than the rational points. Perhaps it is all right for the set of rationals to have probability zero, when we expand our space to include the irrationals. Cantorians know that the reals are uncountable, so that sigma additivity does not let us add up the probabilities of the points in the expanded space to get the conclusion that the whole space has probability zero. Sigma coherence—but not strict coherence—appears to have been rescued by a more generous conception of the points on the circumference of our wheel of fortune (see Grünbaum, 1952, 1968).

But there are still problems for sigma coherence in this setting, as shown by a more subtle form of Zeno's argument due to Giuseppe Vitali (1905). Consider the relation between real numbers x, y, defined by: $x - y$ is a rational number. Notice that this is an equivalence relation: (i) $x - x$ is rational (ii) if $x - y$ is rational then so is $y - x$ (iii) if $x - y$ is rational and $y - z$ is rational then so is $x - z$. Therefore it partitions $[0, 1)$ into equivalence classes. Choose one member from each of these equivalence classes to form a choice set, C. For each rational number $r$ in $[0, 1)$ let $C_r$ be the set gotten by translating each member of C a distance $r$ around the circumference of the wheel of fortune. Since the rationals are countable, the sets $C_r$ form a denumerable partition of $[0, 1)$. Any one of these sets can be gotten by translation from any other, so by translation invariance they must have the same probability. By the argument we saw above, coherence precludes these sets from having positive probability. Then they must each have zero probability. But this conflicts with sigma coherence. For if these sets have probability zero, then sigma additivity leads to the conclusion that their union has probability zero. But by coherence their union (= the whole space) has probability one. On the face of it, it seems that sigma coherence is lost![1]

Measure theoretic treatments of probability avoid this conclusion by a variation on an expedient invented by Aristotle in reply to Zeno—that of restricting the applicability of the notion of measure. Aristotle argued that the notion of measure does not apply to points because points are not properly thought of as constituents of the line. Standard measure theoretic probability has no problem with the points having a well-defined probability of zero. Vitali's sets $C_r$ are another matter. But Vitali's sets are rather cognitively remote entities whose existence is only assured by the axiom of choice. Perhaps we do not need to make judgments about them. Accordingly they are taken to have neither positive probability nor zero probability. They are non-measurable sets, to which the concept of probability simply does not apply. The naive idea (still popular in philosophy of language) that any set of points defines an outcome proposition appropriate for degrees of belief is given up.

Thus, in the measure theoretic framework for probability introduced by Kolmogorov in 1933, there are three components to a probability space. First, there is a set of possible outcomes or possible worlds. Second, there is a set of subsets of the possible outcomes. These can be thought of as the outcome propositions that are legitimate objects of degrees of belief. It is

---

[1] One might suspect the intuitive requirement of translation invariance rather than sigma-additivity as the cause of the problem, especially if one is familiar with the difficulties that its counterpart in three-dimensional space causes in the Hausdorff paradox—even without sigma-additivity. However, the demonstration of the existence of a non-measurable set for sigma-additive measure can be carried out without any assumption of translation invariance. These matters fall outside the scope of this chapter, but I discuss them in "Zeno's Paradox of Measure" (1983a).

definitely not assumed that every set of possible outcomes is an outcome proposition. However, to get a rich enough set of outcome propositions on which to build the theory, those propositions are required to form a Boolean sigma algebra, which is to say that they are closed under countable Boolean operations. Third, there is a probability measure defined on the outcome propositions. This maps every outcome proposition to a real number in the interval from 0 to 1 inclusive, such that the probability of a tautological outcome is equal to 1 and the probabilities are sigma additive. There is an illuminating alternative way in which the postulate of sigma additivity can be stated: as an axiom of continuity. This is, in fact, the way in which Kolmogorov introduces it in 1933. A sequence of outcome propositions, each member of which entails the preceding ones and the infinite conjunction of which is inconsistent, must have probabilities that approach 0 in the limit.

To illustrate the Kolmogorov setup in our example, we might—for instance—consider the Borel outcome propositions which correspond to the smallest sigma algebra of sets of points that contain the open intervals.[2] And we might take the probability of an outcome proposition corresponding to an interval as equal to its length, and use sigma additivity to extend this probability measure to all the Borel outcome propositions. This gives us—as desired—a sigma-coherent, translation invariant, probability measure defined on a rich algebra of outcome propositions. This is the Lebesgue probability measure. As an illustration of continuity, consider the sequence of open intervals (0, 1), (1/2, 1), (3/4, 1), whose intersection is the null set and whose probabilities approach 0 in the limit. In this illustration, point sets are measurable and point outcome propositions have probability zero, as do outcome propositions corresponding to countable unions of point sets—for example, the proposition that the outcome is a rational point. Thus the standard 1933 Kolmogorov approach fails to deliver strict coherence and buys sigma coherence at the cost of introducing non-measurable sets which are not legitimate objects of belief. The status of non-measurable sets deserves some philosophical attention. Different positions are possible. For example, de Finetti asks whether we ought not to be able to have degrees of belief about any outcome set: "is

---

[2] These are the Borel-measurable sets. For a somewhat richer notion of outcome proposition, we could consider the Lebesgue-measurable sets, but I will not go into the details of their definition here.

there any justification for this discrimination between sets of different status: the orthodox which we are permitted to consider and the heretical which must be avoided at all costs?" (de Finetti, 1974: 230). If one is willing to give up sigma-coherence, it is consistent with coherence to make all sets measurable (by the Hahn–Banach extension theorem). In our example the sets, $C_r$, would then each have probability zero by finite additivity and translation invariance, but their union would have probability one. This is the approach advocated by de Finetti. On the other hand, some theorists who only impose finite additivity, and thus have the mathematical elbow room available to make all sets measurable, still express reservations about non-measurable sets: "To go further and take seriously comparisons between sets that are not Lebesgue measurable, or even between those that are not Borel measurable, seems to me to be without any implication bearing on reality" (Savage, 1972: 42). I will end this section with a little puzzle for someone who does accept the standard 1933 Kolmogorov theory. Suppose that your degrees of belief in our example correspond to Lebesgue measure on the Borel propositions, as described above. Suppose that you are given the information that the outcome is a rational point. What should your new degrees of belief be? The information that I suppose you to have gotten is a Borel outcome proposition in which you initially had degree of belief zero. So it is a legitimate proposition, but not one where conditional probability gives you a natural way in which to revise your degrees of belief. Still, you haven't learned anything that should upset your initial judgment of translation invariance. But now we are back to the pre-Pythagorean problem with which this section began. You cannot maintain both the symmetry of translation invariance and countable additivity.

## 3. Infinitesimals

Why can't we have strict coherence in our example? Strict coherence requires that we spread positive probability over all the domain of the probability function (except the null set). If you can't cover the wall with the paint in your bucket, perhaps you need more paint.

Zeno's argument uses the Archimedean property of the real numbers. Given a positive probability, E, assigned to the points there is some finite integer, N, such that NE, the probability that one of the N points is the outcome, is greater than one. One way out is to consider probabilities that take their values not in the real numbers, but rather in some non-Archimedean ordered field. This was, in fact, the route favored by Carnap in a manuscript written in 1960 and published posthumously in 1980.[3]

There are various ways to do this. The most elegant is to use non-standard measure theory. The basic construction of infinitesimals comes from Abraham Robinson's (1966) non-standard analysis. Leibniz—at least at one point—thought of infinitesimals as ideal elements which obey the same laws as the real numbers. But the infinitesimals cannot obey literally all the same laws, or we would not be able to distinguish them from real numbers. The question as to which statements about the reals remain true for the infinitesimals was left hanging. Robinson found a way to use model theory to give a very nice answer. Robinson showed how a non-standard model of first-order analysis could incorporate infinitesimals and therefore that the elements of this model must obey all the first-order laws which govern the real numbers.

The crucial property of first-order languages that Robinson uses is compactness: if a set of sentences is such that every finite subset of it has a model, then the whole set in question must have a model. Compactness of first-order languages depends on their limited logical resources—that the logical constants are limited to truth-functions, identity and first-order quantifiers, and the sentences are of finite length. It does not depend on the language's being denumerable. Thus we can consider a first-order language that contains a logical constant for every real number, which is nevertheless compact. (We should note at this point that the proof of compactness in this case is highly non-constructive.) Compactness fails for second-order logic given the 'natural' interpretation of second-order quantifiers having as their domain the power set of the domain of first-order quantifiers. However, if we allow Henkin's (1960) general models in which higher-order quantifiers are allowed to have as their domain arbitrary subsets of their natural domain, higher-order quantification theory is also compact.

We can now sketch the leading idea of the method by which we get a non-standard model of analysis that includes infinitesimal elements. Consider a rich, non-denumerable first-order language which for every real number, $r$, contains a name $O_r$; a relational symbol for every relation on the reals; and an operation symbol for every operation on the reals. Let the theory of analysis consist of all the true sentences of this language and consider that theory, which is the union of the theory of analysis with the set of all sentences of the form $O_r < y$ for each real $r$. Each finite subset of this theory has a model in the reals, so by compactness this theory does as well. Such a model—there are many—is a non-standard model of the real numbers.

It has a much richer structure than that of the real numbers. First, we note that it contains as a substructure, the structure of the reals. The $\star$-function which maps each real number, $r$, onto $o^\star$, the denotation in the non-standard model of its name, is an isomorphism. Each non-standard model contains an isomorphic copy of the reals. When working within the non-standard model, we can simply call these the standard reals. The denotation of the less-than relation in this model totally orders the non-standard reals since the axioms of total order are first order. According to that order, the element that the model assigns to the denotation of y is an infinite element; it is greater than any of the standard reals. There is a first-order sentence which says that every number has a reciprocal and that if x is greater than y then the reciprocal of x is less than the reciprocal of y. Since the non-standard model makes these sentences true, there must be an element of the model that is the reciprocal of the infinite element and less than any positive standard real. This is an infinitesimal element. A rich structure of infinitesimals follows from the fact that they obey all true first-order statements about the reals.

Carnap's hope was that infinitesimal probabilities could be used to preserve strict coherence in infinite probability spaces. In our example, each point on the circumference of the wheel of fortune should get the same infinitesimal probability. Bernstein and Wattenberg (1969) show how this can, indeed, be done. I will again just sketch some of the leading ideas.

Here we have to consider a higher-order language of analysis where we have the resources to refer not only to numbers but also to sets of numbers, and have at our disposal appropriate predicate and operation symbols. The non-standard model of this general structure will be a general model in the sense of Henkin. There is a predicate—*finite*—which in the standard model has as its extension just the finite sets of real numbers. A set which is in the extension of this predicate in the non-standard model will be called a *\*finite* set. Some such sets are, in fact, infinite but they have all the properties of finite sets expressible in our language. In particular, such a set must have a (non-standard) integer as its cardinality. This raises the prospect of doing measure theory just as if we were operating with finite sets.

The general strategy will be as follows: First, pick a *finite* subset of the non-standard reals in the unit interval. Such a subset will be called a sample. Then, using this sample, every subset, A, of the standard reals is assigned a sample measure equal to the proportion of the number of points in the sample that are also in the non-standard counterpart of $A$.[4] The sample measure is constructed from the sample simply by counting—in the non-standard way. The sample can be chosen such that every standard real number is in it. Then the sample will have an infinite non-standard integer, $w$, as its cardinality and a set containing just one real number—that is, an outcome proposition corresponding to a point on our wheel of fortune will have infinitesimal probability of $1/w$. Bernstein and Wattenberg show that the sample can be chosen so that the sample measure also has the other desired properties to a large degree. There is a non-standard probability measure defined on all subsets of the standard reals, such that each non-empty set gets positive probability, and the measure is invariant up to an infinitesimal with respect to translation by any standard real. This probability measure is finitely-additive, but cannot be sigma additive. It is infinitesimally close to Lebesgue measure on the Borel-measurable sets.[5]

Let us take stock of what has been achieved so far. By allowing our probability measure to take values in the richer structure of the non-standard reals, we are able to assure strict coherence and to make all sets measurable. In particular, the Vitali sets of the last section get infinitesimal probability. We can get infinitesimally close to the intuitive requirement of translation invariance. But we cannot have sigma-additivity. The sum of the probabilities of any finite number of Vitali sets is infinitesimal, but the probability of their union is equal to one. So the probability of their union cannot be the limit of the sequence of partial sums. In fact, that limit does not exist!

---

[4] That is to say, let S be the sample. S is *finite* and so has a non-standard cardinality. Now let $A$ be a subset of the standard reals. Its non-standard counterpart, *$A$, is internal, that is to say it is in the domain of the higher-order quantifiers in the non-standard model. Then the intersection of *$A$ with S must also be *finite* and have a non-standard cardinality. The ratio of the latter cardinality to that of S is the non-standard probability assigned to A.

[5] It can be shown in non-standard models of analysis that every non-standard real is infinitesimally close to a unique standard real. Call the second the standard part of the first. Then taking the standard part of a non-standard probability measure of the type described above, we get a finitely additive extension of Lebesgue measure as was described in section 2.

What about sigma coherence? Recall that the connection between sigma-additivity and sigma coherence was only established under the assumption that all the betting quotients and payoffs are real-valued. Suppose that a non-standard bookie offers to sell contracts which pay off $1 if the outcome is in a certain Vitali set, nothing otherwise for the infinitesimal price of $1/$w$. He will sell such a contract for any Vitali set, and for as many as you please. A standard cunning bettor buys one such contract for each Vitali set, thus guaranteeing herself a sure win of $1. But how much does she owe the bookie for the denumerable number of bets? The standard cunning bettor may reason that since any finite number of bets has by the bookie's own lights a price less than any real number, she can give him a penny for all of them and tell him to keep the change—for a Dutch Book profit of 99 cents. But the non-standard bookie will insist on *finite *summation, and so will insist that the total price for the bets is just the dollar won.

Allow me to return to the puzzle with which I ended section 2. In the current setting, it is perfectly reasonable to ask what happens when you condition on the proposition that a rational point is the outcome. The intuitive conclusion is that the probability of hitting a rational point in the first half of the wheel, $[0, 1/2)$, should be equal to $1/2$, and so forth. Bernstein and Wattenberg show that this can indeed be arranged. However, guaranteeing that intuitive regularity and invariance conditions hold for conditional probabilities more generally requires more work and leads deeper into the structure of infinitesimals. In this regard see Parikh and Parnes (1974). Hoover (1980) gives a summary of the upshot of this work for the ideas in Carnap's 1960 manuscript.

## 4. Measure Algebras

Why can't we have strict coherence in our example? Strict coherence requires that we spread positive probability over all the domain of the probability function (except the null set). If you can't cover the wall with the paint in your bucket, perhaps you need less wall. We might pursue strict coherence not by fattening the range of the probability function, but rather by shrinking its domain. Such a course was advocated by Kolmogorov himself in 1948. This approach also has interesting implications for sigma coherence.

There is a tradition, going back to Aristotle, which maintains that the outcome propositions of our example make more distinctions than are justified. Can we really distinguish between an outcome in the closed interval [1/2, 1/4], one in the open interval (1/2, 1/4) and one in the half-open interval [1/2, 1/4)? Not by measurements of arbitrarily high finite precision. Perhaps we should not make the distinction. Let us forget about the first component of the 1933 Kolmogorov picture—the points that serve as possible worlds—and pursue a more metaphysically modest algebra of outcome propositions. Suppose we take the Borel outcome propositions of our wheel of fortune example, identify those whose symmetric difference has Lebesgue measure zero, and let the resulting entities inherit the Boolean structure in the natural way. (Mathematically this consists of forming the quotient algebra of the Borel sigma algebra modulo the sigma ideal of sets of measure zero.) Give each element of this quotient algebra probability equal to the Lebesgue measure of the Borel propositions that correspond to it. This probability on the quotient algebra is strictly coherent. All Borel sets of measure zero got absorbed by its null element. Strict coherence can always be gotten by this sort of quotient construction.[6]

In the foregoing we also end up with sigma coherence, but only because we started out with it by assuming Lebesgue measure. Can we find a technique of comparable generality to the quotient construction, which gets us sigma coherence in this setting? Indeed we can. It is a variation on the idea illustrated in section 2, of getting sigma coherence by enlarging the domain of the probability function.

Now we have two ideas that seem to pull in opposite directions. We can pursue sigma coherence by enlarging the algebra of outcome propositions. We can pursue strict coherence by contracting this algebra by taking the quotient algebra. But can we do both, to get beliefs that are both strictly and sigma coherent? Kolmogorov (1948) and Łoś (1955) show in slightly different ways that we can.

Suppose that we start with a finitely-additive, real-valued probability on a Boolean algebra of outcome propositions. By using the quotient construction, we arrive at a strictly coherent, finitely-additive probability measure on a Boolean algebra. This is what Kolmogorov (1948) calls a metric Boolean algebra. If we take as the distance between two elements of this algebra the probability of their symmetric difference, we satisfy the

---

[6] It should be noted, however, that the plausibility of this degree of belief measure comes from starting with a degree of belief measure, which shared sets of measure zero with the natural physical measure of length.

postulates for a metric space. (The probability of an element can be recovered from the metric as the distance from the null element.) This space may not be complete. If not, by standard methods it can be completed such that the set of elements in the original space is dense in the completed space. There is a natural way to extend the finite Boolean operations to countable Boolean operations on the complete metric space. One uses the metric to define convergence in the natural way—that is, to say that a sequence of elements $x_1, x_2, \ldots x_k, \ldots$ converges to $x$ if the distance between $x$ and $x_k$ converges to zero—and then defines the denumerable sum as the limit of the sequence of finite sums. Continuity, and thus its equivalent sigma-additivity, is an immediate consequence of this construction. Infinite outcome propositions have been constructed as limits of finite outcome propositions so that continuity is automatic. The final product of this construction—a Boolean sigma-algebra with a strictly coherent, sigma coherent probability on it is called a measure algebra.

The demands of strict coherence and sigma coherence, which initially seemed as if they might be in conflict, are reconciled in this measure algebra. What about non-measurable sets? In a sense, the question does not arise. The whole construction is in terms of outcome propositions. The 'possible worlds' of the classical 1933 picture have disappeared. Only the outcome propositions remain, with those in the initial Boolean algebra having primary significance and those introduced by the completion of the metric space having the status of ideal limiting elements.

However, in another sense, the classical picture is not far away. By the representation theorem of Stone, every Boolean algebra is isomorphic to a field of sets, and by the representation theorems of Loomis and Sikorski every Boolean sigma-algebra is isomorphic to an algebra gotten from a sigma-field of sets by the quotient construction. It should be noted at this point that these theorems are non-constructive and use the axiom of choice.[7] So from the current perspective, the possible worlds are as remote as the infinitesimals of the preceding section.

In fact, as Łoś (1955) points out, there is an alternative route from a metric Boolean algebra to a Boolean measure algebra, which takes a detour through the space used in the Stone representation theorem. Consider the field of sets

---

[7] The full strength of the axiom of choice is not needed. What is required is the theorem that every filter can be extended to an ultrafilter, which is strictly weaker. This is equivalent to the compactness theorem of first-order logic.

in the Stone space isomorphic to the original metric Boolean algebra. In the Stone space the finitely-additive measure on this algebra always has an extension to a sigma additive measure on the smallest sigma algebra containing the original algebra. The Stone space automatically supplies the structure needed to expand the range of the probability measure in a way that gives sigma coherence. Taking the quotient algebra with respect to sets of probability zero completes the construction. The result is the same—up to isomorphism—as that given by Kolmogorov's 1948 approach.

The points in the Stone space have a natural philosophical interpretation—a fact which is emphasized by Łoś. Mathematically, they are ultrafilters on the original Boolean algebra. They correspond to maximal infinite stories that can be told using propositions of the original Boolean algebra such that each finite substory is satisfiable. The whole story may not be satisfiable in the original measure algebra, but adding these points to the ontology makes it satisfiable. Thus Kolmogorov, commenting critically on his 1933 framework in his 1948 paper:

> The notion of an elementary event is an artificial superstructure imposed on the concrete notion of an event. In reality, events are not composed of elementary events, but elementary events originate in the dismemberment of composite events.

From this point of view, in which possible worlds are constructions from propositions, it is no mystery why not every set of possible worlds should correspond to a proposition.

Finally, let us return to the puzzle from the end of section 2. From the measure algebra approach of this section there is no proposition that the outcome was a rational point, so you can hardly learn it.

## 5. Conclusion

Starting with epistemological questions about kinds of coherence of degrees of belief, we are led into the metaphysics of quantity. Difficulties in implementing strict coherence in the standard setup seem to be a symptom of a mismatch between two kinds of quantity: quantities of belief and quantities that are the objects of belief. Two ways of restoring strict coherence were considered. The first embraces the infinite, and restores strict coherence by introducing infinitesimal probabilities. It solves the classical problem of non-measurable sets whose existence we only know by non-constructive reasoning, by using a non-standard model of a higher-order language of analysis whose existence is only guaranteed by the non-constructive reasoning. It forsakes sigma additivity, essentially because it uses a different notion of infinite sum than that of the limit of a sequence of partial sums. Considerations of learning by conditioning push this approach deep into the structure of infinitesimals.

The second way of restoring strict coherence insists on the primacy of the finite. Countably infinite Boolean operations are introduced into the algebra of outcome propositions as limiting cases in such a way that sigma coherence is a natural consequence. Strict coherence comes from not taking as real differences that make no difference. Outcome propositions rather than possible worlds are taken as basic so that, in a sense, the problem of non-measurable sets does not arise. The classical picture of Kolmogorov (1933) can be recovered via the representation theorems of Stone, Loomis, and Sikorski, but in such a way that features which initially appeared problematic are no longer troubling. However, it should be emphasized that from this point of view, possible worlds are highly theoretical entities whose existence is established by non-constructive means.

This chapter has been only a brief introduction to the field. Many interesting questions have not been discussed. These include the motivations other than coherentist ones for non-Archimedean ordered beliefs, models of uncertain learning which preserve strict coherence in a setting with infinitesimals,[8] the algebraic surrogate for random variables in a measure algebra setting,[9] and the notions of combinatorial possibility implicit in a measure-algebra metaphysics.[10] Any evaluation of the complex of issues involved will have to be sensitive to the interplay between pragmatic, epistemological, and metaphysical considerations.

# Bibliography

Adams, E. (1962) "On Rational Betting Systems," *Archiv fur Mathematische Logik und Grundlagenforschung* 6: 7–18, 112–28.

Bernstein, A. and Wattenberg, F. (1969) "Non-Standard Measure Theory." In W. A. J. Luxemburg (ed.), *Applications of Model Theory: Algebra, Analysis and Probability*, pp. 1171–85. New York: Reinhart & Winston.

---

[8] See Skyrms (1983b).     [9] See Łoś (1955).     [10] See Skyrms (1993).

Carnap, R. (1980) "A Basic System of Inductive Logic, Part 2." In R. C. Jeffrey (ed.), *Studies in Inductive Logic and Probability*. Berkeley: University of California Press.

de Finetti, B. (1937) "La Prévision: Ses lois logiques, ses sources subjectives," *Annales de l'Institut Henri Poincare* 1: 1–68; tr. as "Foresight: Its Logical Laws, Its Subjective Sources," in H. E. Kyburg, Jr. and H. Smokler (eds.), *Studies in Subjective Probability*, 1980. Huntington, NY: Kreiger.

——(1972) *Probability, Induction and Statistics*. New York: Wiley.

——(1974) *Theory of Probability 1*, tr. A. Machi and A. Smith. New York: Wiley.

——(1975) *Theory of Probability 2*, tr. A. Machi and A. Smith. New York: Wiley.

Grünbaum, A. (1952) "A Consistent Conception of the Extended Linear Continuum as an Aggregate of Unextended Elements," *Philosophy of Science* 19: 290–5.

——(1968) *Modern Science and Zeno's Paradoxes*. London: Allen & Unwin.

Halmos, P. R. (1944) "The Foundations of Probability," *American Mathematical Monthly* 51: 497–510.

Henkin, L. (1960) "Completeness in the Theory of Types," *Journal of Symbolic Logic* 15: 81–91.

Hoover, D. N. (1980) "A Note on Regularity." In R. C. Jeffrey (ed.), *Studies in Inductive Logic and Probability*. Berkeley: University of California Press.

Kemeny, J. G. (1955) "Fair Bets and Inductive Probabilities," *Journal of Symbolic Logic* 20: 263–73.

Kolmogorov, A. N. (1933) *Grundbegriffe der Wahrscheinlichkeitsrechnung*. Berlin: Springer; tr. as *Foundations of the Theory of Probability*. New York: Chelsea, 1950.

——(1948) "Algèbres de Boole métriques completes," Zjazd Matematyków Polskich. Appendix to the Annals of the Polish Society of Mathematicians 20: 21–30; tr. Richard Jeffrey as "Complete Metric Boolean Algebras," *Philosophical Studies* 77(1) (1995): 57–66.

Loomis, L. H. (1947) "On the representation of σ-complete Boolean Algebras," *Bulletin of the American Mathematical Society* 53: 757–60.

Łoś, J. (1955) "On the Axiomatic Treatment of Probability," *Colloquium Mathematicum* 3: 125–37.

Parikh, R. and Parnes, M. (1974) "Conditional Probabilities and Uniform Sets." In A. Hurd and P. Loeb (eds.), *Victoria Symposium on Non-Standard Analysis*. New York: Springer Verlag.

Ramsey, F. P. (1931) "Truth and Probability." In R. B. Braithwaite (ed.), *The Foundations of Mathematics and Other Essays*. New York: Harcourt Brace.

Robinson, A. (1966) *Non-Standard Analysis*. Amsterdam: North-Holland.

Savage, L. J. (1972) *The Foundations of Statistics*, 2nd ed. New York: Dover (1st ed., New York: Wiley, 1954).

Shimony, A. (1955) "Coherence and the Axioms of Confirmation," *Journal of Symbolic Logic* 20: 1–28.

Sikorski, R. (1948) "On the Representations of Boolean Algebras as Fields of Sets," *Fundamenta Mathematica* 35: 247–56.

Skyrms, B. (1983a) "Zeno's Paradox of Measure." In R. S. Cohen and L. Lauden (eds.), *Physics, Philosophy and Psychoanalysis: Essays in Honor of Adolf Grünbaum*, pp. 223–54. Dordrecht: Reidel, and Chapter 1 in this volume.

——(1983b) "Three Ways to Give a Probability Assignment a Memory." In John Earman (ed.), *Testing Scientific Theories* (Minnesota Studies in the Philosophy of Science, vol. 10). Minneapolis, MN: University of Minnesota Press.

——(1993) "Logical Atomism and Combinatorial Possibility," *Journal of Philosophy* 90: 219–32, and Chapter 3 in this volume.

Stone, M. H. (1936) "The Theory of Representations for Boolean Algebras," *Transactions of the American Mathematical Society* 40: 37–111.

Vitali, G. (1905) *Sul problema della misura dei gruppi de punti di una retta*. Bologna: Gamberini e Parmeggiani.

# PART II

# Coherent Degrees of Belief

# Introduction

Chapter 5 in Part II, "Higher-Order Degrees of Belief," was written at a time when, at least in some quarters, talk about higher-order subjective probabilities was dismissed as nonsense. The first objective of the essay was to separate issues that were sometimes confused, to clarify the subject, and to delineate those kinds of higher-order probabilities that should really be non-controversial. The second objective was to present a way in which Richard Jeffrey's probability kinematics could be derived by conditioning in a framework of higher-order probabilities. I found out later that I. J. Good had had the same idea. Maximum entropy inference can be analyzed along the same lines, but in a later essay, "Updating, Supposing and MAXENT," I suggest a different view of the matter (see Chapter 8 in this volume).

One of the many justifications for taking rational degrees of belief to have the structure of probabilities is de Finetti's coherence arguments. If you violate the probability structure, you can be "Dutch Booked" or "money pumped" and if you respect it, you can't be money pumped. Various intemperate philosophical objections in the literature can be defused by taking the unit of currency to be your von Neumann–Morgenstern utilities. Doing utility theory at the same time as probability completes the picture in an elegant way. The question then arises whether there is a comparable coherence argument for rules of belief change in the light of new evidence. There were claims in the philosophical literature that this was impossible, but David Lewis produced just such a Dutch Book argument for conditioning on the evidence. Related arguments had already been put forward by Bayesian statisticians. Philosophical doubters replied that this "dynamic," "diachronic" Dutch Book would not work because the incoherent updater would somehow "see it coming" and refuse to bet. The short note "A Mistake in Dynamics Coherence Arguments?" shows that the objection is wrong. If we state Lewis' argument precisely, then under the assumptions of the argument, the feckless incoherent updater will take all the wagers involved in the Dutch Book, regarding each—at the time it is offered—as a way of cutting his losses.

The Dutch Book for conditioning on evidence raises the question as to whether there is also some kind of coherence argument for Richard Jeffrey's belief change by probability kinematics. Probability kinematics is always kinematics with respect to a certain partition—depending on what the uncertain evidence affects. Any coherence argument must then be relative to qualitative conditions on the learning situation that specifies the relevant partition. Then one can, indeed, give appropriate Dutch Book theorems. See Armendt (1980) and Chapter 7 in this volume.

One might wonder whether there might be more general principled rules for updating on uncertain evidence. E. T. Jaynes and others have proposed the principle of maximum entropy (MAXENT) as such a rule. Given a constraint on a posterior, the rule is to choose the posterior satisfying the constraint that minimizes the Kullback–Leibler divergence from the prior. There is no Dutch Book argument supporting this rule, only plausibility arguments. In fact, in an example due to Friedman and Shimony, MAXENT escapes dynamic incoherence by a hair's breadth. In Chapter 8 I argue that the maximum entropy rule has been misconceived as an updating rule (a way of assimilating new evidence) when it is properly a supposing rule (a rule for counterfactual or subjunctive suppositions).

What can one say in general about coherence across time when we lack even the distinguished partitions of probability kinematics? This is the general setting for Jeffrey's philosophy of "radical probabilism." Bas van Fraassen (philosophy) and Michael Goldstein (statistics) provided Dutch Book arguments that showed that coherence requires that one's probabilities today must be one's expectation of one's probabilities tomorrow. Generalizing to many tomorrows gives the Martingale property. Two chapters in this volume—"The Structure of Radical Probabilism" (Chapter 9) and "Diachronic Coherence and Radical Probabilism" (Chapter 10)—discuss the import of Martingale property and of Martingale convergence theorems for the value of knowledge and for inductive skepticism in the context of radical probabilism. The latter chapter, written in memory of Dick Jeffrey, uses arbitrage theory to make diachronic coherence fundamental. Static coherence results are then recovered given extra assumptions. Relaxing the assumptions allows, for instance, the use of dynamic coherence arguments in an intuitionistic setting.

# Bibliography

Armendt, Brad (1980) "Is there a Dutch Book Theorem for Probability Kinematics?" *Philosophy of Science* 47: 583–8.

Good, Irving John (1981) "The Weight of Evidence Provided by Uncertain Testimony or From an Uncertain Event," *Journal of Statistical Computation and Simulation* 13: 56–60.

# 5

# Higher–Order Degrees
# of Belief

It is hardly in dispute that people have beliefs about their beliefs. Thus, if we distinguish degrees of belief, we would not shrink from saying that people have degrees of belief about their degrees of belief. It would then be entirely natural for a degree-of-belief theory of probability to treat probabilities of probabilities. Nevertheless, the founding fathers of the theory of personal probability are strangely reticent about extending that theory to probabilities of higher order. Ramsey does not consider the possibility. De Finetti rejects it. Savage toys with it, but decides against it. I. J. Good (1965) and E. T. Jaynes (1958) put the mathematics of higher-order probability to work, but remain rather non-committal about its interpretation. This reticence is, I believe, ill-founded.

I will argue here that higher-order personal probabilities are legitimate, non-trivial, and theoretically fruitful. In section 1, I will defend the conception of higher-order personal probabilities against charges of inconsistency, illegitimacy and triviality. In section 2, I will illustrate one aspect of their theoretical fruitfulness in connection with the question of the laws of motion for rational belief, and the relations between probability kinematics, the information theoretic approach to statistics, and conditionalization.

## 1. The legitimacy of higher-order
## personal probabilities

The worst suspicion that has been voiced about higher-order probabilities is that they lead to an actual *inconsistency*. Thus, in the development of his theory in terms of conditional probabilities of propositions in *Probability and the Weighing of Evidence*, ch. III, I. J. Good takes pains to exclude higher-order probabilities: "it will be taken that the propositions *E, H, etc.* never involve probabilities or beliefs" (Good, 1950: 19). With regard to this restriction he makes the following comment:

> The development of the abstract theory must follow the rules of ordinary logic and pure mathematics. Hence we could, at this stage, hardly allow the propositions E, F, H, etc. to involve probabilities . . . To what extent this restriction may be relaxed is an interesting question. If it were entirely relaxed . . . the resulting theory would have some convenience, but it would also be confusing and might even be self-contradictory. (Good, 1950: 20)

Good does not spell out the inconsistency that he has in mind, so we can only speculate as to the nature of the perceived danger. It is, of course, possible to blunder into an inconsistency when treating propositions and propositional attitudes. Suppose one maintained that there is a set of all propositions $P$; that for any subset $S$ of that set, there is a proposition to the effect that George believes just the members of $S$; that if $S$ and $S'$ are distinct sets, the propositions to the effect that George believes just the members of these sets respectively are distinct propositions. One would then be maintaining that there is a set $S$, whose power set can be mapped into it, which is impossible. There are various variations one can play on this. In particular, what can be done with belief can, *a fortiori*, be done with probability. The set of probability distributions over a given set of propositions is of greater cardinality than the initial set of propositions. There is some reason to believe that Good has this sort of difficulty in mind. He touches on the matter again in the next chapter. "Perhaps the most obvious method would be to extend the meaning of the word 'proposition' so as to allow it to refer to probabilities, but this course may lead to logical difficulties," a remark which receives the following amplification in a footnote: "it may require a 'theory of types' as in symbolic logic" (Good, 1950: 41).

The moral of this story for those who wish to consider higher-order probabilities is simply, "Be careful." We know how to avoid such contradictions. One can start with some ground-level set of propositions (without any claims to exhaustiveness), and build a language–metalanguage hierarchy on top of it, adding at each level propositions about the probabilities of lower-level propositions. (I take it that this sort of idea is what is behind Good's reference to types.) This is not to say that the story is uninteresting for ontologists who wish to think in some sense about all propositions. And psychological theorists who are interested in propositional attitudes may well draw the conclusion that the hierarchy shouldn't be run up so high that the results won't fit in their subjects' heads. But the fear that considerations of probabilities of probabilities *must* involve presuppositions of the sort that led in our story to an inconsistency is groundless. (For an explicit construction of a system of higher-order personal probabilities, see Gärdenfors (1975).)

Another way in which probabilities of probabilities have been thought to cause logical difficulties is embodied in a paradox due to David Miller (1966). The paradox can be put as follows:

Premiss 1: $Pr(\text{not}-E) = Pr[E$ given that $Pr(E) = Pr(\text{not}-E)]$.
Premiss 2: $Pr[E$ given that $Pr(E) = Pr(\text{not}-E)] = 1/2$.
Conclusion: $Pr(\text{not}-E) = 1/2$.

Since the proof is for any proposition, $E$, we have not just an absurdity, but also an inconsistency with the rules of the probability calculus.

This paradox generated a surprising amount of discussion in the journals, but it really should be transparent to anyone who has paid attention to recent philosophy of language, for it rests on a simple *de dicto–de re* confusion. (Let us remember that the probability contexts at issue are intensional; the probability that the morning star = the evening star may not equal the probability that the morning star is the morning star.) Consider premiss 1. Its plausibility depends on the appropriate *de re* reading of the right-hand expression: '$Pr[E$ given that $Pr(E) = Pr(\text{not-}E)]$'. That is, in Donellan's terminology, the embedded description '$Pr(\text{not-}E)$' is to be thought of *referentially*. If the actual probability of not-$E$ has a certain value, say 3/4, then I think of the embedded description '$Pr(\text{not-}E)$' having as its sole function the designation of this value. There is nothing wrong with:

$$3/4 = PR[E \text{ given that } Pr(E) = 3/4]$$

or indeed with its generalization:

$$a = PR[E \text{ given that } Pr(E) = a]$$

(assume that $PR[Pr(E) = 3/4] \neq 0$, so that the conditional probability is well defined in the standard way) where '$a$' is rigid designator: that is, a name which designates the same numerical value at every point in the space. I will call this principle *Miller's principle*. Those who have followed the development of modal logic will already know that we invite no additional difficulty by universally generalizing Miller's principle to:

$$\text{for any } x, x = PR[E \text{ given that } Pr(E) = x]$$

provided that we restrict universal specification to rigid designators of the type indicated. We shall see that Miller's principle has a genuine significance independent of Miller's paradox.

The second premiss of Miller's paradox depends on a *de dicto* reading for its plausibility. It requires that the description, '$Pr$(not-$E$)' be taken attributively rather than referentially. We are to think of it as designating at a point in the probability space the value of the random variable at that point in the probability space, not as a rigid designator of a numerical value. Likewise for the description '$Pr(E)$'.

It is evident, then, that Miller's paradox is simply a fallacy of equivocation. The plausibility of the first premiss depends on reading 'the probability of $E$' attributively and 'the probability of not-$E$' referentially. The plausibility of the second depends on reading them both attributively. If both are given a uniform attributive reading, and the probability of $E$ is not, in fact, 1/2, then the first premiss is false, and can be derived from Miller's principle only by a fallacious universal specification.

These are the two arguments I know that allege a formal inconsistency in the higher-order probability approach. I would say nothing more about formal inconsistency were it not that some reputable philosophers continue to have suspicions (if not arguments) in these directions. Though it may be a case of bringing out a cannon to swat a fly, I still feel obliged to point out that there is implicit in de Finetti's work a proof of formal consistency for a theory of second-order probabilities: simply interpret *pr* as relative frequency probability (i.e. probability conditional on relative frequency. Indeed any way of explaining *pr* as 'objectified' probability relative to a partition will do. See Jeffrey (1965: ch. 12).) This is not the intended interpretation, but it suffices to settle the question of consistency.

One might, however, hold that, although formally consistent, a theory of higher-order *personal* probabilities is, in some way, *philosophically* incoherent. This appears to be de Finetti's position. De Finetti adopts an *emotive* theory of probability attribution (de Finetti, 1972).

Any assertion concerning probabilities of events is merely the expression of somebody's opinion and not itself an event. There is no meaning, therefore, in asking whether such an assertion is true or false or more or less probable . . . speaking of unknown probabilities must be forbidden as meaningless.

If probability attributions are merely ways of evincing degrees of belief, they do not express genuine propositions and are not capable themselves of standing as objects of probability attribution.

De Finetti's positivism stands in sharp contrast to Ramsey's pragmatism:

> There are, I think, two ways in which we can begin. We can, in the first place, suppose that the degree of belief is something perceptible by its owner; for instance that beliefs differ in the intensity of a feeling . . . of conviction, and that by the degree of belief we mean the intensity of this feeling. This view . . . seems to me observably false, for the beliefs we hold most strongly are often accompanied by practically no feeling at all . . .
>
> We are driven therefore to the second supposition that the degree of belief is a causal property of it, which we can express vaguely as the extent to which we are prepared to act on it.
>
> . . . the kind of measurement of belief with which probability is concerned is . . . a measurement of belief *qua* basis of action. (Ramsey, 1926: 71)

For Ramsey, then, a probability attribution is a theoretical claim. It is evident that on Ramsey's conception of personal probability, higher-order personal probabilities are permitted (and indeed required). (It is perhaps also worth noting that anyone who takes Ramsey's view of degrees of belief, and is willing to accept personal probabilities of propensities, or propensities of propensities, must also accept second-order personal probabilities, for on Ramsey's view personal probabilities *are* a kind of propensity.)

Even from de Finetti's viewpoint, the situation is more favorable to a theory of higher-order personal probabilities than might at first appear. For a given person and time, there must *be*, after all, a proposition to the effect that that person then has the degree of belief that he might evince by uttering a certain probability attribution. De Finetti grants as much:

> The situation is different of course, if we are concerned not with the assertion itself but with whether "someone holds or expresses such an opinion or acts according to it," for this is a real event or proposition. (de Finetti, 1972: 189)

With this, de Finetti grants the existence of propositions on which a theory of higher-order personal probabilities can be built, but never follows up this possibility.

Perhaps this is because of another sort of philosophical objection to second-order personal probabilities, which I think is akin to the former in philosophical presupposition, though not in substance. Higher-order personal probabilities are well defined all right—so this line goes—but they are trivial; they only take on the values zero and one. According to this story, personal probabilities—if they exist at all—are directly open to introspection; so one should be certain about their values. If my degree of belief in $p$ is $x$, then my degree of belief that my degree of belief in $p$ is $x$ will be one, and my degree of belief that my degree of belief in $p$ is unequal to $x$ will be zero. Put so baldly, the objection may seem a bit silly, but I will discuss it because I think that something like it often hovers in the background of discussions of personal probability. But, first, I would like to point out that this objection has a much narrower scope than the previous one. According to the view now under consideration, it is perfectly all right to postulate non-trivial personal probabilities about personal probabilities, if they are my probabilities now about your probabilities now or my probabilities now about my probabilities yesterday or tomorrow. What becomes trivial, according to this view, are my probabilities now about my probabilities (that I am introspecting) now.

The foregoing objection is an expression of a form of positivism which most philosophers would consider a combination of bad psychology and bad epistemology. Ramsey's pragmatism is again good medicine. If we focus on degrees of belief *qua* basis of action rather than the intensity-of-feeling notion, there is much less reason to put so much weight on introspection. (It is perhaps worth a passing remark that those philosophers who argue that personal probabilities don't exist because they can't introspect them are relying on the same positivistic preconceptions.) For a dispositional sense of belief, the status of my beliefs about my beliefs now is not so different in principle from the status of my beliefs now about my beliefs yesterday, or indeed about the status of my beliefs now about your beliefs now (although there will typically be differences in degree). In a word, the dispositional sense of belief makes sense of the possibility that someone may not *know his own mind* with certainty, and thus makes sense of this last disputed case. (See Jeffrey (1974) for a discussion of second-order preferences, desires, and probabilities.)

I should mention at this point that some philosophers do adopt a pragmatic, dispositional sense of belief but do so in such a rigid operationist way that they are led to have verificationist doubts about the case in question. The following argument has been made to me in conversation:

Probability is a disposition to bet in certain ways. To test his second-order degrees of belief, we must get him to bet on his first-order degrees of belief. To determine the payoff on this bet we must test his first-order degrees of belief. To do this we must get him to bet on ground-level propositions. But the ratios at which he bets on these propositions may be distorted by his efforts to protect his previous higher-order wagers.

To this objection there is both an internal and external reply. The internal reply is that we can ameliorate the bias by making the first-order bets small with respect to the second-order bets. The external reply is that one surely need not be so rigidly operationist as to assume that the *only* way that one can gain evidence for a degree of belief is by making a wager. The pragmatic notion of probability that Ramsey espouses in "Truth and Probability" is by no means so rigid. Ramsey thinks of personal probabilities as theoretical parts of an imperfect but useful psychological model, rather than as concepts given a strict operational definition. Ramsey's point of view is, I think, infinitely preferable to either the left-wing positivism implicit in the objection just discussed, or the right-wing positivism of the one preceding it.

There is some psychological evidence, however, which suggests that even Ramsey's modest claims of approximate truth for the theory of personal probability as a psychological theory may be overstated. Actual preferences often appear to be ill-defined, or, where defined, incoherent. Depending on how bad things really are (I will not try to evaluate that here), it may be better to stress the normative rather than the descriptive aspect of the theory of personal probability. According to this view, the theory of personal probability is a prescription for coherence, just as the theory of deductive logic contains prescriptions for consistency. It is this strand of thought that is really fundamental, I think, in "Truth and Probability" and it remains even if the average man proves more incoherent than Ramsey expected. Let us notice now that if the theory of personal probabilities is conceived of as medicine, then we need second-order medicine for our second-order degrees of belief just as we need first-order medicine for our first-order degrees of belief. Higher-order personal probabilities remain a natural and indeed an inescapable part of the theory of personal probability.

I hope that in the preceding I have been able to sweep away some of the philosophical debris that has played a part in blocking the development of a theory of higher-order personal probabilities. But even when one is convinced that the conception is consistent and philosophically legitimate, then the question remains as to whether they are of any special interest. Savage's brief discussion in *The Foundations of Statistics* is along these lines:

there seem to be some probability relations about which we feel relatively "sure" as compared with others. When our opinions, as reflected in real or envisaged action, are inconsistent, we sacrifice the unsure opinions to the sure ones . . . There is some temptation to introduce probabilities of a second order so that the person would find himself saying such things as "the probability that $B$ is more probable than $C$ is greater than the probability that $F$ is more probable than $G$." But such a program seems to meet insurmountable difficulties . . .

If the primary probability of an event $B$ were a random variable $b$ with respect to secondary probability, then $B$ would have a "composite" probability, by which I mean the (secondary) expectation of $b$. Composite probability would then play the allegedly villainous role that secondary probability was intended to obviate, and nothing would have been accomplished.

Again, once second order probabilities are introduced, the introduction of an endless hierarchy seems inescapable. Such a hierarchy seems very difficult to interpret, and it seems at best to make the theory less realistic, not more.

Finally, the objection concerning composite probability would seem to apply, even if an endless hierarchy of higher order probabilities were introduced. The composite probability of $B$ would here be the limit of a sequence of numbers, $E_n$ $(E_{n-1} ( \ldots E_2(P_1(B)) \ldots ))$, a limit that could scarcely be postulated not to exist in any interpretable theory of this sort . . .

The interplay between the "sure" and "unsure" is interestingly expressed by de Finetti thus: "The fact that a direct estimate of a probability is not always possible is just the reason that the logical rules of probability are useful. The practical object of these rules is simply to reduce an evaluation, scarcely accessible directly, to others by means of which the determination is rendered easier and more precise". (Savage, 1972: 57–8)

In this passage, Savage appears to have two rather different motivations in mind for higher-order probabilities. The first is the consideration that he begins with: that there is a second-order aspect of our beliefs, i.e. 'sureness' about our first-order beliefs, which is not adequately reflected in the first-order probability distribution alone. The second is the idea that second-order distributions might be a *tool* for representing vague, fuzzy, or ill-defined first-order degrees of belief with greater psychological realism than a first-order distribution would provide. This second motivation is implicit in the discussion of the "insuperable difficulties," and becomes even clearer in a footnote to the second edition:

One tempting representation of the unsure is to replace a person's single probability measure $P$ by a set of such measures, especially a convex set. (Ibid., 58)

I think that it is very important to carefully distinguish these two lines of thought. Savage's "insuperable difficulties" are serious objections against the suggestion that second-order distributions provide a good mathematical representation of vague, fuzzy, or ill-defined first-order beliefs. Indeed, an apparatus of second-order distributions presumes more structure than conventional first-order distributions rather than less, and the first-order structure can be recovered as an expectation (provided we have Miller's principle: see Skyrms, 1980: Appendices 0 and 1). But *however* we wish to model vague or fuzzy first-order degrees of belief, we shall, given beliefs about beliefs, wish to model vague or fuzzy second-order degrees of belief as well. Interval valued, fuzzy logical, and convex set representations of imprecise first-order degrees of belief are not *competitors* with second-order probabilities; they are aimed at a different problem. If we then return to Savage's first motivation, we find that vis-à-vis this problem, the "insuperable objections" are not objections at all. The extra structure of higher-order probabilities is just what is wanted. That two second-order distributions for $pr(p) = x$ can have the same mean but different variance gives us a representation of the intuitive phenomenon with which Savage broached the discussion: two people may have the same first-order probabilities, but different degrees of sureness about them.

There is one further strand in the passage from Savage that invites comment. Savage speculates that the notion of sureness may give us some insight into probability *change*: "When our opinions, as reflected in real or envisaged action are inconsistent, we sacrifice the unsure opinions to the sure ones." One version of Savage's first objection might hold that everything that we can know about probability change is already encoded in the first-order conditional probabilities, so that any second-order information must be either redundant or irrelevant. Such a position rests on several questionable premises; but there is one in particular to which I would again like to call attention. That is, that second-order probabilities should only be treated *instrumentally*, i.e. that the relevant inputs and outputs of probability change must always be first-order. Once we take the philosophical position that higher-order probabilities can refer to something as real as first-order probabilities, it opens up the possibility of conditionalizing at a higher level, e.g. conditionalizing on some statement about the first-order probability distribution. It therefore opens up possibilities that simply do not exist as we restrict ourselves to the first-order setup. I believe that these possibilities do indeed illuminate questions of probability change. I will give a brief illustration of this in section 2 of this chapter.

## 2. Higher-order personal probabilities and the question of the laws of motion for rational belief

The 'rational' in 'rational belief' refers to *coherence*. The idea of justifying the probability calculus as embodying laws of *static* coherence for degrees of belief occurred independently to Ramsey and de Finetti. Each had the idea that qualitative constraints could lead to a representation theory for probability. And each had the idea of a Dutch Book theorem; a theorem to the effect that if probabilities are taken as betting quotients, then someone who violates the laws of the probability calculus would be susceptible to a system of bets, each of which he considers fair or favorable, such that he would suffer a net loss no matter what happened. A great deal turns on the significance of these theorems, and indeed this has been the subject of some philosophical dispute. I think that the way in which Ramsey states the Dutch Book theorem is enlightening:

> If anyone's mental condition violated these laws, his choice would depend on the precise form in which the option were offered him, which would be absurd. He could then have a book made against him by a cunning bettor and would then stand to lose in any event. (Ramsey, 1926: 84)

It is clear that what is important for Ramsey about coherence, and what makes it for him a kind of consistency, is that someone who is incoherent is willing to bet on the same betting arrangement at two different rates, depending on how that arrangement is described to him. The remark about the cunning bettor is simply a striking corollary to this fundamental theorem. Thus, let the criterion of individuation of a *betting arrangement* be the schedule specifying the *net payoff* on each possible outcome. The additivity law for probability is then justified by the observation that the same betting arrangement may either be described as a bet on a disjunction of two mutually exclusive propositions, or as the upshot of separate bets on each of the two propositions. The condition that the betting arrangement be evaluated consistently, no matter which advertising brochure accompanies it, is just that the probability of the disjunction be equal to the sum of the probabilities of the disjuncts. Along the same lines, de Finetti provides a justification for the customary definition of conditional probability:

$$Pr(q \text{ given } p) = Pr(p\&q)/Pr(q)$$

via the notion of a conditional bet. A bet on $q$ conditional on $p$ is called off if $p$ is false, otherwise won or lost depending on the truth value of $q$. Again such a conditional betting arrangement can be redescribed as the upshot of separate bets on $p$ & $q$ and against $p$, with the consequence that coherence *requires* the foregoing treatment of conditional probability.

I find these arguments very compelling. And I think that some philosophers who fail to find them compelling fail to do so because they focus on the striking corollary about the cunning bettor rather than on the fundamental theorem. "Must the rational man always behave," they ask, "as if the world were a cunning bettor, lying in wait to make a Dutch Book?" Asking the question in this way appears to make the subjective theory of probability rest on a kind of methodological paranoia that is usually associated only with the theory of games. This is, I think, the wrong way to look at the question. Of course there are situations in which a little incoherence won't hurt you, just as there are situations in which a little deductive inconsistency won't hurt you. (Remember, it is Ramsey's remark that he believes each of his beliefs but believes that at least one of his beliefs is false.) Of course there are situations in which it would be too costly to remove an incoherence to be worth it, just as there are situations in which it would be too costly to remove a deductive inconsistency to be worth it. Ramsey's pragmatism is not William James' pragmatism! But this is all, I think, beside the point. At a deeper level, Ramsey and de Finetti have provided a way in which the fundamental laws of probability can be viewed as pragmatic consistency conditions: conditions for the consistent evaluation of betting arrangements no matter how described.

The question naturally arises as to whether there is any analogous coherence argument for ways of *changing* degrees of belief. Ramsey strongly suggests that he believes that there *is* such an argument for conditionalization:

Since an observation changes (in degree at least) my opinion about the fact observed, some of my degrees of belief after the observation are necessarily inconsistent with those I had before. We have therefore to explain how exactly the observation should modify my degrees of belief; obviously if $p$ is the fact observed, my degree of belief in $q$ after the observation should be equal to my degree of belief in $q$ given $p$ before, or by the multiplication law to the quotient of my degree of belief in $pq$ by my degree of belief in $p$. When my degrees of belief change in this way we can say that they have been changed *consistently* by my observation. (Ramsey, 1926: 94)

but does not explicitly set out any such argument. Hacking (1967) doubts if there can be such an argument, and regards it as a serious failing of Bayesian theory that this "dynamic assumption" lacks a justification. Nevertheless, David Lewis has produced a coherence argument for conditionalization (reported in Teller (1973). See also Freedman and Purves (1969)). I would like to give the leading idea of Lewis' argument here, so that it may be compared with the static coherence arguments. Suppose that I am about to find out whether a certain proposition, $p$, is true or false (e.g. the result of a certain experiment is about to come in); that I have a rule or disposition to change my degrees of belief in a certain way upon learning that $p$ is true; that $PR$ represents my degrees of belief just before learning whether $p$ is true or not and $PR_p$ the degrees of belief that I would have according to the rule (or disposition) upon learning that $p$ is true. The key point is this: prior to finding out about $p$, *the rule or disposition to change my beliefs in a certain way upon learning $p$ is tantamount to having a set of betting ratios for bets conditional on $p$.* (Someone can achieve a betting arrangement for a bet on $q$ conditional on $p$ with me, at the betting ratio $PR_p(q)$, just by reserving a sum of money which he will bet on $q$ with me *after* I change my degrees of belief if $p$ turns out true, and which he will not bet at all if $p$ turns out false.) But we also know from de Finetti's observation that $PR$ alone commits us to betting ratios for conditional bets in a different way, with those betting ratios being reflected in the conditional probabilities of $PR$ (assuming $PR(p) \neq 0$). For the conditional betting ratios arrived at in these two ways to coincide, $PR_p$ must come from $PR$ by conditionalization on $p$ (i.e. for all $q$, $PR_p(q) = PR(p \& q)/PR(p)$). (Obviously, the same argument can be repeated for $PR_{\sim p}$, and for the more general case where the experimental report may consist of any one of a set of mutually exclusive and exhaustive propositions.)

This observation yields a Dutch Book theorem as a corollary. If someone does not change his degree of belief by conditionalization, then someone who knows how he does change his belief can exploit the different betting ratios for bets conditional on $p$ to make a Dutch Book conditional on $p$, which can then be turned into an unconditional Dutch Book by making an appropriate small side bet against $p$.

We can only speculate as to whether Ramsey had this sort of argument in mind. But it is clear that the Lewis argument is quite in the spirit of Ramsey, and rests on the same conception of pragmatic consistency as the static consistency arguments of Ramsey. It is, I think, undeniable that it establishes a special status for conditionalization as a law of motion for rational belief in the cases which satisfy the conditions of the argument. But what of cases in which these conditions are not met? In particular, what about those cases to which Ramsey alludes, in which observation changes *in degree* my opinion about the fact observed, but where that change is not a change to probability 1 of some observation proposition? Richard Jeffrey (1965) introduces *probability kinematics* for just this purpose. Suppose that an observational interaction autonomously changes the probability of some proposition, *p*, but does not change it to 1. In such a situation we might plausibly decide to take as our final probability distribution a mixture (weighted average) of the probability distribution we would get by conditionalizing on *p*, and the probability distribution that we would get by conditionalizing on not-*p*. Then, for any *q*:

$$PR_{final}(q) = PR_{final}(p)PR_{initial}(q \text{ given } p) \\ + PR_{final}(\sim p) PR_{initial}(q \text{ given } \sim p).$$

Under these circumstances, we say that the final probability distribution comes from the initial probability distribution by probability kinematics on *p*. More generally,

*Probability Kinematics*: Let $Pr_i$ and $Pr_f$ be probability functions on the same field of propositions and let $\{p_j: j = 1, \ldots, n\}$ be a partitioning of that field such that $Pr_i(p_j) \neq 0$ and $Pr_f(p_j) = a_j$. $Pr_f$ is said to come from $Pr_i$ by *probability kinematics on* $\{p_j\}$ iff:

For all propositions, *q*, in the field:

$$Pr_f(q) = \Sigma_j a_j Pr_i(q \text{ given } p_j)$$

This is equivalent (Jeffrey, 1965: ch. 11) to:

For all *q* and *j* : $Pr_f(q \text{ given } p_j) = Pr_i(q \text{ given } p_j).$

Conditionalization on *p* is a special case of probability kinematics where the partitioning consists of [*p*, ~*p*] and the final probability of *p* is 1. Probability kinematics takes a certain special kind of constraint on the final probability distribution as its input, the constraint as to the final probabilities of the $p_j$s. E. T. Jaynes, the originator of the information theoretic approach to statistical mechanics, suggests a more generally applicable rule (Jaynes, 1957): Maximize the relative entropy in the final distribution relative to the initial distribution subject to the stated constraints. Jaynes' maxim can be put roughly as: Be as modest as possible about the amount of information you have acquired. Several writers have recently pointed out that probability kinematics is a special case of Jaynes' Rule (May and Harper, 1976; Shafer, 1979; van Fraassen and Domotor, Zanotti and Graves in not yet published papers). But neither the maximum entropy rule in general nor the special case of probability kinematics has the kind of Ramsey–de Finetti justification that Lewis supplied for conditionalization. True modesty is, no doubt, an epistemic virtue but false modesty is not, and the question is now to distinguish true modesty from false.

If only we had some proposition in our language which summed up the content of our imperfect observation, we could simply conditionalize on it. But the assumption that every observation can be interpreted as conferring certainty to some observational proposition leads to an unacceptable epistemology of the given. There is, however, another, entirely natural way in which the sorts of cases under consideration can be assimilated to conditionalization. Within the framework of second-order personal probabilities, we can answer that in the case of probability kinematics there was, after all, something that we did learn for certain from the observation. We learned the values of the final probabilities of the members of the partition. The same remark generalizes to other cases in which Jaynes' Rule of maximizing relative entropy relative to a set of constraints on the final distribution applies. In the higher-order probability setup, we can conditionalize on statements specifying those constraints (by conditionalizing on random variables on the second-order probability space). I would like to proceed to discuss the relation between second-order conditionalization and the first-order generalizations of conditionalization suggested by Jeffrey and Jaynes. I will start with the case of probability kinematics, but much of what I have to say will carry over to maximum relative entropy inference as well.

I would first like to set out the formal connection between first-order probability kinematics and second-order conditionalization, and then discuss the interpretation of this connection in the light of what I have said about higher-order personal probabilities. First, the framework for second-order probabilities:

Let $L_1$ consist of some field of propositions. We extend $L_1$ to $L_2$ by adding every proposition of the form: $pr(p) \in S$ where $p$ is a proposition of $L_1$ and $S$ is a subinterval of the unit interval, and closing under finite truth-functional combination. (We could iterate this process as far as you please.) I will here only discuss a probability distribution $PR$ on $L_2$ with English being the language of discussion.

Suppose that $[p_i : i = 1, \ldots, n]$ is a partition such that $PR[p_i] \neq 0$ and let $[a_i : i = 1, \ldots, n]$ be numerical values such that $PR[\wedge_i pr(p_i) = a_i] \neq 0$. Under what conditions does conditioning on the second-order proposition, $\wedge_i pr(p_i) = a_i$, which specifies probability values for every member of the partition, have the same effect at the first-order level as probability kinematics on that partition $[p_i]$? By the characterization (Jeffrey 1965: ch. 11) of probability kinematics on $[p_i]$ as a change which leaves the probabilities of propositions conditional on members of the partition unchanged, it follows that

Conditionalization on $\wedge_i pr(p_i) = a_i$ is equivalent at the first-order level to probability kinematics on the partition $[p_i]$ if and only if:
(SUFFICIENCY CONDITION): $PR$ ($q$ given $p_j$ and $\wedge_i pr(p_i) = a_i$) = $PR$ ($q$ given $p_j$) for all first-order propositions, $q$, and all elements, $p_j$, of the partition.

For conditionalization on $\wedge_i pr(p_i) = a_i$ to also be a change which leads to each member of the partition $[p_i]$ having as its final probability the corresponding $a_i$, we must also have:

(GENERALIZED MILLER): $PR(p_j$ given $\wedge_i pr(p_i) = a_i) = a_j$ for all elements, $p_j$, of the partition.

(The special case of the foregoing observation, for probability kinematics on a partition consisting of $[p, \sim p]$, is discussed in Skyrms (1980: Appendix 1).)

This bit of mathematics is open to more than one interpretation. One could, for instance, use it to argue for probability kinematics in cases in which one, by reflection, comes to know his own mind a little better. But, here, I would like to focus on the sort of interpretation for which it was designed. Here, *pr* signifies the final probabilities that are the upshot of an observational interaction. Under this interpretation it is plausible that there should be a wide range of first-order propositions for which the sufficiency condition holds.

One is almost tempted to think of the sufficiency condition as a methodological postulate. My degrees of belief with regard to the $p_i$s are irrelevant to the probability of $q$ in the presence of the truth about the world regarding the $p_i$s (i.e. $p_j$). This, however, would be going too far. Notice that the sufficiency condition would not be plausible if we allowed second-order propositions to take the place of the $q$. But we can think of examples of first-order propositions which are highly correlated with the second-order final probability propositions in question, and for these the sufficiency condition may fail too. (E.g. my current probability that I will sweat at the moment of arriving at my final probability, conditional on the fact that Black Bart will not really try to gun me down *and* that my final probability that he will try to kill me will be 0.999, is *not* equal to my current probability that I will sweat, conditional on the fact that he will not really try to gun me down. The sweating is highly correlated with my final degree of belief rather than the fact of the matter.) So we must make do with the more modest claim that in typical situations there is a wide range of first-order propositions for which the sufficiency condition holds. When our first-order language consists of such propositions (relative to the probability measure and partition in question) we shall have probability kinematics on that partition as the first-order consequence of second-order conditionalization.

The generalized Miller condition is also highly plausible under this interpretation, though for different reasons. Here the plausibility depends on the interpretation of *pr* as my *final* probability, after the observational interaction. Under the assumption that my final probability is to be arrived at by conditionalization on $\wedge_i pr(p_i) = a_i$ and under the assumption that *pr* is to be interpreted as final probability, the generalized Miller principle says that conditional on the final probability of $p_j$ having a certain value (and a few other things), it has that value. Of course, we can invent cases where these assumptions do not hold. I might have reason, for instance, to believe that my final probabilities would not be reached by conditionalization, but rather would be distorted and biased in a foreseeable way by an evil force. Contemplating that sort of final probability distribution from my antecedent, clear-headed state, I would not have probabilities [PR] which exemplify Miller's principle, but rather probabilities which compensate for the projected bias in [pr]. The point I would like to make here is that the approach by way of higher-order probabilities both shows us why probability kinematics is the right approach in a wide variety of cases, and enables us to isolate "pathological" cases in which it would give the wrong results. Furthermore, in the cases in which it is correct, it appears not merely as a successful ad hoc method, but rather as a special case of second-order conditionalization.

I will close this section with a brief discussion of the relation higher-order conditionalization and maximum entropy inference. I rely on Halmos and Savage (1949), Kullback and Leibler (1951), and Kullback (1959). The question is there treated in a very general setting. We deal with abstract probability spaces, $\langle X, S, \mu_i \rangle$, where $X$ is a set, $S$ a sigma algebra of subsets of $S$, and $\mu_i$ a measure on $S$. The relative information of $\mu_1$ with respect to $\mu_2$ is defined as:

$$I(1:2) = \int f_1(x)\ln[f_1(x)/f_2(x)]\mathrm{d}\lambda(x)$$

where $f_1$ and $f_2$ are generalized probability density functions whose existence is guaranteed under mild conditions of continuity. (We need only assume that $\mu_1$ is absolutely continuous with $\mu_2$. Then we can take $f_1(x)$ as the Radon–Nikodym derivative of $\mu_1$ with respect to $\mu_2$. $f_2(x)$ then equals 1, since it is $\mathrm{d}\mu_2/\mathrm{d}\mu_2$, so in this case $I(1:2) = \int f_1(x)\ln[f_1(x)]\mathrm{d}\mu_2(x)$; see Kullback (1959: 28–9). We can then take the information theoretic version of statistical inference as follows: starting from an initial probability distribution, $\mu_2$, and a constraint of the form $\int T(x)f_1(x)\mathrm{d}\lambda(x) = \theta$, and a set of eligible candidates for final probability distribution with respect to which $\mu_1$ is absolutely continuous, infer that final probability distribution $\mu_2$ such that among the candidates for final distribution which meet the constraint it minimizes the relative information, $I(1:2)$. Here $T(x)$ is a measurable statistic, either real or vector valued, and $\theta$ is a constant. For example: (1) suppose $T(x)$ is the characteristic function of measurable set, $s$; $\mu_2(s) > 0$; $\theta = 1$; and we take every $\mu_1$ with which $\mu_2$ is absolutely continuous as eligible. Then the final probability, $\mu_1^\star$, which minimizes $I(1:2)$, comes from $\mu_2$ by conditionalization on $s$. (2) Just as (1), except that $\theta = a$ for some $0 \leq a \leq 1$. Then $\mu_1^\star$ comes from $\mu_2$ by probability kinematics on the partition $[s, \bar{s}]$ (see Kullback, 1959: example 2.3, pp. 42–3). (3) As before except that $T(x) = \langle c_1(x) \ldots c_n(x) \rangle$, where each $c_i$ is the characteristic function of an element, $p_i$, of a finite partition of $X$; $\mu_2(p_i) > 0$; $\theta = \langle a_1 \ldots a_n \rangle$ with $0 \leq a_i \leq 1$. Then $\mu_1^\star$ comes from $\mu_2$ by probability kinematics on the partition $[p_i]$. (4) As (3), except that the partition may be countably infinite. Then $\mu_1^\star$ still comes from $\mu_1$ by probability kinematics, in a sense that I will explain. (5) However, the random variables are not limited to characteristic functions, or vectors whose components are characteristic functions, but may be any measurable functions, or vectors whose components are measurable functions.

To discuss the relation of probability kinematics to the maximum relative entropy (minimum relative information) rule, we need an equally general formulation of probability kinematics. Suppose that we have a countably infinite partition, $[p_i]$, such that $\mu_2(p_i) > 0$ for all $p_i$. Then we can say that $\mu_1$ comes from $\mu_2$ by generalized probability kinematics on the partition, $[p_i]$, if and only if for each element of the partition, $p_i$, the ratio of the posterior to the prior density at each point in $p_i$, $f_1(x)/f_2(x)$, is equal to the ratio of the posterior to the prior probabilities of that element, $\mu_1(p_i)/\mu_2(p_i)$. That is, the criterion of constancy of probability, conditional on members of the partition in the finite case, is simply generalized to constancy of conditional density. Given this generalized definition, my remark under (4) above holds. Strictly speaking, I should add the qualification: *modulo* a set of points of measure zero in $\mu_2$. In fact, the generalized probability distribution functions we have been using are only determined to within a set of measure zero in $\mu_2$. This qualification should be understood to hold throughout. If $\langle X, S, \mu_1 \rangle$ comes from $\langle X, S, \mu_2 \rangle$ by probability kinematics on the countable partition, $[p_i]$, in the way indicated, we say that the partition is *sufficient* for $\langle \mu_1, \mu_2 \rangle$ because in this case measuring the relative information with respect to the partition $\Sigma_i\mu_1\ln$ $[\mu_1(p_i)/\mu_2(p_i)]$ gives the relative information, $I(1:2)$. If a partition is not sufficient, i.e. if $\mu_2$ does not come from $\mu_1$ by kinematics on that partition, then the information with respect to the partition is less than $I(1:2)$; measuring information relative to an insufficient partition causes loss of information (Kullback, 1959: corollary 3.2: 16). It follows that if a constraint consists in specifying the final probabilities of each member of a countable partition each of whose members have positive prior probability, then the final probability measure comes from the initial one by minimizing relative information *if and only if* it comes from the initial one by probability kinematics on that partition.

For a fully general formulation of probability kinematics, we need to remove the restrictions on the partition. Any statistic (measurable function) on a probability space *induces a partition* on that space, with the elements of the partition being the inverse images of the values of the statistic (e.g. if I have a probability space of baskets and the statistic 'number of eggs in,' the statistic induces a partition of baskets such that two baskets are members of the same element of the partition if and only if they contain the same number of eggs. Notice that a vector-valued statistic induces the partition that is the common refinement of the partitions induced by its components). Conversely, any partition whose elements are measurable sets is induced by some statistic. (Note: I have not made any limitation as to the types of values that statistics can take.) So we can have full generality if we formulate probability kinematics relative to a statistic. Let $T$ be a statistic, with domain $X$ and range $Y$, and let $R$ be the class of measurable subsets of $Y$ (i.e. $G \in R \leftrightarrow; T^{-1}(G) \in S$). Then starting with a probability space, $\langle X,S,\mu \rangle$, and a statistic, $T$, we can consider an associated probability space $\langle Y,R,\upsilon \rangle$ where the measure $\upsilon$ is derived from $\mu$, by $\upsilon(G) = \mu(T^{-1}(G))$. Then $\upsilon(G) = \int_G g(Y)\mathrm{d}_\gamma(Y)$ where $\gamma(G) = \lambda(T^{-1}(G))$. The associated probability space can be thought of as representing the effect of consolidating the elements of the partition induced by the statistic into single elements. Let $g_1$ and $g_2$ be the generalized probability density functions for the spaces $\langle Y,R,\upsilon_1 \rangle$; $\langle Y,R,\upsilon_2 \rangle$ which corresponds to $\langle X,S,\mu_1 \rangle$; $\langle X,S,\mu_2 \rangle$ under the statistic $T$. (We may take them as the Radon–Nikodym derivatives of $\mu_1$ and $\mu_2$ with respect to $\mu_2$.) Then we will say that $\langle X,S,\mu_1 \rangle$ comes from $\langle X,S,\mu_2 \rangle$ by *generalized probability kinematics on the statistic* $T$ (or, if you please, on the partition induced by $T$) if and only if $f_1(x)/f_2(x) = g_1 T(x)/g_2 T(x)$. This is equivalent to saying that the conditional density conditional on $T(x) = y$, i.e. $f(x)/gT(x)$, remains the same before and after the change, and is thus clearly the correct statement of probability kinematics for this general case. If $\langle X,S,\mu_1 \rangle$ comes from $\langle X, S,\mu_2 \rangle$ by generalized probability kinematics on the statistic $T$, we shall say that $T$ *is a sufficient statistic*, relative to them. Just as in the countable case, we have the result that the relative information measured on the partition, $I$ $(1{:}2, Y)$, is less than or equal to the relative information, $I(1{:}2, X)$, with equality if and only if the statistic is sufficient (Kullback and Leibler, 1951: theorem 4.1; Kullback, 1959: theorem 4.1). A sufficient statistic is one which loses no information. It follows from this that, if the satisfaction of a certain constraint is a function of the posterior values of $g(y)$ (i.e. the posterior values of the conditional expectation of $f(x)$ given that $T(x) = y$), then the posterior distribution that comes from the prior by minimizing relative information subject to that constraint comes from the prior by generalized probability kinematics on $T$. For consider the posterior distribution of values of $g(y)$ in the minimum relative information posterior. By the hypothesis that the satisfaction of the constraint is a function of the posterior values of $g(y)$, any posterior distribution with these values satisfies

the constraint. Thus the posterior which comes from the prior by probability kinematics on $T$ with this final distribution for $g(\gamma)$ satisfies the
constraint. And, by the previous theorem, it must be the minimum relative
information posterior.

But the constraints considered in the maximum entropy (minimum
relative information) formalism are all of this character! Remember that the
constraints all consisted in specifying the posterior expectation of a statistic:

$$\int T(x)f_1(x)\mathrm{d}\lambda(x) = \theta.$$

This can now be rewritten as:

$$\int \gamma g_1(\gamma)\mathrm{d}\gamma(\gamma) = \theta.$$

So $T$ is a sufficient statistic relative to a prior and a posterior which
minimizes relative information subject to the constraint that the posterior
expectation of $T$ has a certain value. (See Kullback, 1959: 43–4; van
Fraassen has also discussed a special case of this in a recent unpublished
paper.) We have just established a theorem, which can be roughly put as:

## Jaynes implies Jeffrey

That is, if we start with a prior and move to that posterior (among those
with respect to which the prior is absolutely continuous and which satisfy
the constraint that a statistic $T$ has a certain posterior expected value)
which minimizes relative information, then the posterior comes from
the prior by generalized probability kinematics on the statistic, $T$. Conversely, we can say that if a posterior comes from a prior by generalized
probability kinematics on $T$, then it minimizes relative information subject
to the constraint that $g(\gamma)$ has those posterior values. In the finite or
countable case, we could always put that constraint in Jaynes' form by
considering a statistic $T'$ which is a vector of characteristic functions of
elements of the partition induced by $T$. But in the general cases it is not
clear that we can always put the constraint in Jaynes' form (unless we use
the same trick and countenance vectors of uncountable dimension). So it is
only with some qualification that we can assert that Jaynes implies Jeffrey.

The point I made about the relation of higher-order probabilities to
probability kinematics carries over to this general setting. Let me explain
why I called the sufficiency condition:

$$PR\big(q \text{ given } p_j \text{ and } \wedge_i pr(p_i) = a_i\big) = PR(q \text{ given } p_i)$$
$$\text{for all first order } q \text{ and all } j$$

by that name. Given that the change from the initial distribution to the final distribution is to be by conditionalization on $\wedge_i pr(p_i) = a_i$, the condition can be rewritten as:

$$PR_{final}(q \text{ given } p_j) = PR_{initial}(q \text{ given } p_j)$$
$$\text{for all first order } q \text{ and all } j$$

which means that if we look at the first-order probability space, we have the condition for $[p_j]$ to be a sufficient partitioning for $(PR_{initial}, PR_{final})$.

It should be clear from the foregoing discussion that we can carry all this over to abstract probability spaces and generalized probability density functions. So we will be able to say in general that second-order conditionalization results in first-order probability kinematics on a partition if and only if such a sufficiency condition is satisfied.

It would be of some interest to investigate the full structure of minimum relative information inference from the same point of view. That is, we look at a second-order distribution where we can conditionalize on the constraint that the final expected value of a statistic has a certain value, and identify the characteristics that the second-order distribution must have for such conditionalizing to coincide at the first-order level with minimum relative information inference. We have some of the answers already, but not all. It is a necessary condition for minimum relative information that we have generalized probability kinematics on $T$, the statistic of the constraint. We have this if and only if the second-order probability distribution satisfies the proper sufficiency condition. To ensure that conditionalizing at the second-order level leads us to a distribution in which the constraint is in fact met requires a further generalization of the generalized Miller condition. But there will be further requirements necessary to guarantee that the final density over the elements of the partition induced by $T$ satisfies the minimum relative information principle. (See Kullback (1959: ch. 3) for derivation and discussion of the exponential solutions.) (See also Chapter 8 in this volume.)

# 3. Conclusion

If I end with more questions open than closed, I hope this will only reinforce the point that second-order personal probabilities are not only legitimate, but also theoretically interesting. They provide a perspective from which the scope of applicability of first-order generalizations of conditionalization can be assessed. Counter-instances to the sufficiency condition are counter-instances both to probability kinematics and the minimum relative information principle. The scarcity and peculiar nature of such counter-instances explains the wide range within which probability kinematics can be plausibly applied. An analogous determination of the range of applicability of minimum relative information inference calls for further study.

I would like to thank Zoltan Domotor, Glenn Shafer, and Bas van Fraassen for letting me see copies of papers not yet published. Each of these illuminates some of the issues discussed here, and each represents a different philosophical viewpoint. I would also like to thank Richard Jeffrey for discussion of some of these ideas.

# Bibliography

Carnap, R. (1952) *The Continuum of Inductive Methods*. Chicago: University of Chicago Press.

de Finetti, B. (1972) *Probability, Induction and Statistics*. London: Wiley.

Domotor, Z., Zanotti, M., and Graves, G. (1980) "Probability Kinematics," *Synthese* 44: 421–42.

Field, H. (1978) "A Note of Jeffrey Conditionalization," *Philosophy of Science* 45: 171–85.

Freedman, D. and Purves, R. (1969) "Bayes Method for Bookies," *Annals of Mathematical Statistics* 40: 1177–86.

Gärdenfors, P. (1975) "Qualitative Probability as Intensional Logic," *Journal of Philosophical Logic* 4: 171–85.

Good, I. J. (1950) *Probability and the Weighing of Evidence*. London: Charles Griffin.
——(1965) *The Estimation of Probabilities*. Cambridge, MA: MIT Press.
——(1971) "The Probabilistic Explication of Information, Evidence, Surprise, Causality, Explanation and Utility." In V. P. Godambe and D. A. Sprott (eds.), *Foundations of Statistical Inference*. Toronto: Holt, Rinehart & Winston.

Hacking, I. (1967) "Slightly More Realistic Personal Probability," *Philosophy of Science* 34: 311–25.

Halmos, P. R. and Savage, L. J. (1949) "Application of the Radon–Nikodym Theorem to the Theory of Sufficient Statistics," *Annals of Mathematical Statistics* 20: 225–41.

Hintikka, J. (1971) "Unknown probabilities, Bayesianism and de Finetti's representation theorem." In *Boston Studies in the Philosophy of Science*, vol. 8. Dordrecht: Reidel.

Jaynes, E. T. (1957) "Information Theory and Statistical Mechanics," *Physical Review* 106: 620–30.

——(1958) *Probability Theory in Science and Engineering*. Dallas: Socony Mobil Oil Co. Field Research Laboratory.

——(1965) *The Logic of Decision*. New York: Wiley.

——(1974) "Preference among Preferences," *Journal of Philosophy* 63: 377–91.

——(1979) "Where Do We Stand on Maximum Entropy?" In R. D. Levine and M. Tribus (eds.), *The Maximum Entropy Formalism*, pp. 115–18. Cambridge, MA: MIT Press.

Kullback, S. and Leibler, R. A. (1951) "On Information and Sufficiency," *Annals of Mathematical Statistics* 22: 79–86.

——(1959) *Information Theory and Statistics*. New York: Wiley.

May, S. and Harper, W. (1976) "Toward an Optimization Procedure for Applying Minimum Change Principles in Probability Kinematics." In W. L. Harper and C. A. Hooker (eds.), *Foundation of Probability Theory, Statistical Inference and Statistical Theories of Science*, vol. I. Dordrecht: Reidel.

Miller, D. (1966) "A Paradox of Information," *British Journal for the Philosophy of Science* 17: 59–61.

Raiffa, H. and Schlaifer, R. (1961) *Applied Statistical Decision Theory*. Boston, MA: Harvard Business School.

Ramsey, F. P. (1926) "Truth and Probability." In D. H. Mellor (ed.), *Foundations*, pp. 58–100. 1978. London: Routledge and Kegan Paul.

Savage, L. J. (1972) *The Foundations of Statistics*, 2nd ed. New York: Dover.

Shafer, G. (1979) "Jeffrey's Rule of Conditioning," *Technical Report 131*, Department of Statistics, Stanford University.

Skyrms, B. (1975) *Choice and Chance*, 2nd ed. Belmont, CA: Wadsworth.

——(1980) *Causal Necessity*. New Haven, CT: Yale University Press.

Teller, P. (1973) "Conditionalization and Observation," *Synthese* 26: 218–58.

# 6

# A Mistake in Dynamic Coherence Arguments?

## 1. Static Coherence of Degrees of Belief

The person whose degrees of belief are being tested for coherence acts as a bookie. She posts her fair prices for wagers corresponding to her degrees of belief. Her degrees of belief are *incoherent* if a cunning bettor can make a Dutch Book against her with a finite system of wagers—that is, there is a finite set of wagers individually perceived as fair, whose net payoff is a loss in every possible future. Otherwise her degrees of belief are *coherent*. De Finetti ([1937] 1980) proved the following theorem: *Degrees of belief are coherent if and only if they are finitely additive probabilities.*

Obviously, if a Dutch Book can be made with a finite number of fair transactions, it can be made with a finite number of uniformly favorable transactions. The bettor pays some small transaction premium $e$ to the bookie for each of the $n$ transactions where $ne$ is less than the guaranteed profit that the bettor gets under the Dutch Book based on fair prices. Let us bear in mind that this point applies equally well in what follows.

## 2. Dynamic Coherence for Updating Rules

The epistemologist acts as bookie. Her updating rule is public knowledge. Today she posts her fair prices, and does business. Tomorrow she makes an observation (with a finite number of possible outcomes each of which has positive prior probability) and updates her fair prices according to her updating rule. The updating rule is thus a *function* from possible observations to revised fair prices. The day after tomorrow she posts prices again, and does business. The pair consisting of (1) her fair prices for today and (2) her updating function will be called the bookie's *epistemic strategy*.

The bookie's *epistemic strategy* is *coherent* if *there is no* possible bettor's strategy which makes a Dutch Book against him (the bettor's strategy being a pair consisting of (1) a finite number of transactions today at the bookie's posted prices and (2) a function taking possible observations into a finite number of transactions the day after tomorrow at the prices that the bookie will post according to her epistemic strategy). Lewis (reported in Teller, 1973) proves that *the epistemologist's strategy is coherent only if her degrees of belief today are finitely additive probabilities and her updating rule is Bayes' Rule of conditioning*. The 'only if' can be strengthened to 'if and only if' (see section 4). (For generalizations of this theorem, see van Fraassen, 1984 and Skyrms, 1987, 1990.)

Notice that the relevant notions of coherence and incoherence here apply not just to the *pair* of degrees of belief for today and the day after tomorrow, but rather to an *epistemic strategy*, which is a more complicated object. A focus on the former notion leads understandably to skepticism regarding dynamic coherence, as in Hacking (1967), Kyburg (1978), and Christensen (1991).

## 3. The Dynamic Dutch Book

Coherence of degrees of belief today is the static case. It remains to show that for any non-Bayes updating rule, there is a bettor's strategy which makes a Dutch Book. Let the conditional probability of A on $e$, that is $\Pr(A \& e)/\Pr(e)$, be symbolized as usual, as $\Pr(A|e)$, and let the probability that the updating rule gives $A$ if $e$ is observed be $\Pr_e(A)$. If the predictor's rule disagrees with conditioning, then for some possible evidential result $e$ and some A, $\Pr_e(A)$ is not $\Pr(A|e)$. Suppose that $\Pr(A|e) > \Pr_e(A)$. (The other case is similar.) Let the discrepancy be $\delta = \Pr(A|e) - \Pr_e(A)$. *Here is a bettor's strategy which makes a Dutch Book:*

TODAY: Offer to sell the bookie at her fair price:
1: [$1 if A & e, 0 otherwise]
2: [$Pr(A|e) if not-$e$, 0 otherwise]
3: [if $e$, 0 otherwise]
DAY AFTER TOMORROW:
If $e$ was observed, offer to buy [$1 if A, 0 otherwise] for its current fair price, $\Pr_e(A) = \Pr(A|e) - \delta$.

Then in every possible situation, the bookie loses $\$\delta \Pr(e)$.

## 4. The Converse

If the bookie has the strategy of updating by Bayes' Rule of conditioning, then every payoff that a bettor's strategy can achieve can be achieved by betting only today (see Skyrms, 1987). This reduces our case to the static case. Thus, by de Finetti's result, if the epistemologist's prior degrees of belief are finitely additive probabilities and her updating rule is Bayes's Rules of conditioning, then she is dynamically coherent.

## 5. Sequential Analysis 1: A Mistake in the Dynamic Coherence Argument?

Maher's (1992 a,b) objection is that the bookie will see it coming and refuse to bet. This is made precise by modeling the bookie's situation as a sequential choice problem, as shown in Figure 1. The bookie sees that if she bets today and $e$ occurs, then at decision node 2, she will find the cunning bettor's offer fair according to her revised probability, $Pr_e(A)$. Thus she sees that betting today leads to a sure loss. Since she prefers net gain of zero to a sure loss, she refuses to bet today—frustrating the cunning bettor who goes home unable to execute his plan.

The first thing that must be said about 'Maher's objection' is that it is misleading to represent it as showing a 'mistake' in the dynamic coherence theorem. Under the conditions of the theorem the bookie posts her fair prices for today and honors them. There is no provision for changing one's mind when approached by a cunning bettor who discloses his strategy, nor indeed any mention of a requirement that the cunning bettor disclose his strategy prior to the initial transaction. But Maher might be read as suggesting a different conception of dynamic coherence in this setting:

The epistemologist acts as bookie. Her updating rule is public knowledge. Today she posts her tentative fair prices, but in fact does business only with bettors who disclose their strategies in advance, and does so on the basis of sequential decision analysis. Tomorrow she makes an observation (with a finite number of possible outcomes each of which has positive prior probability) and updates her probabilities according to her updating rule. The day after tomorrow she posts prices again, and does business according to those prices.

She is *coherent* if *there is no* possible bettor's strategy which makes a Dutch Book against her. This is an interesting modification of the usual notion of dynamic

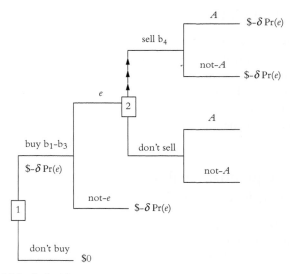

**Figure 1** Maher's decision tree

coherence, and it merits investigation. Is it a better motivated conception of dynamic coherence? What differences does it make?

# 6. Sequential Analysis 2: A Mistake in the Mistake?

A natural reaction to Maher's line might be to say that the redefinition unfairly prejudices the case against dynamic coherence arguments. It is therefore of some interest to see that the dynamic Dutch Book still goes through under the revised scenario.

There is a gratuitous assumption in the analysis presented in Figure 1. Why is it assumed that the cunning bettor will just go home if the bookie refuses to bet today? The bettor's strategy which I presented says otherwise. The bettor will make an offer the day after tomorrow if $e$ was observed. So the branch of the decision tree where the bookie refuses transactions today cannot simply be assumed to have payoff of zero, but requires further analysis. This is done in Figure 2.

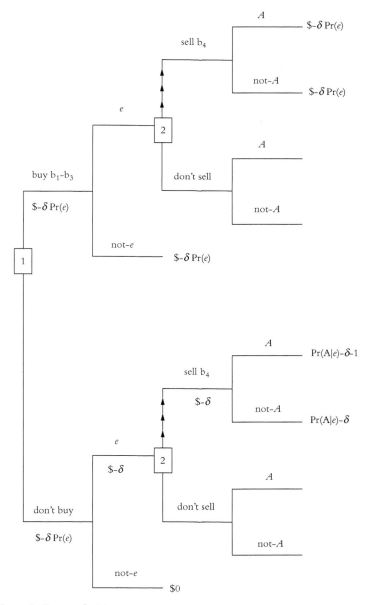

**Figure 2** Correct decision tree

Note that the bookie knows that if *e* is observed, she will accept the offer the day after tomorrow for the same reason on the lower path as on the upper. Deciding now not to bet ever is not an option. If the offer the day after tomorrow is accepted but the offer today was not and *e* and *A* both happen, then the net payoff is the price the cunning bettor paid, \$Pr (A|e)− $\delta$, less the lost bet, \$− 1, as shown. If *e* occurs but *A* does not, the net payoff is just \$Pr(A|e)− $\delta$. For the bookie's current analysis of this decision tree, to get the relevant expectation over *A* occurring or not we average, using as weights her current conditional probabilities, Pr(A | e) and Pr(−A|e). Thus the value at the node where the bookie refused to bet today and where *e* is observed tomorrow is

$$\Pr(A|e)\$[\{\Pr(A|e) - \delta\} - 1] + [1 - \Pr(A|e)]\$[\Pr(A|e) - \delta] = \$ - \delta$$

Then the value at the node where the bookie refused to bet today is not 0 but rather \$−$\delta$ Pr(*e*). This is just the same as the value at the node where the bookie agrees to bet today.

In fact, if we consider the version of the Dutch-Book strategy where the bettor adds an *e* premium for each transaction, the upper branch involves four transactions and the lower branch involves only one, so the upper branch has a higher payoff than the lower branch. *Even though the bookie sees it coming, she will prefer the sure loss of the upper branch because doing so looks strictly better to her than the alternative.*

# 7. Sequential Analysis 3: What Makes the Cunning Bettor Tick?

Why did the cunning bettor adopt a strategy of staying around if the bookie decided not to bet today? The official answer in sections 2–3 is "Don't ask." *Any* bettor's strategy which makes a Dutch Book will prove incoherence. But, as Levi (1991) points out, that sort of analysis proceeds in strategic normal form rather than in extensive form. Might it be that the cunning bettor's strategy described would have to be *sequentially irrational*? That is to say, might it not be that staying around and betting the day after tomorrow if the bookie decided not to bet today would not maximize expected utility for the cunning bettor in the belief state he would have in that case the day after tomorrow? If this could be shown, then the cunning bettor's strategy that I have described would have to rest on a non-credible threat, and the significance of the analysis of the previous section would be called into question. (For discussion of such non-credible threats in extensive form games and of sequential rationality, see Selten, 1975 and Kreps and Wilson, 1982.)

But such is not the case. Suppose that the bettor is a Bayesian; that he starts out with exactly the same degrees of belief as the bookie; and that he updates by conditioning. If $e$ is observed tomorrow—whether or not the bookie accepted the bet today—he conditions on $e$ and the day after tomorrow his fair price for $b4$ is $pr(A|e)$. But his strategy only commits him to offering to pay the bookie's fair price, $pr(A|e) - \delta$, to buy back $b4$ for what he perceives as a net gain in expected utility of $\$\delta$. This bettor's threat to stick around and bet the day after tomorrow if $e$, even if the bookie declines to bet today, is perfectly credible and consistent with sequential rationality. If he is called upon to carry out the threat, he maximizes expected utility by doing so.

## 8. Strategic Rationality

Let us explicitly model the bookie's choice of an updating strategy. The bookie and the bettor start out with identical priors. The bettor updates by conditioning. First the bookie chooses an updating strategy. Then the bettor bets, the evidence comes in, the bookie updates according to her updating rule, and the bettor bets again. The bookie's initial strategy is either to choose updating by conditioning or not.

If the bookie chooses the strategy of updating by conditioning, then the fair prices of the bookie and bettor agree at all times. Thus either no transactions are made, or any transactions have net change in expected utility of 0 for both players. The bookie's expected utility of choosing the strategy of updating by conditioning is zero. If, however, the bookie chooses an updating strategy at variance with conditioning then, for the bettor, the expected utility of betting is greater than that of not betting (section 7) and the net expected utility for the bookie is negative (section 6). At the first choice point the bookie is strictly better off by choosing the rule of updating by conditioning.

Thus the strategy combination in which the bookie updates by conditioning and the bettor does not bet at all is an *equilibrium* in the sense that no player will perceive it in his or her interest at any decision node to deviate from that strategy. But no strategy combination in which the bookie chooses a strategy at variance with conditioning is such an equilibrium.

## 9. The Bottom Line

Two ways of strengthening the requirements for a dynamic Dutch Book were suggested by the discussions of Levi and Maher: (1) We require the cunning bettor to disclose his strategy, and allow the bookie to use knowledge of that strategy in a sequential analysis when deciding whether to bet today or not, and (2) we require that the cunning bettor's strategy itself be sequentially rational. The somewhat surprising result is that the additional restrictions made no difference. The bookie whose epistemic strategy is at odds with conditioning is also subject to a Dutch Book in this stronger sense. 'Seeing it coming' does not help. It is at the very least a noteworthy property of the rule of conditioning that, in this sort of epistemic situation, it alone is immune from a Dutch Book under either the original or strengthened requirements.

## 10. Postscript: Conditioning, Coherence, and Rationality

Many of the concerns of Levi and Maher have not been addressed in the foregoing. Levi is concerned to resist the doctrine of "confirmational tenacity", according to which the only legitimate way in which to update is by conditioning. Maher wishes to resist the doctrine that rationality requires dynamic coherence at all costs. Does the foregoing show that conditioning is the only coherent way to ever update one's probabilities? Does it show that rationality requires coherence at all costs?

I agree with Levi and Maher in answering 'no' to both questions. With regard to the first, let me emphasize that the Lewis proof takes place within the structure of a very special epistemic model. In that context it shows that the rule of conditioning is the unique dynamically coherent updating rule. It does not show that one must have an updating rule. It does not apply to other epistemic situations which should be modeled differently. The modeling of a variety of epistemic situations and the investigation of varieties of dynamic coherence in such situations is an ongoing enterprise (in which I take it that both Levi and I are engaged; see Skyrms (1990) for further discussion).

Maher is concerned that an uncritical doctrine of "dynamic coherence at all costs" could lead one to crazy belief changes and disastrous actions. Should Ulysses have changed to his prior probability of safe sailing conditional on hearing the Sirens' song so that subsequently his belief change would be in accordance with the rule of conditioning? Nothing in the foregoing implies that he should. In the first place, there is something a little odd in thinking that one achieves dynamic coherence by changing the original prior $pr_1$ to the revised prior $pr_2$ so that the change to $pr_3$ will agree with conditioning. What about the change from $pr_1$ to $pr_2$? But, more fundamentally, I would agree with Maher that rationality definitely does not require coherence *at all costs*. Where costs occur they need to be weighed against benefits. There are lucid discussions of this matter in Maher (1992a, b). These things said, it remains that in the Lewis epistemic model under the 'sequentialized' notion of dynamic coherence, the unique coherent updating rule is the rule of conditioning.

## Bibliography

Christensen, D. (1991) "Clever Bookies and Coherent Beliefs," *Philosophical Review* 100: 229–47.

de Finetti, B. ([1937] 1980) "Foresight: Its Logical Laws, Its Subjective Sources," translated in H. E. Kyburg, Jr. and H. Smokler (eds.), *Studies in Subjective Probability*. (Originally published as "La Prévision: Ses lois logiques, ses sources subjectives," *Annales de l'Institut Henri Poincaré* 7: 1–68.) Huntington, NY: Kreiger, pp. 93–158.

Earman, J. (1992) *Bayes or Bust: A Critical Examination of Bayesian Confirmation Theory*. Cambridge, MA: MIT Press.

Hacking, I. (1967) "Slightly More Realistic Personal Probability," *Philosophy of Science* 34: 311–25.

Kreps, D. and Wilson, R. (1982) "Sequential Equilibria," *Econometrica* 50: 863–94.

Kyburg, H. (1978) "Subjective Probability: Criticisms, Reflections and Problems," *Journal of Philosophical Logic* 7: 157–80.

Levi, I. (1987) "The Demons of Decision," *The Monist* 70: 193–211.

——(1991) "Consequentialism and Sequential Choice." in M. Bacharach and S. Hurley (eds.), *Foundations of Decision Theory*, pp. 92–146. Oxford: Basil Blackwell.

Maher, P. (1992a) *Betting on Theories*. Cambridge: Cambridge University Press.

——(1992b) "Diachronic Rationality," *Philosophy of Science* 59: 120–41.

Selten, R. (1975) "Reexamination of the Perfectness Concept of Equilibrium in Extensive Form Games," *International Journal of Game Theory* 4: 25–55.

Skyrms, B. (1987) "Dynamic Coherence and Probability Kinematics," *Philosophy of Science* 54: 1–20.

——(1990) *The Dynamics of Rational Deliberation.* Cambridge, MA: Harvard University Press.

Teller, P. (1973) "Conditionalization and Observation," *Synthese* 26: 218–58.

van Fraassen, B. (1984) "Belief and the Will," *Journal of Philosophy* 81: 235–56.

# 7

# Dynamic Coherence and Probability Kinematics

## 1. Dynamic Coherence

Frank Ramsey introduces the notion of static coherence of degrees of belief—coherence at a given time—as a kind of pragmatic consistency property:

> These are the laws of probability, which we have proved to be necessarily true of any consistent set of degrees of belief... If anyone's mental condition violated these laws, his choice would depend on the precise form in which the options were offered him, which would be absurd. He could have a book made against him by a cunning bettor and would then stand to lose in any event. (Ramsey, 1931: 182)

Ramsey rightly treats the possibility of a Dutch Book as a symptom of deeper pathology. The bettor who violates the laws of the probability calculus leaves himself open to having a book made against him because he will consider two different sets of odds as fair for an option depending on how that option is described; the equivalence of the descriptions following from the underlying Boolean logic.

Ramsey (and following him, de Finetti and Savage) argued for the representation of coherent degrees of belief at a time as a finitely additive probability measure on a Boolean algebra of propositions. However, the argument can be extended in a natural way to justify countable additivity of the probability measure on a Boolean sigma–algebra of propositions (Adams, 1962). Protection against a Dutch Book resulting from a finite number of bets perceived as fair requires finite additivity; protection against one resulting from a countable number of bets perceived as fair requires countable additivity. We will assume countable additivity.

Later in the same essay, Ramsey discusses *changes* in degrees of belief:

Since an observation changes (in degree at least) my opinion about the fact observed, some of my degrees of belief after the observation are necessarily inconsistent with those I had before. We have, therefore, to explain exactly how the observation should modify my degrees of belief; obviously if $p$ is the fact observed, my degree of belief in $q$ after the observation should be equal to my degree of belief in $p$ before, or by the multiplication law to the quotient of my degree of belief in $pq$ by my degree of belief in $p$. When my degrees of belief change in this way we can say that they have been changed consistently by my observation. (Ramsey, 1931: 192)

Ramsey is describing the process of belief change by *conditionalization* on $p$, "the fact observed":

$$Pr_{new}(q) = Pr_{old}(q/p) = Pr_{old}(p\&q)/Pr_{old}(p).$$

The relevant conditional probabilities are often calculated by means of Bayes' theorem, in which case the rule of updating & by conditionalization is known as *Bayes' Rule*. Ramsey's use of the word "consistently" in the foregoing passage might suggest that he has in mind a coherence argument to justify this rule parallel to the argument he used to justify the laws of the probability calculus as rules for consistent degrees of belief at a fixed time. But no such argument is given, either in this essay or elsewhere in his published writings. We are left to speculate as to whether he considered the argument too obvious to put down or whether he had no such argument.

There is a coherence argument, given explicitly by de Finetti, for the ratio definition of conditional probability:

$$Pr_{old}(q/p) = Pr_{old}(p\&q)/Pr_{old}(p).$$

This involves conditional bets. A bet on $q$ conditional on $p$ is won if $p$ and $q$ are both true, lost if $p$ is true and $q$ false, and called off if $p$ is false. Conditional bets can be compounded from unconditional bets. A bet on $p\&q$ that wins $c$ if $p\&q$ and loses $d$ otherwise and a bet on not-$p$ that wins $d$ if not-$p$ and loses $f$ otherwise taken together give net payoff of a bet on $q$ conditional on $p$ that has zero payoff if the condition $p$ is not realized, wins $c - f$ if $p\&q$, and loses $d + f$ if $p\&$not-$q$. Coherence requires that conditional probabilities as fair betting ratios for conditional bets mesh with fair betting ratios for unconditional bets, as in the standard definition of conditional probability. None of this in itself, however, gives us a coherence argument for the rule of conditionalization for *changing* degrees of belief.

In an essay examining Savage's system, Ian Hacking points to the rule of conditionalization as an implicit assumption. He calls it the *dynamic assumption* of personalism:

The idea of the model of learning is that $Prob(h/e)$ represents one's personal probability after one learns $e$. But formally the conditional probability represents no such thing. If, as in all of Savage's work, conditional probability is a defined notion, then $Prob(h/e)$ stands merely for the quotient of two probabilities. It in no way represents what I have learned after I have taken $e$ as a new datum point. It is only when we make the dynamic assumption that we can conclude anything about learning from experience. (Hacking, 1967: 315)

Hacking argues that no dynamic Dutch Book argument is possible:

a man knowing $e$ would be incoherent if the rates offered on $h$ unconditionally differed from his rates on $h$ conditional on $e$. But no incoherence obtains when we shift from the point before $e$ is known to the point after it is known . . . since the man announces his post-$e$ rates only after $e$ is discovered, and simultaneously cancels his pre-$e$ rates, there is no system for betting with him which is guaranteed success in the sense of a Dutch book. (Ibid.)

Given the way Hacking structures the problem, with the bettor simply betting at two different times with someone whose degrees of belief at each of those times are statically coherent, it is clear why he thinks that no Dutch Book is possible. But the problem can be given more structure.

Indeed, any plausible treatment of the case must give it more structure, for there must be some way of indicating in the statement of the problem that the man in question learns only $e$, rather than $e$ together with some extra information. Furthermore, it is of some importance that we are discussing coherence not of separate degree-of-belief states but of a *rule* or *strategy* for changing such states upon receiving a proposition as input.

Let us consider a perfect model situation for the application of such rules. Suppose that our bookie has at time 1 a prior probability assignment, $Pr_1$, over a probability space, and there is a countable partition of that space, $\{e_i\}$, such that each member of that partition has positive prior probability. At time 2, the true member of the partition is announced and the bookie moves to a posterior probability, $pr_2$, according to a strategy that treats the announced member of the partition as total input. Such a strategy is a *function*, STRAT, which maps members of $\{e_i\}$ onto posterior probability distributions. The strategy of conditionalization maps $e_i$ onto the posterior probability, $Pr_2$, such that $Pr_2(q) = Pr_1(q/e_i)$ for all $q$. There are many other possible strategies. We will allow a cunning bettor to bet with our bookie at each time. He must make bets that the bookie considers fair or favorable (non-negative expected utility) at the time. He is allowed to know the bookie's probabilities at the times of the bets and he is allowed to know the bookie's *strategy*. Formally, the bettor's strategy consists of a pair of functions. The first maps the pair consisting on the bookie's ($Pr_1$, STRAT) onto bets to be made at $t_1$ that for the bookie have non-negative expected utility at $t_1$ according to his $pr_1$; the second maps ($Pr_1$, STRAT, $e_i$) onto bets to be made at $t_2$ that for the bookie have non-negative expected utility at $t_2$ according to his $pr_2 = $ STRAT ($e_i$). Let us say that the bettor makes a *dynamic Dutch Book* against the bookie, if no matter what the true member, $e_i$, of the partition, the bettor's strategy leaves him at $t_2$ with a finite number of bets whose net payoff is positive for every point in $e_i$. And we will say that the bookie's strategy is *dynamically coherent* if no bettor's strategy makes a dynamic Dutch Book against it.

Now there is an argument, due to David Lewis,[1] which shows that in the type of situation under consideration a dynamically coherent strategy must proceed by conditionalization:

THEOREM I (LEWIS). *If the bookie's strategy does not proceed by conditionalization on the evidence, he leaves himself open to a dynamic Dutch Book.*

*Proof.* Suppose that for some proposition (measurable set), $q$, in the bookie's probability space, and some member of his evidential partition, $e$, $Pr_1(q/e)$ unequal to $Pr_e(q)$ where $Pr_e$ is the $Pr_2$ onto which STRAT maps $e$. Then either (1) $Pr_1(q/e) < Pr_e(q)$ or (2) $Pr_1(q/e) > Pr_2(e)$. If the first, let $d = Pr_e(q) - Pr_1(q/e)$. The bettor can now proceed as follows: At $t_1$ he proposes (i) the conditional bet to the effect that if $e\&q$ the bookie pays him $\$Pr_1$ (not-$q/e$); if $e\&$not-$q$ he pays the bookie $\$Pr_1(q/e)$; if not-$e$ the bet is called off; and (ii) the sidebet on not-$e$ such that if $e$, he pays the bookie $\$d$ $Pr_1$ (not-$e$); if not-$e$, the bookie pays him $\$d$ $Pr_1(e)$. The bookie judges these bets as fair at $t_1$. At $t_2$ if a member of the evidential partition other than $e$ was revealed, the conditional bet is canceled and the cunning bettor wins the sidebet and gains $\$d$ $Pr_1(e)$. If $e$ was the member of the evidential partition revealed at $t_2$, then the bettor

---

[1]  Reported in Teller (1973, 1976). Anyone who doubts the value of this argument because of qualms about the existence of a suitable prior should consider the arguments in Freedman and Purves (1969).

proposes an additional bet (iii) on $q$ such that if $q$, he pays the bookie $Pr_e$(not-$q$); if not-$q$, the bookie pay him $Pr_e(q)$. The bookie regards these as fair, according to $Pr_e$. The net result of (i) and (iii) is then that the bettor wins $d$ no matter whether $q$ or not-$q$. He has lost $d$ $Pr_1$(not-$e$) on the sidebet (ii), giving him again a net gain of $Pr_1(e)$ on (i), (ii), and (iii). Case (2) is similar.

In the dynamic case, as in the static one, the possibility of a Dutch Book is the result of an underlying pragmatic inconsistency. If the bookie has a rule for changing degrees of belief of the kind under discussion, and is in a situation such as we have described where the rule is applicable, then the bettor can achieve the effect of a bet on $q$ conditional on a member, $e$, of the evidential partition in one of two ways. He can make the conditional bet at $t_1$ either directly or by making a finite number of unconditional bets that achieve the same effect. Or he can simply resolve to wait until $t_2$ and make the bet on $q$ at the revised rates if and only if $e$ is the member of the partition announced. The second possibility is foreseeable by the bookie; it is based on his own rule for revising his degrees of belief. For the bookie to evaluate conditional bets consistently, his strategy must update his degrees of belief by conditionalization on the evidence.

## 2. Probability Kinematics

Can we build an adequate theory of evidence in which conditionalization is the only rule for updating degrees of belief? There is a tradition in epistemology that goes back to the Stoics that is favorable to an affirmative answer. According to this general view, there is a kind of evidence that is the foundation for all knowledge. When in possession of such evidence one is unmistakably led to certainty in the appropriate evidential proposition; that proposition bears 'the mark of truth' that compels unqualified assent. All other propositions are evaluated in relation to these foundational ones. Various versions of this view have surfaced since Hellenistic times, with the mark of truth being conferred by the senses or intuition or some combination; the most recent version being promulgated by one wing of the logical positivist movement. On such a view, one simply updates by conditionalization as new evidence comes in. If one's ultimate prior were also somehow given by intuition or reason, all of epistemology would be grounded in certainty. Such was, in its essentials, the program of Carnap's inductive logic, at least in the beginning.

But even leaving aside the question of the grand prior, it is hard to swallow the view that evidence comes as neatly packaged as the Stoics claim it does. Their doctrine was forcefully opposed in their own time by the academic skeptics who held that all knowledge is 'probable' rather than certain, and in our own time by epistemologists as diverse as J. L. Austin, Sir Karl Popper, and Wilfrid Sellars. According to the strict skeptical view, conditionalization is *never* justified. One need not be a complete skeptic, however, to doubt that conditionalization is always the appropriate model. Even a positivist who believed in the possibility of an adequate language of sense data might not have that language in hand yet. Everyone has an interest in how belief revision in the light of evidence that does not render any proposition in the agent's language certain should be handled.

Addressing this problem, Richard Jeffrey (1965) suggested a generalization of the rule of conditionalization as a way to deal with some cases of uncertain evidence. Suppose $\{e_j\}$ is a partition all of whose members have positive initial probability, $Pr_i$. A subsequent probability, $Pr_f$, is said to *come from $Pr_i$ by probability kinematics on $\{e_j\}$* iff:

$$Pr_i(q/e_j) = Pr_f(q/e_j) \text{ for all } j \text{ and all } q.$$

Jeffrey uses the name "probability kinematics" to suggest the absence of informational forces that might deform the probabilities conditional on members of the partition. In statisticians' language the partition $\{e_j\}$ is a *sufficient partition* for the class of probability distributions that can come from $Pr_i$ by probability kinematics on $\{e_j\}$, and a measurable function whose set of inverse images in the partition is a *sufficient statistic* for that class of probability distributions. (For a nice discussion, see Diaconis and Zabell, 1982.)

Belief revision by probability kinematics is a natural generalization of conditionalization. The partition must, of course, be one appropriate to the evidence; the evidential event should give us information relevant only to the relative probabilities of members of the partition. If the information gives one member of the partition final probability of one, we have belief change by conditionalization on that member of the partition. The set of probabilities that can come from a prior that gives every member of $\{e_j\}$ positive probability, by probability kinematics on $\{e_j\}$, is a convex set of which the probability measures that come by conditionalization on a member of $\{e_j\}$ are the extreme points.

There is an obvious question to ask: "Is there a dynamic coherence argument for probability kinematics?" The answer is not quite obvious, because the whole point of probability kinematics is to deal with the sort of situation where there is no proposition in the agent's language that represents the epistemic input of the evidential experience. How, then, do we represent his strategy for changing degrees of belief? Let us consider these questions in the context of an example of the sort of situation that Jeffrey had in mind.

# 3. The Observation Game

Player A (the bookie) is shown a jellybean under dim light, and on the basis of this observational event may revise his prior probabilities of its color. Subsequently, he is told its true color by the gamemaster. Player A has three salient probability distributions: $Pr_1$ (before the observation); $Pr_2$ (after the observation); $Pr_3$ (after the gamemaster announces the true color); over a discrete probability space whose points represent ⟨color, flavor⟩ pairs. Sets of points in this space can be thought of as representing propositions about the bean in question. (I will use the ampersand, '&', for set intersection and the dash, '−', for set complement.) Player B (the cunning bettor) can make bets with player A at any of the corresponding times, $t_1$, $t_2$, $t_3$, regarding the color and flavor of the bean. Player B doesn't get to make any observations, but at each time he is allowed to know player A's probability measure over this space at that time. He also gets to know player A's *strategy* for changing degrees of belief.

## 3.1 Strategies

Allow me to begin with some heuristic considerations that motivate the definition of strategies. Player A comes into the game with an initial probability, $Pr_1$, which is modified in response to the observation to yield $Pr_2$. If the information that the observational event supplied were just that the true situation were in some set in his probability space, then we could require that his strategy specify his $Pr_2$ as a function of that given set (as in the strategy of conditionalization). But we are here interested in the case in which information conveyed by observation cannot be captured in this way. We suppose that the light is too dim, the probability space too crude, to allow for this possibility. Lacking such an observational proposition, we require at this point only that player A's strategy specify a class of possible $Pr_2$'s that he takes to be permissible.

At $t_3$ player A learns just the color of the jellybean, and here he does have a set, COLOR, which captures what he learns. His strategy must specify his output, $Pr_3$, as a function of his $\langle Pr_2, \text{COLOR} \rangle$. We need, however, some way of building into the specification of his strategy that his observation at $t_2$ is relevant only to the partition of colors; of ruling out that he cheats by perhaps sniffing the bean when he is supposed to be only observing its color. If the change from $Pr_1$ to $Pr_2$ reflects only the acquisition of information about color, then when at $t_3$ player A is told the true color of the jellybean, this should supersede whatever imperfect information about color he obtained by the act of observation in dim light. We build in the prohibition against extra illicit information by requiring that $Pr_3$ be a function of COLOR alone.

We will assume for simplicity that player A's $Pr_1$ and $Pr_2$ must give each atom of the probability space positive probability and that his $Pr_3$ gives each flavor positive probability. Player A must believe the gamemaster: $Pr_3(C) = 1$ for the color, $C$, that the gamemaster announced. Player A's strategy must address the possibility that any color may be the one announced whatever his $Pr_2$. [(iv) below.]

Formally, *Player A's strategy* may be taken to be a set, STRAT, of quadruples: $\langle Pr_1, Pr_2, \text{COLOR}, Pr_3 \rangle$ such that: (o) $Pr_1$, the prior that player A brings to the situation, is the same in each quadruple and gives each atom positive probability. (i) In each quadruple $Pr_2$ gives each atom positive probability and $Pr_3$ gives each flavor positive probability. (ii) The $Pr_3$ of a quadruple gives the color, which is the third component of that quadruple, probability 1. (iii) If two quadruples in STRAT agree on COLOR, they agree on $Pr_3$. (iv) For every $Pr_2$ that occurs as the second coordinate of a quadruple in STRAT and every COLOR, there is a quadruple in STRAT whose second and third coordinates are, respectively, that $Pr_2$ and that COLOR.

Player B specifies a strategy that tells him what to bet at $t_1$, $t_2$, $t_3$ given player A's strategy and player A's probability measures up to the appropriate time. At any time, he can make a finite number of bets that player A considers fair or favorable at the time; or he may refrain from betting.

Formally, *Player B's Strategy* is an ordered triple of partial functions (partial because player B may decide not to bet), $\langle F_1, F_2, F_3 \rangle$, where $F_1$ where defined maps player A's STRAT onto a finite number of bets with non-negative expectation for A according to A's $Pr_1$; $F_2$ where defined maps $\langle$STRAT, $Pr_2\rangle$ pairs onto a finite number of bets with non-negative expectation according to $Pr_2$; $F_3$ where defined maps $\langle$STRAT, $Pr_2$, COLOR, $P_3\rangle$ quadruplets onto a finite number of bets that have non-negative expectation according to $Pr_3$. A *Sequence of play* is a septuplet, $\langle Pr_1, B_1, Pr_2, B_2, \text{COLOR}, Pr_3, B_3\rangle$ where $\langle Pr_1, Pr_2, \text{COLOR}, Pr_3\rangle$ is in player A's strategy, and $B_1$, $B_2$, and $B_3$, respectively, are the bets or absence of bets that this quadruple elicits in the obvious way from player B's strategy. Let us say that player B's strategy *scores against* that of player A if (1) there is a sequence of play in which player B ends up at $t_3$ with bets whose net result is positive for him for all flavors (a Dutch Book against A), and (2) for every sequence of play, player B's winnings are non-negative for every flavor. We will say that player A's strategy is *bulletproof* if no strategy for player B will score against it.

*3.2 Bulletproof Strategies and Sufficient Partitions*

We will say that the partition of colors is *Sufficient for A's Strategy*, or in Jeffrey's terminology that *A's strategy proceeds by probability kinematics on the partition of colors* just in case for each $\langle Pr_1, Pr_2, C, Pr_3\rangle$ in A's STRAT, each color, $C$, and flavor, $F$:

$$Pr_1(F/C) = Pr_2(F/C) = (\text{where defined})Pr_3(F/C).$$

THEOREM II. *It is a necessary condition for A's strategy in the Observation Game to be bulletproof that A's strategy proceed by probability kinematics on the partition of colors.*

*Proof (1).* Suppose that A's strategy set has as a member a quadruple, $\langle Pr_1, Pr_2, C, Pr_3\rangle$ such that there is a flavor, $F$, such that $Pr_1(F/C)$ is unequal to $Pr_3(F/C)$. Then either $Pr_1(F/C)$ is less than $Pr_3(F/C)$ or $Pr_1(F/C)$ is greater than $Pr_3(F/C)$. Consider the first case, and let $e = Pr_3(F/C) - Pr_1(F/C)$. Player B can then end up at time $t_3$ with a Dutch Book against player A. At $t_1$ he makes a complex betting arrangement with player A: He proposes that if $C\&F$, player A pay him $\$Pr_1(F/C)$; if $C\&- F$, he pays player A $\$Pr_1(F/C)$; if $- C$, then the bet is called off. (ii) He proposes in addition that if $C$, he pays player A $\$ePr_1(- C)$; if $- C$, player A pays him $\$ePr_1(C)$. Player A regards both bets (i) and (ii) as fair according to his $Pr_1$. (The conditional bet, (i), can be constructed from a finite number of unconditional bets that he considers fair, as pointed out in section 2.) Then player B waits until time $t_3$. If the gamemaster announces that the color is something other than $C$, (i) requires no payment and player B receives $\$ePr_1(C)$ as a consequence of winning (ii). If, on the other hand, the color $C$ is announced, he then makes a further arrangement with player A: (iii). If $C\&F$, he pays player A $\$Pr_3(-F/C)$; if $C\& - F$, player A pays him $\$Pr_3(F/C)$. Player A, by the lights of his current $Pr_3$, will regard (iii) as fair because his current $Pr_3$ must be the same as the one in the quadruple we started with by the requirement that $Pr_3$ be a function of color alone. The net result of (i) together with (iii) is that player B wins $\$e$ no matter whether $F$ or $-F$. He has lost $\$ePr_1(-C)$ on (ii) reducing his winnings to $\$ePr_1(C)$ as before. The argument for case (ii) is similar, with player B taking the opposite ends of bets (i) and (iii).

*Proof (2).* Suppose that player A's STRAT contains a quadruple, $\langle Pr_1, Pr_2, C, Pr_3 \rangle$ such that there is a flavor, $F$, such that $Pr_2(F/C)$ is unequal to $Pr_3(F/C)$. Player B then waits until $t_2$. If the $Pr_2$ of the quadruple is not present at $t_2$, player B does not bet. However, if it is present, he can end up at $t_3$ with a Dutch Book against player A by betting just as in Proof (1) with $Pr_2$ substituted for $Pr_1$ and $t_2$ substituted for $t_1$ everywhere.

*Proof (3).* Suppose that player A's STRAT contains a quadruple $\langle Pr_1, Pr_2, C, Pr_3 \rangle$ such that there is a flavor, $F$, such that $Pr_1(F/C)$ is unequal to $Pr_2(F/C)$. Then either (i) $Pr_1(F/C)$ is unequal to $Pr_3(F/C)$ or (ii) $Pr_2(F/C)$ is unequal to $Pr_3(F/C)$ or (iii) $Pr_3(F/C)$ is undefined. In cases (i) and (ii), we have seen how the cunning bettor should bet under proofs (1) and (2), respectively. In case (iii), player A's STRAT must contain another quadruple with the same $Pr_1$ and $Pr_2$ in which $Pr_3(F/C)$ *is* well defined by the definition of a STRAT. This quadruple brings us back under case (i) or (ii).

Player B's strategy is this: He searches player A's STRAT for a quadru-plet of the kind described under proof (1). If he finds one, he takes the first one that he finds and bets relative to it as described under (1). If not, he searches for a quadruplet as described under (2). If he finds one, he takes the first one that he finds and bets as described under (2). If not, he does not bet at all. If player A's strategy does not proceed by probability kinematics on the partition of colors, player B's strategy will score against him. Player B will either find a quadruple of the kind described under proof (1) or one of the kind described under (2). If the first, he surely ends up with a Dutch Book against player A at $t_3$; if the second, he either ends up with a Dutch Book at $t_3$ or makes no bet at all.

Inspection of the proof of the foregoing theorem shows that player B knows the magnitude, $e$, of the discrepancy between player A's strategy and probability kinematics before he makes his first bet; at $t_1$ in case 1 and at $t_2$ in case 2. He could, then, modify the strategy given by inflating the stakes by a factor of $\$N/e\, Pr_1(C)$ to fit the $e$ and $C$ involved, where $N$ is an arbitrarily large positive real. Such a modified strategy for player B yields him a payoff of $\$N$ in each course of play in which he bets at all. In case 1, he is assured of such a payoff. In case 2, he is assured of such a payoff if the offending $Pr_2$ assignment appears, and does not bet otherwise.

### 3.3  Bulletproof Strategies and Potential Centering

Because we allow player A to pick his set of possible $Pr_2$'s in the specification of his strategy, there is another way in which his strategy can fail to be bulletproof. He might, for example, choose his possible $Pr_2$'s such that for each one, $Pr_2(C\&F)$ is less than $Pr_1(C\&F)$, for some particular color–flavor pair. In that case, player A's probability for $C\&F$ would have to move in a foreseeable direction, a fact that player B could exploit by betting against $C\&F$ at $t_1$ and buying back the bet at a profit at $t_2$.

If player A's strategy is such that for some proposition, $Q$, in the color–flavor space, $Pr_1(Q)$ greater than $Pr_2(Q)$ for all $Pr_2$'s allowed by the strategy, we will say that player A's strategy is *OUT*. If his strategy is such that for some $Q$ in the color–flavor space, there is a positive $e$ such that $Pr_1(C\&F) - Pr_2(C\&F)$ not less than $e$ for all $Pr_2$'s, we will say that his strategy is *DISTANT*. If his strategy is such that for some such $Q$, for some $Pr_2$, $Pr_1(Q)$ is greater than $Pr_2(Q)$ and for no $Pr_2$ is $Pr_1$ less than $Pr_2(Q)$, we will say that his strategy is *NOT-IN*.

> LEMMA. *If player A's strategy is* DISTANT, *player B can always end up with a Dutch Book at $t_2$ which assures him of whatever payoff he chooses in advance at $t_1$. If his strategy is* OUT *player B can always end up at $t_2$ with a Dutch Book against him. If his strategy is* NOT–IN, *player B's strategy can score against his.*

Proof is obvious.

Being *NOT-IN, OUT,* and *DISTANT* are increasingly serious defects for player A's strategy, the least serious of which still prevents his strategy from being bulletproof. If the $pr_1$ of player A's strategy can be represented as a mixture of the $pr_2$'s of his strategy, his strategy cannot be *OUT* or *DISTANT*. If his strategy has a finite number of $pr_2$'s, and the $pr_1$ of his strategy can be represented as a mixture of his $pr_2$'s in which each $pr_2$ has positive weight, then his strategy isn't *NOT-IN* (because if it were *NOT-IN*, the hypothesized mixture would give $Q$ probability less than $pr_1$). The question of centering will be raised again in a context where it is possible to bet on the $pr_2$'s.

# 4. Higher-Order Probabilities and Absolute Dutch Books

The foregoing discussion of the observation game focused on the concept of a *bulletproof strategy*. The state of being bulletproof is a strong coherence property, that is, a guarantee against a certain kind of conditional Dutch Book. A *conditional Dutch Book* is a set of bets such that they result in a net loss to the bookie (player A) if the condition is realized, and result in zero net transaction otherwise. A conditional Dutch Book on a condition of positive probability can always be turned into an unconditional Dutch Book by making the appropriate sidebet against the condition; but in the observation game, the conditions in question include the specification of an observational probability distribution, $pr_2$. If player A has well-defined probabilities over courses of play in the game, the conditions of the conditional Dutch Books that constitute *scores* against his strategy may well for him have probability zero. I did not assume in the foregoing discussion that the observer in the observation game had any such probabilities. The question arises as to what more can be said if he does. (The subsequent discussion owes much to the important work of Armendt (1980).)

## 4.1 Probability Kinematics

If for every sequence of play, player B's strategy results in bets at $t_3$ whose net result is positive for him for all flavors, we will say that player B's strategy constitutes an *unconditional dynamic Dutch Book* against that of player A. Under reasonable conditions, we can show that a strategy of belief change by probability kinematics on the observational partition almost everywhere (with respect to $Pr_1$) is a necessary condition for avoiding an unconditional Dutch Book.

Let us modify the observation game to get a version with higher-order probabilities as follows: Player A's three probability measures, $Pr_1$, $Pr_2$, and $Pr_3$, are over an enlarged probability space. This space is the product of (a) the original discrete space of color–flavor pairs of 'The Observation Game' and (b) the space of probability measures over space (a) with Lebesgue measurable sets in the appropriate $n$-space serving as the measurable sets. (These probability measures are to be interpreted as player A's $Pr_2$

about which player A is uncertain at $t_1$.) We assume that player A has a fixed initial probability, $Pr_1$. Since $Pr_3$ is a function of COLOR, we can take a set specified by a given $Pr_2$ and color as tantamount to a specification of a quadruple, $\langle Pr_1, Pr_2, \text{COLOR}, Pr_3 \rangle$, in player A's strategy. We will speak loosely of probabilities of sets of quadruples in this sense.

Let us call a quadruple, $\langle Pr_1, Pr_2, \text{COLOR}, Pr_3 \rangle$, in Player A's strategy VULNERABLE if there is a color, $C$, and flavor, $F$, such that $Pr_i (F/C)$ is defined for $i = 1, 2, 3$ and it is not the case that it takes on the same value for $i = 1, 2, 3$.

LEMMA 1. *If the set of VULNERABLE quadruples in player A's strategy has positive probability, player B can make an unconditional Dutch Book against player A.*

*Proof.* We showed that if in the Observation Game a VULNERABLE quadruple is played out by player A, player B ends up with a Dutch Book at $t_3$ that guarantees him fixed positive winnings, $\$K$, no matter what the flavor turns out to be. If the set of VULNERABLE quadruples has positive measure, then player B could guarantee himself an unconditional Dutch Book by making a sidebet against the set of vulnerable quadruples, $V$. He offers to pay player A $\$K Pr_1 (-V)$ if $V$, if player A will pay him $\$K Pr_1(V)$ if $-V$, guaranteeing himself winnings of $\$K Pr_1(V)$.

A quadruple disagrees with probability kinematics—is UNKINE-MATIC—if for some color, $C$, and flavor, $F$, $Pr_1(F/C)$ is unequal to $Pr_2(F/C)$, or $Pr_2(F/C)$ is unequal to $Pr_3(F/C)$, or both. The UNKINE-MATIC quadruples are the VULNERABLE ones together with ones in which $Pr_1(F/C)$ is unequal to $Pr_2(F/C)$ but $Pr_3(F/C)$ is undefined.[2] We must deal with the case in which player A gives his set of UNKINE-MATIC quadruples positive probability and gives his set of VULNER-ABLE quadruples zero $Pr_1$. Note that in this case, the agent has the optimistic belief ($Pr_1 = 1$) that nature will render him invulnerable to the consequences of any lack of kinematicity ($Pr_1(F/C)$ unequal to $Pr_2(F/C)$) by conveniently canceling the conditional bets by producing a color other than $C$ at $t_3$. He cannot square this with the requirement of the game that each $Pr_2$ in player A's strategy give each $Pr_2$ positive probability.

LEMMA 2. *If player A gives his set of UNKINEMATIC quadruples positive $Pr_1$, but gives his set of VULNERABLE quadruples zero $Pr_1$, then player B can make an unconditional dynamic Dutch Book against him.*

---

[2] Because some other color is the third coordinate of the quadruplet.

*Proof.* Since there are only a finite number of colors, if the set of unkinematic quadruples has positive measure and the set of vulnerable quadruples has zero measure, then there must be some particular color, $C$, such that the set of unkinematic quadruples with $Pr_1(F/C)$ unequal to $Pr_2(F/C)$ for some $F$ has positive measure and such that the subset of quadruples that contain $C$ has zero measure. Call these sets $UNK_C$ and $VUL_C$, respectively. If $UNK_C$ has positive measure, then there is some positive number, $e$, such that the set of quadruples that contain $Pr_2(C)$ at least as great as $e$ has positive measure,[3] since the observation game requires that for each color, each $Pr_2$ gives it positive measure. Call this set $UNK'_C$ and the subset in which $C$ does come up, $VUL'_C$. Now consider the following fair-bet strategy: At $t_1$ B proposes (1) that player A pay him \$1 if $VUL'_C$ and that he pay player A nothing if not. Player A considers this fair since he gives $VUL'_C$ zero $Pr_1$. If at $t_2$ player A is in $UNK'$ player B offers (2) to sell back bet 1 for \$$e$. Player A now considers this fair or favorable. B's strategy so far constitutes a Dutch Book conditional on $UNK'_C$. But since $UNK'_C$ has positive $Pr_1$, this can be turned into an unconditional Dutch Book by a suitable sidebet (3) against $UNK'_C$ at $t_1$ as before.

We will say that player A's strategy *proceeds by probability kinematics almost everywhere in $Pr_1$* if his $Pr_1$ gives his set of UNKINEMATIC quadruples probability zero. Lemmas 1 and 2 do not quite establish that this property is a necessary condition for avoiding an unconditional dynamic Dutch Book because nothing has been said that requires these sets to be measurable. However, it is most reasonable to add the requirement that these sets be measurable if we regard player A's strategy not just as a set theoretical entity, but as a strategy that is specifiable in an effective manner.

THEOREM III. *If player A's sets of VULNERABLE and UNKINEMATIC quadruples are measurable and his strategy does not proceed by probability kinematics almost everywhere in $Pr_1$, player B can make an unconditional dynamic Dutch Book against him.*

### 4.2 Centering

In the present context we can say more about centering. Goldstein (1983) and van Fraassen (1984) both argue that coherence requires that $pr_1$ be

---

[3] We use countable additivity here.

equal to the prior expectation of $pr_2$ considered as a random variable. That is, $pr_1$ must be the 'center of mass' of the possible $pr_2$'s where $pr_1$ is taken as the measure of mass. I will take some liberties in adapting their arguments to the present setting.

Consider first the case in which there are a finite number of possible $pr_2$'s, each with positive $pr_1$:

THEOREM IVA (VAN FRAASSEN). *The bookie's prior, $pr_1$, must be such that for any proposition, Q, of the color–flavor space, and any number, a, such that $pr_1[pr_2(Q) = a]$ is positive:*
$pr_1[Q/pr_2(Q) = a] = a$
*or the bettor can make an unconditional dynamic Dutch Book against him.*

*Proof.* Suppose that $pr_1[Q/pr_2(Q) = a] = a - e$ for some positive $e$. Then at $t_1$, (i) the bettor makes a conditional bet with the bookie to the effect that if $pr_2(Q) = a\&Q$, the bookie pays him $\$1 - (a - e)$; if $pr_2(q) = a\& - Q$, he pays the bookie $\$a - e$; if it is not the case that $pr_2(Q) = a$, the bet is called off. (ii) In addition, he makes a sidebet to the effect that if $pr_2(Q) = a$, he will pay the bookie $\$e\, pr_1[ - pr_2(Q) = a]$; if $ - pr_2(Q) = a$, the bookie will pay him $\$e$ $pr_1[pr_2(Q) = a]$. Then he waits until $t_2$. If it is not the case that $pr_2(Q) = a$, the conditional bet (i) is canceled and he wins the sidebet (ii). If it is the case that $pr_2(Q) = a$, then (iii) he bets on Q such that if Q, he pays the bookie $\$1 - a$; if $ - $ Q the bookie pays him $\$a$. Then the net effect of (i) and (iii) is that he wins $\$e$ no matter whether Q or not, which is reduced by his loss of the sidebet (ii). In any event, his net gain from (i), (ii), (iii) is $\$e\, pr_1[pr_2(Q) = a]$. If $pr_1[Q/pr_2(Q) = a] = a + e$ for some positive $e$, the bettor takes the other end of bets (i) and (iii). It follows immediately that $pr_1(Q) = E_1[pr_2(Q)]$; that the prior probability of any proposition in the color–flavor space is the prior expectation of its posterior probability. To get the same result in a more general setting, we need to bet on $pr_2$ falling within an interval.

THEOREM IVB (GOLDSTEIN). *The bookie's prior, $pr_1$, must be such that for any proposition, Q, of the color–flavor space, and any closed interval, I, such that $pr_1[pr_2(Q)$ in $I]$ is positive:*
$pr_1[Q/pr_2(Q)$ in $I]$ in $I$
*or the bettor can make an unconditional dynamic Dutch Book against him.*
*Proof.* As in IVA.

The principles that figure in these theorems are sometimes referred to in the philosophical literature as 'Miller' principles. One or both are discussed in Goldstein (1983), Skyrms (1980a, 1980b), and van Fraassen (1984).

# 5. Converse Dynamic Dutch Book Arguments

A dynamic Dutch Book argument shows that if you have a rule for updating probabilities in a certain type of situation, and your rule does not meet certain standards, some kind of Dutch Book can be made against you. David Lewis' Dutch Book argument for conditionalization and my generalization of that argument to probability kinematics are examples. Converse Dutch Book arguments show that if the standards are met, no such Dutch Book can be made. A Dutch Book theorem has little force if its correlative converse is not true. For the *dynamic* case, converse Dutch Book arguments have not been pursued in the philosophical literature.

## 5.1 Conditionalization

Consider the conditions for Lewis' dynamic Dutch Book argument for conditionalization. The bookie has a prior at time 1 such that every member of a finite partition, $p_i$, has positive prior probability. At time 2, he learns the true member of the partition and changes his probability assignment. His rule for change is a function that maps the pair ⟨prior, member of the partition learned⟩ to his posterior. A bettor gets to know the bookie's strategy, gets to know the true member of the partition, when the bookie does, and gets to make a finite number of bets at each time that the bookie considers fair at that time. The bettor's strategy is a pair of functions, one from the bookie's probability assignment at time 1 to a finite set of bets that the bookie considers fair at that time, and a second from the revealed member of the partition and the bookie's probability at time 2 to a finite set of bets that he considers fair at that time. The bookie's strategy, together with that of the bettor, determine a *payoff function*, which gives the net payoff of all bets for each state of the world. Lewis' argument shows that if the bookie's strategy is not to update by conditionalization, the bettor can choose a strategy such that the two yield a payoff function for the bettor that is positive everywhere.

> THEOREM V. *If the bookie's strategy is to update by conditionalization, then there is no bettor's strategy that constitutes a Dutch Book against him.*

*Proof.* Any payoff function that the bettor can achieve against the conditionalizing strategy by betting at $t_1$ and $t_2$ can be achieved by an alternative strategy that relies only on a finite number of bets all made at time 1. For every bet that the bettor's original strategy makes at $t_1$, the modified strategy will make at $t_1$. For every bet on $Q$ that the bettor's original strategy makes at $t_2$, if $P_i$ is the true member of the partition, the modified strategy substitutes a bet on $Q$ conditional on $P_i$ made at $t_1$, (which can be attained by a finite number of unconditional bets made at $t_1$). Given that the bookie is a conditionalizer and that the true member of the partition is announced at $t_2$, the payoff must be the same. A dynamic Dutch Book can therefore be made against the conditionalizer only if a static Dutch Book can be made against him at $t_1$ by a finite number of bets that he considers fair. This we know to be impossible given that he respects the probability calculus at $t_1$ since the expectation of the sum of a finite number of random variables, each with zero expectation, is zero; while the expectation of a betting arrangement which constitutes a Dutch Book must be negative.

### 5.2 Probability Kinematics

In the discussion of the Observation Game, it is shown that the bookie's strategy must proceed by probability kinematics on the partition, to be 'bulletproof.' This is somewhat weaker than an unconditional Dutch Book. The converse would then be somewhat stronger than the converse to a Dutch Book; that is, that belief change by probability kinematics is 'bulletproof.'

Consider first the case of "coarsegrained observation by candlelight" where the bookie in the observation game has only a finite number of $pr_2$'s possible. We will argue that if the bookie has a strategy of belief change by probability kinematics on the partition of colors, and if his strategy meets an INTERIOR condition, we can embed the observation game in a bigger Lewis game such that the bookie's strategy in the original game fails to be bulletproof only if a strategy of conditionalization in the Lewis game can have a dynamic Dutch Book made against it. This is impossible by the results of the previous section.

The larger game is constructed along the lines suggested by section 4. The bookie has a larger probability space, which is the product of a space of $N$ elements $\langle p_1, \ldots, p_n \rangle$ (for the $N$ possible $Pr_2$'s over the color–flavor space) with the original color–flavor space. The bookie has a prior over this space that gives each atom positive probability. At time $t_2$ a $p_i$ is announced and the bookie must move to a new probability, $pr_2$, by a rule which makes $pr_2$ a function of the announced $p_i$. $Pr_2$ must be a non-zero for each color–flavored pair. At time $t_3$ a color is announced and the bookie must move to a new probability, $Pr_3$, by a rule that makes $Pr_3$ a function of $Pr_2$ and COLOR. This larger game is the composition of two Lewis games for the move from $t_1$ to $t_2$ and the move from $t_2$ to $t_3$, for which we know that the strategy of conditionalization is both a necessary and sufficient condition for immunity from Dutch Book.

The possible probability assignments over a discrete space of $m$ objects can be thought of as represented by the points in an $m - 1$ dimensional polyhedron in $m$ dimensional space. The $n$ $p_i$'s that are considered by the bookie's strategy in the original game to be possible $pr_2$'s are to be thought of as $n$ points in the interior of such a polyhedron (the interior because they must all give each color–flavor pair non-zero probability). The INTER-IOR condition on the bookie's strategy in the original game is that his $pr_1$ over the color–flavor space be in the interior of the convex hull of the $p_i$'s. If the INTERIOR condition is met, it follows that the bookie's $pr_1$ can be represented as a non-trivial mixture of his $p_i$'s, that is, one which gives each $p_i$ non-zero mixing coefficient.

The bookie's $pr_1$ in the smaller game is extended to $PR_1$ over the probability space of the bigger game as follows:

(1) Let $PR_1(C\&F/p_i) = p_i(C\&F)$ for each $C$, $F$, $i$.[4]
(2) Distribute $PR_1$ over the $p_i$'s such that each $p_i$ gets non-zero probability and $PR_1(C\&F) = pr_1(C\&F)$ for each $C$, $F$; that is, represent $pr_1$ as a non-trivial mixture of the $p_i$'s.

Notice that we then have:

$$\begin{aligned}
(3)\quad PR_1(F/Cp_i) &= PR_1(p_i)PR_1(F\&C/p_i)/PR_i(p_i)PR_i(C/p_i) \\
&= PR_1(F\&C/p_i)/PR_i(C/p_i) \\
&= p_i(F\&C)/p_i(C) \quad by\ (1) \\
&= p_i(F/C) \\
&= pr_i(F/C) \text{because the } p_i\text{'s figure in a strategy} \\
&\qquad\text{of belief change by probability kinematics} \\
&\qquad\text{on the partition of colors in the} \\
&\qquad\text{original game.} \\
&= PR_i(F/C) \text{ by (2).}
\end{aligned}$$

((3) and its relation to probability kinematics are discussed in Armendt (1980), Good (1981), and Skyrms (1980a, 1980b).)

---

[4] In a slight abuse of notation, '$p_i(C\&F)$' is used for '$pr_2(C\&F)$ according to the $i^{th}$ possible $pr_2$.' The construction models the random variable $pr_2$ as probability conditional on the partition of the $p_i$s.

Now let a bookie's strategy in the big game be belief change by conditionalization. His behavior vis-à-vis the color–flavor space will be indistinguishable from that of a bookie pursuing a strategy of belief change by probability kinematics in the smaller game. The initial probabilities at $t_1$ are the same by (2). At $t_2$ when the $p_i$ resulting from the observation interaction becomes known the probabilities are the same by (1). At $t_3$ when the true color becomes known as well, the probabilities are the same by (3). Consequently, a bettor's strategy that will *score* against a strategy of belief change by probability kinematics that meets the INTERIOR condition in the observation game will *score* against the strategy of conditionalization in the bigger game. But a *score* against the conditionalizing strategy in the bigger game could be turned into an unconditional dynamic Dutch Book if the course of play leading to that *score* has positive prior probability, by making a suitable sidebet against that course of play in the standard way. Each course of play does have positive prior probability. $PR(p_i)$ is positive by (2). $PR_1(C/p_i)$ is positive by (1) together with the requirement of the observation game that each possible probability at $t_2$ gives each atom of the color–flavor space positive probability. We know that a bettor's strategy that constitutes an unconditional dynamic Dutch Book against the conditionalizationing strategy in the larger game is impossible from the previous section. So we have shown:

THEOREM VI. *In the case in which the bookie has a finite number of possible $pr_2$'s in the observation game, if his strategy proceeds by probability kinematics on the partition of colors and meets the INTERIOR condition, his strategy is bulletproof.*

What can we say about the general case where the bookie's strategy may recognize infinitely many $pr_2$'s as possible? Call a strategy *catholic* if it contains $pr_2$'s that distribute probabilities among the colors in every possible way consistent with giving each color non-zero probability. If we idealize our observer so that he has no trouble dealing with arbitrary real numbers, a catholic strategy will be for him a sign of open-mindedness about what observation will bring. For each possible $pr_1$ (which gives each atom of the color–flavor space positive probability) there is a unique *catholic probability kinematics* strategy for the bookie. (The quadruples have the given $pr_1$ as first coordinate. The second coordinate is a $pr_2$ determined by an arbitrary $pr_2$ for color, extended to flavor by probability kinematics.

The third coordinate is an arbitrary color. The fourth coordinate is a $pr_3$ gotten from the second coordinate by conditionalization on the third.)

THEOREM VII. *A catholic strategy of belief change by probability kinematics in the observation game is bulletproof.*

*Proof.* Suppose that it is not bulletproof. Then some bettor's strategy can score against it. The bettor's strategy scores against that of the bookie if (1) there is a sequence of play in which the bettor ends up at $t_3$ with bets whose net payoff is positive for him (negative for the bookie) for every flavor, and (2) for every sequence of play, the bettor's winnings are non-negative for every flavor. So if a bettor's strategy will score against the bookie's infinite strategy, it will score against any finite substrategy of that strategy that includes (one of) the quadruples of the type described under (1). Let $q = \langle pr_1, pr_2, C, pr_3 \rangle$ be such a quadruple relative to the hypothesized score against the infinite strategy. There is a finite substrategy of the original strategy that meets the INTERIOR condition. Since $pr_1$ gives each color-flavor atom non-zero probability, it is in the interior of the convex hull of the probabilities that can be gotten from $pr_1$ by conditionalization on a color. Consider the probability measures that can be gotten by from $pr_1$ by 'almost conditionalizing' on colors, that is, by probability kinematics on the partition of colors that gives the color 'almost conditionalized on' probability $1 - e$. Call these the $V$'s. Given $pr_1$ we can choose $e$ small enough so that $pr_1$ is in the interior of the convex hull of the $V$'s. As our possible $pr_2$'s of the finite substrategy, we take the $V$'s together with the $pr_2$ of the quadruple $q$. The finite substrategy consists of all the quadruples in the original strategy having one of these $pr_2$'s. This is a finite number because there are only a finite number of possible colors, $C$, and $Pr_3$ is a function of $C$. So, if the bettor's strategy will score against the original infinite strategy, it will score against this finite substrategy, but this is impossible by the previous theorem.

## 6. Diachronic Coherence and Probability Kinematics

Conditionalization is such a natural way for updating degrees of belief that Hacking needed to remind us that it required a justification. When it is regarded as a *rule* or *strategy* applicable to a certain sort of situation that is commonly approximated by our experience, a justification is forthcoming. In such situations, adoption of any alternative rule, strategy, or habit leads an agent to dynamic incoherence regarding conditional bets. In effect, he adopts two distinct fair betting quotients for conditional bets depending on how they are described, where the equivalence of the descriptions is a simple consequence of Boolean logic together with his own rule. In such situations, adoption of the rule of conditionalization guarantees coherence.

But not every learning situation is of the kind to which conditionalization applies. The situation may not be of the kind that can be correctly described or even usefully approximated as the attainment of certainty by the agent in some proposition in his degree of belief space. The rule of belief change by probability kinematics on a partition was designed to apply to a much broader class of learning situations than the rule of conditionalization. In those situations for which it was designed, it preserves the virtues of conditionalization.[5] It is coherent and any rule which conflicts with it is not.

This is not to say that we can build an adequate epistemology solely on the rule of belief change by probability kinematics. That rule has its own limits of applicability; its justification here occurs within the context of the observation game. Other models of learning situations are possible, and each poses the question: "What rule or rules for belief change are dynamically coherent for this sort of situation?"

# Bibliography

Adams, E. (1962) "On Rational Betting Systems," *Archive für Mathematische Logik und Grundlagenforshung* 6: 7–29, 112–28.

Armendt, B. (1980) "Is There a Dutch Book Argument for Probability Kinematics?" *Philosophy of Science* 47: 583–8.

Diaconis, P. and Zabell, S. (1982) "Updating Subjective Probability," *Journal of the American Statistical Association* 77: 822–30.

de Finetti, B. (1937) "La Prévision: Ses lois logiques, ses sources subjectives," *Annales de l'Institut Henri Poincaré* 7: 1–68. (Translation published as "Foresight: Its Logical Laws, Its Subjective Sources," in *Studies in Subjective Probability*, Henry E. Kyburg, Jr. and H. Smokler (eds.), Huntington, NY: Krieger, 1980.)

---

[5] This includes some other virtues, in addition to dynamic coherence. See Teller (1973, 1976).

Freedman, D. A. and Purves, R. A. (1969) "Bayes Method for Bookies," *Annals of Mathematical Statistics* 40: 1177–86.

Goldstein, M. (1983) "The Prevision of a Prevision," *Journal of the American Statistical Association* 78: 817–19.

Good, I. J. (1981) "The Weight of Evidence Provided by Uncertain Testimony or from an Uncertain Event," *Journal of Statistical Computation and Simulation* 13: 56–60.

Hacking, I. (1967) "Slightly More Realistic Personal Probability," *Philosophy of Science* 34: 311–25.

Jeffrey, R. (1965) *The Logic of Decision*. New York: McGraw-Hill. Second edition. Chicago: University of Chicago Press, 1983.

Ramsey, F. P. (1931) "Truth and Probability," in R. B. Braithwaite (ed.), *The Foundations of Mathematics and Other Essays*. New York: Harcourt Brace. (Reprinted in *Studies in Subjective Probability*, Henry E. Kyburg, Jr. and H. Smokler (eds.), Huntington, NY: Krieger, 1980.)

Skyrms, B. (1980a) *Causal Necessity*. New Haven, CT: Yale University Press, Appendix 2.

—— (1980b) "Higher-Order Degrees of Belief," in *Prospects for Pragmatism*, D. H. Mellor (ed.), Cambridge: Cambridge University Press.

Teller, P. (1973) "Conditionalization and Observation," *Synthese* 26: 218–58.

—— (1976) "Conditionalization, Observation, and Change of Preference," in W. Harper and C. Hooker (eds.), *Foundations of Probability Theory, Statistical Inference, and Statistical Theories of Science*, pp. 205–53. Dordrecht: D. Reidel.

van Fraassen, B. (1984) "Belief and the Will," *Journal of Philosophy* 81: 235–56.

# 8

# Updating, Supposing, and MAXENT

## 1. Introduction

Updating subjective belief to assimilate a given bit of information and supposing what the world would be like were that bit of information true, are distinct mental processes for which distinct rules are appropriate. A Warrenite asked to update on the piece of information that Oswald didn't kill Kennedy would come to the conclusion that someone else did; but when asked to suppose what the world would be like had Oswald not killed Kennedy will not suppose that someone else would have. The difference is often marked in ordinary language by the distinction between indicative and subjunctive mood. The Warrenite will assert: "If Oswald didn't kill Kennedy, then someone else did" but deny: "If Oswald hadn't killed Kennedy, then someone else would have."[1]

Given an initial probability measure and a constraint on possible final probability measures, one moves to a final probability by the rule of MAXENT if one chooses from among the final probabilities which satisfy the constraint, the one which has minimum information or (equivalently) maximum entropy relative to the initial probability. This rule was intro-duced as "the principle of minimum discrimination information" by Kull-back and Leibler[2] and as the rule of maximum entropy by Jaynes.[3] It has found application in a wide variety of fields,[4] but its logical status remains a matter of controversy.

---

[1] The example is due to Adams (1970). See also the discussion in Lewis (1976).
[2] Kullback and Leibler (1951); the rule is extensively studied in Kullback (1959).
[3] Jaynes (1957, 1963, 1967, 1974, and 1980).
[4] E.g. statistical mechanics (Jaynes, 1957; image enhancement Frieden, 1972).

Some supporters of MAXENT go so far as to give it the status of a principle of Bayesian *logic*, on a par with additivity of probability or Bayes' rule of conditioning.[5] Some of its detractors claim that it is almost inconsistent with Bayesian methodology.[6] Much of the debate appears to proceed on the assumption, tacit or explicit, that MAXENT is an *inductive* rule, i.e. a rule for *updating* subjective probabilities.[7] I want to suggest that this is the wrong way to look at MAXENT. Properly viewed, MAXENT is a rule for *stochastic hypothesizing*; a rule for *supposing*.

In section 2, I will discuss dynamic coherence requirements for Bayesian updating. The framework will be broad enough to cover cases in which Bayes' rule of conditionalization does not directly apply, including cases in which MAXENT is construed as a rule of updating. In section 3, I will introduce the Stalnaker logic of supposing and adapt it to the case where the possible situations are stochastic; i.e. statistical models. Section 4 will develop a few technical facts about the relation of MAXENT, exponential families and sufficient statistics. With the stage thus set, the next two sections will analyze MAXENT alternatively as an updating rule and as a supposing rule. Section 5 will find it wanting as a generally valid rule for Bayesian updating for essentially the reasons put forward by Shimony and his co-workers. Section 6 will argue that MAXENT properly applied as a Bayesian *supposing* or *hypothesizing* rule is perfectly legitimate.

## 2.  Updating Subjective Probability

Bayesians update subjective probabilities by *Bayes' Rule: Condition on the evidence!* That is, when presented with new evidence, e, which has positive prior probability, revise your subjective probabilities such that:

$$\text{NEWPR}(q) = \text{OLDPR}(q|e) = \text{OLDPR}(q\ e) / \text{OLDPR}(e)$$

Why use Bayes' Rule for such situations, rather than some other? It is a necessary and sufficient condition for *dynamic coherence* that one do so.

Thus, suppose that you have an initial probability at time $t_1$; that there is a partition, $E$, of your probability space each of whose members has

---

[5] Jaynes, Shore and Johnson (1980), Williams (1980), Cheesman (1983).

[6] Friedman and Shimony (1971), Shimony (1973), Dias and Shimony (1981), Shimony (1985), Seidenfeld (1986).

[7] At least insofar as one can tell from the discussion.

positive initial probability; that then you are to be told the true member of the partition and are to move to a final probability at time $t_2$ by some epistemic rule for updating probability. A bettor who knows your rule can make a finite number of bets with you at time $t_1$ according to your probabilities at $t_2$. He will be said to make an unconditional dynamic Dutch Book against you if he has a strategy which always leaves him at $t_2$ with a system of bets whose net gain to him is positive in every possible situation. *You are not open to an unconditional dynamic Dutch Book if and only if your epistemic rule is Bayes' Rule.*

The foregoing updating model presumes that two things are given: (1) a learning situation in which the input is just the information that the true state of affairs is in some designated member of the partition, $E$, and (2) a initial probability distribution which gives the relevant conditional probabilities: $\Pr(q|e)$. The model may not apply in many cases of interest because we do not have the nice package of (1) and (2). What sort of theory is possible if these assumptions are weakened?

Non-Bayesian statisticians (Fisher, Neyman) question (2). Suppose we have a statistical model with an observation space, $X$, with chances depending on a parameter, $\theta$. In Bayes' method, we assume a prior over the parameter space, calculate pr $(\theta|x)$ by Bayes' theorem, and update on our observation by Bayes' rule. But what if we don't have a prior on the parameter space? Suppose we have some rule assigning probabilities to the parameter values after an observation. Call this rule *chance coherent* if it always assigns posterior probabilities which are immune from a *Dutch Book in chance*, i.e. a finite system of bets which have a negative chance expectation for every value of $\theta$. Cornfield (1969) and Freedman and Purves (1969) show that our updating rule is chance coherent just in case it coincides with Bayes' method applied to some prior or other over the parameter space.

Epistemologists (Austin, Sellars, Jeffrey) question (1). Various modified versions of the learning situation are possible. Can we say anything general enough to cover them all? Suppose you have at time $t_1$ an initial probability and will update it at time $t_2$ to a probability revised in the light of some sort of learning experience. Suppose that you have at time $t_1$ initial probabilities over one's possible revised probabilities. Assume for the moment that one has only a finite number of possible revised probabilities, each with positive initial probability. A bettor can bet with you at times $t_1$ and $t_2$. If we give the learning situation only this much structure, what can we say about dynamic coherence? It is a necessary and sufficient condition for coherence that your initial probability, $\text{pr}_1$, satisfy principle $M$:[8]

$$M : \text{pr}_1(q|\text{pr}_2 = \text{pr}^\star) = \text{pr}^\star(q)$$

If we give the learning situation additional structure, $M$ remains necessary for coherence but may not be sufficient. Notice that in the presence of $M$ the move to an enlarged probability space with $\text{pr}_2$ as a random variable formally embeds our 'black box' learning situation in a conditioning model.

It appears that Bayes' rule of conditioning has greater scope in the theory of updating subjective probability than some of its critics have been willing to concede. Very substantial generalizations of the setting for updating carry the consequence that dynamic coherence requires embeddability in a conditioning model.

## 3. Statistical Supposition

*Supposing* as a branch of logic has been developed as the theory of subjunctive conditionals. This may seem rather remote from the subject matter at hand, but I urge the reader to be patient. Subjunctive conditionals were a problem for logical empiricists; a puzzle knot in the hands of Nelson Goodman; and only became a branch of logic when Stalnaker (1968) cut the knot. Stalnaker's idea was to introduce a *selection function, f*, which maps an ordered pair $\langle w,s \rangle$ where $w$ is a possible world and $s$ is a supposition onto a world $w'$. The idea is that according to that selection function, starting in world (or situation) $w$ and supposing $s$ takes you to $w'$. Then, a subjunctive conditional "If $s$ were the case, $q$ would be" is true in $w$ just in case $q$ is true in $f\langle w,s \rangle$; false otherwise. Stalnaker required a selection function to have certain properties: (i) supposition $s$ indeed holds in $f\langle w,s \rangle$; (ii) If $s$ holds in $w$, then $f\langle w,s \rangle = w$; (iii) If $s'$ holds in $f\langle w,s \rangle$ and $s$ holds in $f\langle w,s' \rangle$, then $f\langle w,s \rangle = f\langle w,s' \rangle$. The second and third conditions are motivated by the idea that $f\langle w,s \rangle$ should be the most similar world to $w$ in which $s$ holds. (There is a fourth condition which requires impossible

---

[8] The Dutch Book is constructed in Goldstein (1983) and van Fraassen (1984). For further discussion of principle $M$ and its generalizations, see Gaifman (forthcoming) and Skyrms (1987a, b).

presuppositions to take one to an impossible world where everything is true, but the treatment of impossible presuppositions need not concern us here.) Stalnaker then studied the logic of subjunctive conditionals that holds for every such selection function. Stalnaker's account was generalized by Lewis who challenges the assumptions of existence and uniqueness for "the world minimally different from $W$ in which $S$ holds," and suggests an extension of the Stalnaker semantics to the cases where these assumptions fail.

How can these ideas apply to statistics? Let us shrink the grandiose philosophical notion of a possible world to the more modest one of a possible situation, and let us make that situation stochastic. Then what we have is a chance distribution over some outcome space. A set of chance distributions over some outcome space $X$, indexed by some parameter space $W$—i.e. a statistical model—is a natural domain of application for a stochastic Stalnaker selection function. Stochastic hypotheses will be taken as consistent constraints on the chances (which may undetermine the chance distribution). The game here is to find some interesting sense of "the chance distribution most similar to $w$ which satisfies constraint $S$."

Note that in this setting the difference between *supposing* and *updating* is mathematically clear-cut. In a typical Bayesian updating situation one is uncertain about the chances, and so one's subjective probability distribution on the outcome space is a mixture of the possible chance distributions. Updating is an operation which typically takes one from one point in the interior of the convex closure of the chance distributions to another; supposing moves from one chance distribution to another.

## 4. Maxent

Let us start with the simplest case, where our outcome space, $X$, contains only a finite number of points, $x_1, x_2, \ldots x_n$. Then the *entropy* of a probability, $P$, on this space is:

$$-\Sigma_i P(x_i) \log P(x_i)$$

and the *information* is the negative of the entropy. The minimum information or maximum entropy probability is the one which makes the states equiprobable: $P(x_i) = 1/n$.

Suppose that one has some requirements about what the probability on this space should look like in the form of what expectations it should give to some random variables. These constraints might very well underdetermine the probability measure. In the absence of any further information or desiderata about what the probability should look like, it might seem natural to choose among the probabilities satisfying the constraints that which has the minimum information.[9] This is the rule MAXENT, suggested by Jaynes (1957) and others.

For a simple example, consider an outcome space with just three points, $x_1$, $x_2$, $x_3$. You can think of these as the outcome of the roll of a three-sided die. Consider the random variable $f(x_i) = i$, (the number of spots showing on the die). The MAXENT probability gives $P(x_i) = 1/3$, and $E(f) = 2$. Choosing the MAXENT probability under the constraint that $E(f)$ have a different value has the following results (courtesy of E. T. Jaynes' Basic program, MAXENT 1.16):

| $E(f)$ | $P(x_1)$ | $P(x_2)$ | $P(x_3)$ |
|--------|----------|----------|----------|
| 1   | 1        | 0        | 0        |
| 0.1 | 0.907833 | 0.084333 | 0.007834 |
| 0.2 | 0.826297 | 0.147407 | 0.026297 |
| 0.3 | 0.751567 | 0.196866 | 0.051567 |
| 0.4 | 0.681867 | 0.236267 | 0.081867 |
| 0.5 | 0.616204 | 0.267592 | 0.116204 |
| 0.6 | 0.553972 | 0.292055 | 0.153972 |
| 0.7 | 0.494780 | 0.310440 | 0.194780 |
| 0.8 | 0.438371 | 0.323257 | 0.238271 |
| 0.9 | 0.384586 | 0.330829 | 0.284586 |
| 2.0 | 0.333333 | 0.333333 | 0.333333 |
| 2.1 | 0.284586 | 0.330829 | 0.384586 |
| 2.2 | 0.238372 | 0.323257 | 0.438370 |
| 2.3 | 0.194780 | 0.310440 | 0.494780 |
| 2.4 | 0.153972 | 0.292055 | 0.553972 |
| 2.5 | 0.116204 | 0.267592 | 0.616203 |
| 2.6 | 0.081867 | 0.236267 | 0.681867 |
| 2.7 | 0.051567 | 0.196866 | 0.751567 |
| 2.8 | 0.026297 | 0.147407 | 0.826296 |
| 2.9 | 0.007834 | 0.084332 | 0.907834 |
| 3.0 | 0        | 0        | 1        |

[9] Uniqueness is guaranteed by strict convexity of the entropy as a function of $P$

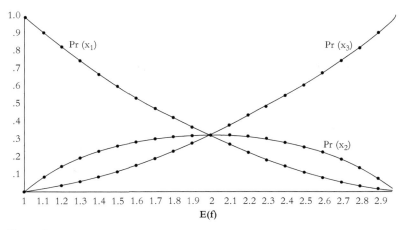

**Figure 1**

These results are plotted in Figure 1. Notice that this family of probabilities is not closed under mixing. E.g. an equal mixture of $\langle 1,0,0 \rangle$ and $\langle 0,0,1 \rangle$ is $\langle 1/2,0,1/2 \rangle$ but that is not in the family.

To extend these ideas to the general case, the notion of information needs to be generalized to the Kullback–Leibler discrimination information. Suppose that we start with a prior probability, $P$, and move to a posterior $Q$ which satisfies certain constraints. For a countable space, $W$, the discrimination information in $Q$ with respect to $P$ is:

$$I(Q, P) = \Sigma_w Q(w) \log [Q(w)/P(w)]$$

The finite sample space is a special case with $P$ making the points equiprobable.

More generally, let $\langle W, X_1, \mu_1 \rangle$ be a probability space, with $\mu_1$ being our initial probability measure. Let $\mu_2$ and $m$ be probability measures on this space such that $\mu_1$ and $\mu_2$ are both absolutely continuous with respect to $m$. Then the Radon–Nikodym derivatives $P = d\mu_1/dm$ and $Q = d\mu_2/dm$ exist and the discrimination information in $\mu_2$ with respect to $\mu_1$ is:

$$I(\mu_2, \mu_1) = \int_w Q(w) \log [Q(w)/P(w)]dm^{10}$$

---

[10]   Or, letting $m = P$, $\int_W Q \log Q \, dP$.

The principle of minimizing this quantity subject to constraints was put forward and extensively studied by Kullback and Leibler (1951); Kullback (1959).

The notion of a chance supposition or constraint in the most general form imaginable would be just a set of possible chance probability measures. If the constraint is a *convex* set, then if a MAXENT solution exists, it is unique since $I(Q, P)$ is strictly convex in $Q$. Constraints taking the form of the specification of the desired expectation of a random variable specify such a convex set. Topological conditions on the constraint set which guarantee the existence of a MAXENT solution are given in Csizar (1975).[11]

Consider simple constraints consisting of the specification of the expectation of a random variable, $E(f) = a$; where the MAXENT solution exists. For fixed $f$, letting $a$ vary *the solutions forms an exponential family for which $f$ is a sufficient statistic passing through the initial probability P.* This family has $m$ density:

$$P(x) \exp [kf(x)]/N(k)$$

(Here $P$ is the $m$ density of the initial probability. If we let $m = P$, it is unity, $k$ is adjusted to give the value of $a$ required by the constraint. $N$ is a normalizing factor.) If a member of the constraint set has this density it is the MAXENT solution. Moreover, if $\mu_1$ is the initial probability and $\mu_2$ is the MAXENT solution, then for any probability, $m$, in the constraint set:

$$(\text{MDI}) \ I(m, \mu_1) = I(m, \mu_2) + I(\mu_2, \mu_1)$$

MAXENT solves the problem of selecting a member of the constraint set by using the initial probability and the statistic of the constraint to generate in a canonical way a statistical model which contains just one member of the constraint set. Essentially the same thing happens in the general case.[12] The exponential family of MAXENT solutions for the three-sided die is graphed in Figure 2.

---

[11] The constraint set being a convex set closed in the topology of variational distance guarantees the existence of a MAXENT solution.

[12] See Kullback (1959); Csizar (1975). In particular the minimum discrimination information equation, (MDI), holds in general for the MAXENT solution it exists in. We will use this fact in section 6.

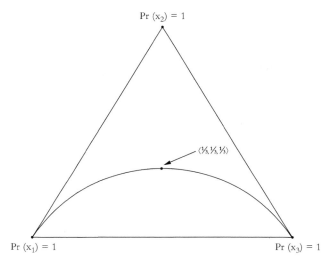

Figure 2

## 5. MAXENT as Bayesian Updating

As we say in section 2, *coherence* gives a special place in the theory of updating subjective probability to Bayes' rule of conditioning. Bayes' rule is a special case of MAXENT. Let the random variable $I_c$ be the indicator function which takes the value 1 in the set $c$ and the value 0 outside $c$. Let $c$ be a set with non-negative initial prior probability. And let the constraint be $E(I_c) = 1$. Then the MAXENT solution is the same as that gotten by updating by Bayes' rule, i.e. conditioning on $c$. This follows immediately from Kullback's theorem (noted in section 3) that the statistic of the constraint is a sufficient statistic for the exponential family of MAXENT solutions. This means that probabilities conditional on $c$ must be the same in all members of the family, including the initial probability. Sufficiency together with the fact that in the final probability $E(I_c) = 1$ determine that the final probability comes from the initial one by conditioning on $c$.

Kullback's sufficiency theorem also leads immediately to the result that Richard Jeffrey's (1965) generalization of Bayes' rule is also a special case of MAXENT. Suppose there is a finite partition, $\{p_i\}$, each of whose members have positive probability. Jeffrey says that a final probability comes from an initial probability by *probability kinematics on the partition*

$\{p_i\}$, just in case the probabilities conditional on members of the partition remain the same during the change. The MAXENT solution for a finite number of constraints of the form $E[Ip_i]$ = Final probability $(p_i)$ is just the change by probability kinematics which results in those final probabilities for members of the partition. Jeffrey's rule has a connection with dynamic coherence, although it is a little more delicate than that of Bayes' rule because of the relativity to a partition.[13] One way of putting the matter is by embedding Jeffrey's rule in a conditioning model as in section 2. That is, take the initial 'small' probability space and enlarge it by adding final probability as a random variable. Say that $\{p_i\}$ is subjectively sufficient for belief change if in the initial probability, PR $[r \mid \wedge_i \wedge_i \mathrm{pr}_f(p_i) = a_i \& p_j]$ = PR $[r \mid p_j]$ for all $r$ in the small space and all members of the partition. Then a necessary condition for dynamic coherence is that it be by belief change by probability kinematics on all partitions subjectively sufficient for belief change.[14]

The connection between MAXENT and the updating rules of Bayes and Jeffrey have led to speculation that MAXENT may be a generally valid rule for updating subjective probability.[15] Much of the critical discussion of the MAXENT rule has also cast it in this role.[16] A consideration put forward in 1971 by Friedman and Shimony shows that it is difficult to maintain this point of view.

Consider the case of the three-sided die which we have been using as a simple illustration. Suppose that you are a MAXENT updater and that your initial subjective probabilities are 1/3 for each side. The desired final expected number of spots, $E_f(g) \in [1,3]$, is for you information that you will somehow acquire before updating. Consider your initial probability over possible values of the desired expectation. They are tantamount to initial probabilities over your possible final probabilities since for you the MAXENT rule associates a unique final probability. It might occur to you to take the flat prior (with respect to Lebesgue measure) on [1, 3]. But this choice would be *dynamically incoherent*! The prior probability would not

[13]  There is an extensive discussion in Skyrms (1987a).

[14]  See Skyrms (1980a, b) and Good (1981).

[15]  E.g. Williams (1980) "the purpose of the principle is to assist in the rational modification of beliefs" (132, fn. 1). See also Shore and Johnson (1980); Domotor (1980); Cheesman (1983).

[16]  Van Fraassen (1980, 1981); Shimony (1973); Dias and Shimony (1981); Friedman and Shimony (1971).

equal the expectation of posterior probability, and a dynamic Dutch Book could be made against you. All right, you needn't make that application of the principle of insufficient reason. What do your initial probabilities on the value of the desired expectation need to be in order to escape the dynamic Dutch Book? You must concentrate probability 1 on the desired expectation being 2! This is the only way in which the initial expectation of the final probability of 2 spots can equal the initial probability of 2 spots, because the final probability of 2 spots under the MAXENT revision rule is a strictly concave function of the desired expected number of spots, taking its maximum at the initial probability of 2 spots, 1/3. This is easily seen in Figures 1 and 2. But this is just the case in which under MAXENT the initial probability is not revised. It appears that the MAXENT updater in this case can only be coherent if he believes with probability one that the rule will not lead to any substantive belief revision. This is hardly a desideratum for a rule for updating subjective probability.

There have been attempts to discount the Shimony–Friedman example, but I do not think that they are successful. Williams (1980) claims that the rule does not violate static coherence:

> According to the present interpretation, the probabilities emerging from the principle of minimum information are not conditional probabilities associated with the prior distribution but unconditional probabilities of a new and entirely different distribution, unrelated to the prior distribution by the normal 'synchronic' probability calculus. This is to be understood even in the case corresponding to Bayesian conditionalization. If this is accepted, objections of the type raised by Friedman and Shimony (1971) are not applicable.

I think that the discussion of dynamic coherence in section 2 shows that this response to the example is inadequate. It might be argued that you might not have probabilities over the possible values of the constraint; but if such values are incoming data, I see no reason why a Bayesian should not be able to have probabilities on them. It might be argued that the constraint isn't data, but rather something quite different. In a sense I think that this is correct, but this is really to give up maintaining that MAXENT is a rule for Bayesian updating and to assert that it is a rule for something else.

Notice that the Friedman–Shimony example applies to a wide range of 'minimal revision' rules for updating; not just MAXENT. Any rule which provides a solution satisfying the constraint must agree with MAXENT for $E(g) = 1$ and $E(g) = 3$. Any rule which gives a unique minimal revision must agree with MAXENT on $E(g) = 2$ since it takes no revision to satisfy this constraint. If in addition the rule makes a monotonic transition in final probability of 2 spots from $E(g) = 2$ to the extremes, the Friedman–Shimony reasoning applies.

In fact, let us suppose that for whatever reason, your initial probabilities for the desired value of the constraint are concentrated on the values 1, 2, 3. Why shouldn't they be? Then any minimal revision rule which calls for no revision if the constraint is actually satisfied will be subject to the Friedman–Shimony analysis.

To understand what is happening, it is instructive to embed the problem in several alternative Bayesian settings:

EXAMPLE 1 (*Determinism*). You are sure that the die is a trick die which will always come up the same way, but are unsure which is the favored side with probabilities 1/3, 1/3, 1/3. A friend will conduct a large number of independent trials (to all intents and purposes infinite) and report to you the sample mean. Your initial probabilities for $E(g) = 1, 2, 3$ are 1/3, 1/3, 1/3. If he reports $E(g) = 2$, your final probability for two spots should be 1, rather than the 1/3 prescribed by MAXENT.

EXAMPLE 2 (*Determinism or No Information*). As above, but there is a one-in-four chance that your friend will forget to perform the experiment, in which case he will also report $E(g) = 2$. Then your initial probabilities for $E(g) = 1, 2, 3$ are respectively 1/4, 1/2, 1/4. A report of $E(g) = 2$ has ambiguous significance. Upon receiving such a report you should change your final probability of 2 spots showing to 2/3.

EXAMPLE 3 (*Uncertain Chance*). You believe that the die is a chance device with uncertain chance, and your initial probabilities for the chances are given by the measure uniform with respect to Lebesgue measure in Euclidean space (see Figure 3). The data is a report of the true chance expectation. The data $E(g) = 2$ should lead you to revise your probability upward to 1/2.

In Examples 1–3 the report $E(g) = 2$, although compatible with your present probability, is nevertheless grounds for Bayesian revision. MAXENT gives different results in these cases because it interprets $E(g) = 2$ as 'no news' and no reason for revision. In the extreme case in which MAXENT is compatible with conditioning, i.e. where the initial probability of $E(g) = 2$ is one, the data that $E(g) = 2$ really is no news in the sense

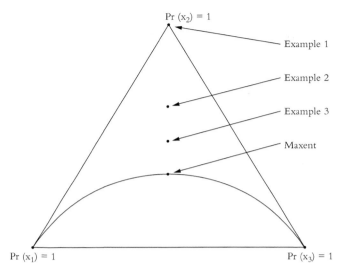

**Figure 3**

of Bayes' rule. The probabilities conditional on it must be the same as the unconditional probabilities. But this is hardly the typical setting for Bayesian updating. MAXENT is not a generally valid updating rule.

## 6. MAXENT as Supposition

Suppose we have a given chance model; for instance the equiprobable chance probability on the three-sided die, and want to hypothesize about the chance probability which satisfies a certain constraint and is in some interesting sense most similar to our given chance model. To do this systematically, we would like something like a Stalnaker selection function for chance models. It is just this that MAXENT gives us, at least for certain well-behaved hypotheses.

In the general case, a constraint set of probabilities will be considered a well-behaved hypothesis with respect to an initial probability if it is a convex, closed set of probabilities absolutely continuous with respect to the initial probability. For such hypotheses the MAXENT solution exists and is unique, so on the domain of well-behaved hypotheses, the MAXENT method determines a MAXENT SELECTION FUNCTION.

It is easy to see that the MAXENT selection function is STALNAKER, i.e. it satisfies Stalnaker's three conditions listed in section 3:

(1) By definition of the MAXENT solution it is in the constraint set, so $f(w,s) \in s$.

(2) Since the information in the initial probability with respect to itself is minimal and the Kullback-Leibler $I(\mathrm{pr}_f, \mathrm{pr}_i)$ is strictly convex in $\mathrm{pr}_f$, it follows that if $\mathrm{pr}_i$ satisfies the constraint, it is the MAXENT solution, i.e. if $w \in s$ then $f(w, s) = w$.

(3) Show that $f(w, s) \in s'$ and $f(w, s') \in s$ then $f(w, s) = f(w, s')$: By hypothesis and the MDI equality of section 4, we have both:

$$I(f\langle \mathrm{pr}_i, s' \rangle, \mathrm{pr}_i) = I(f\langle \mathrm{pr}_i, s' \rangle, f\langle \mathrm{pr}_i, s \rangle) + I(f\langle \mathrm{pr}_i, s \rangle, \mathrm{pr}_i)$$

and

$$I(f\langle \mathrm{pr}_i, s \rangle, \mathrm{pr}_i) = I(f\langle \mathrm{pr}_i, s \rangle, f\langle \mathrm{pr}_i, s' \rangle) + I(f\langle \mathrm{pr}_i, s' \rangle, \mathrm{pr}_j).$$

Since all terms are nonnegative:

$$I(f\langle \mathrm{pr}_i, s \rangle, f\langle \mathrm{pr}_i, s' \rangle) = I(f\langle \mathrm{pr}_i, s' \rangle, f\langle \mathrm{pr}_i, s \rangle) = 0$$

By strict convexity, $f\langle \mathrm{Pr}_i, s \rangle = f\langle \mathrm{Pr}_i, s' \rangle$ as required.

Notice that it is just these properties which qualify MAXENT as defining a Stalnaker selection function for well-behaved hypotheses which caused trouble for it as a method of Bayesian updating. (In the examples where the initial probability was concentrated on $E(2) = 1, 2, 3$, the trouble can be gotten from Conditions (1) and (2) alone.) Any stochastic Stalnaker selection function will get into Friedman–Shimony difficulties if it is applied as a rule for updating subjective probabilities.

This has a certain general significance, because there is a whole family of minimal revision rules which can be made to yield Stalnaker selection functions for chance models, several of which have been considered as possible rules for mechanical updating of subjective probability. One can minimize the variational distance, the Hellinger distance, etc.[17] Each of these should be thought of as defining a different selection function for

---

For a quick survey, see Diaconis and Zabell (1982) sections 5 and 6. The point applies generally to minimization of any $f$-divergence in the sense of Csizar (1975). Diaconis and Zabell show that the variational distance and Hellinger distances are both $f$-divergences. See also May and Harper (1976).

well-behaved hypotheses or suppositions rather than as rules for updating subjective probability.

## 7. Supposing as Conditioning

MAXENT gives us one selection function among many possible ones. Is there anything specially interesting about this one? There is a deep connection with the concept of *sufficiency*, and with conditioning after all in the one limiting case in which MAXENT is consistent with conditioning.

As Jaynes (1979) notes,[18] the MAXENT solution gives us the exponential families as the Darmois–Koopman–Pitman theorem. Consider the exponential family: $PR(X) = P(X) \exp [a\ T(X)]/N$. $T$ is a sufficient statistic. Furthermore, for multiple IID (independent identically distributed) trials the sum $\Sigma_i\ T(X_i)$ is a sufficient statistic. Darmois–Koopman–Pitman is the converse. If the sum is a sufficient statistic, then we have the functional equation:

$$PR_a[T(X_1)]PR_a[T(X_2)] \ldots = PR_a[T(X_1) + T(X_2) + \ldots]$$

which under mild regularity conditions has the exponential solution.[19]

If the members of the family are the physical probabilities, then in a typical case of uncertainty about the true physical probabilities, degree of belief will be a mixture of the members of the family. In the product space if the physical probabilities make the trials independent, then the degrees of belief will be exchangeable. De Finetti's theorem shows how to go the other way. An exchangeable sequence of random variables has a unique representation as a mixture of independent ones. If in the degree of belief probabilities $T$ is a sufficient statistic such that the sum is a sufficient statistic for multiple trials, then Darmois–Koopman–Pitman can be combined with de Finetti to characterize the extreme points: the 'physical probabilities' which are implicit in the degree of belief probabilities. They consist of exponential families of the statistic.[20] This means that for a subjectivist who regards chances or physical probabilities as artifacts of the de Finetti

---

[18] "An interesting fact which may have some deep significance as not yet seen, is that the class of maximum entropy functions is, by the Pitman–Koopman theorem, identical with the class of functions admitting sufficient statistics" (Jaynes 1979: 87).

[19] There is a whole family of theorems of this nature. One can consider multidimensional sufficient statistics, and one can consider refinements of the regularity conditions. See Koopman (1936), Hipp (1974).

[20] See Freedman (1962) and Diaconis and Freedman (1985).

representation theorem: *if T is for him such an additive sufficient statistic then MAXENT applied to constraints of the form $E_f(T) = b$ is for him a way of moving from one possible physical probability to another.*

Typically Bayesian conditioning is applied to update subjective probability by moving from one non-trivial mixture of possible physical probabilities to another. As we saw in section 5, MAXENT fails to be embeddable in a conditioning model in such contexts. Suppose, however, that your subjective probability is concentrated on one possible physical probability; e.g. you are sure that the three-sided die is fair and multiple trials are independent. You now expect with limiting probability one that the average number of spots showing in a long series of trials will be 2. Suppose that you now get the information that this empirical average on a long sequence of trials *including trial i* was different from 2, say *b*. Conditional on the evidence, your probabilities of outcomes on trial *i* will change. Taking as the limit of these probabilities that the number of trials goes to infinity, we get the probability distribution that is given by applying MAXENT to the constraint $E_f(T) = b$. More generally, under suitable regularity conditions if *T* is a sufficient statistic, for an IID sequence of random variables conditioning on an empirical average $1/n \sum_i T(X_i) = b$ gives in the limit the same result as applying MAXENT to $E_f T(X_1) = b$.[21] Conditioning on a biased mean of a sufficient statistic can be used to give us a supposing or hypothesizing rule; a way of moving from one statistical hypothesis to another. *MAXENT gives us a selection function with the remarkable property of agreement with the rule of conditioning on a biased mean of a sufficient statistic.*

# 8. Conclusion

The philosophical controversy concerning the logical status of MAXENT may be in large measure due to the conflation of two distinct logical roles: (1) a general inductive principle for updating subjective probabilities; (2) a supposing rule for moving from one chance probability to another. When judged under standards of dynamic coherence appropriate to (1), MAXENT is found wanting. When judged in terms of the logic appropriate to (2), MAXENT yields for convex closed constraint sets a reasonable selection function with interesting connections with sufficiency and conditioning.

---

[21]  See van Campenhout and Cover (1981); Tjur (1974); Zabell (1974).

Indeed it is just the features of MAXENT which make it appropriate for (2) which make it inappropriate for (1). MAXENT can be thought of as part of Bayesian logic. But it is part of the logic of supposition rather than the logic of induction.[22]

# Bibliography

Adams, E. (1962) "On Rational Betting Systems," *Archive für mathematische Logik und Grundlagenforschung* 6: 7–29, 112–28.

——(1970) "Subjunctive and Indicative Conditionals," *Foundations of Language* 6: 89–94.

——(1975) *The Logic of Conditionals*. Dordrecht: D. Reidel.

Armendt, B. (1980) "Is There a Dutch Book Argument for Probability Kinematics?" *Philosophy of Science* 47: 583–8.

Cheesman, P. (1983) "A Method of Computing Generalized Bayesian Probability Values for Expert Systems." In Alan Bundy (ed.), *Proceedings of the Eighth International Joint Conference on Artificial Intelligence*, pp. 198–202. Karlsruhe, West Germany and San Francisco, CA: Morgan Kaufman.

——(1985) "In Defense of Probability," *Proc. AAAI* 85: 1002–9.

Csizar, I. (1975) "I-Divergence Geometry of Probability Distributions and Minimization Problems," *Annals of Probability* 3: 146–58.

Dawid, A. P. and Stone, M. (1972) "Expectation Consistency of Inverse Probability Distributions," *Biometrika* 59: 486–9.

——(1973) "Expectation Consistency and Generalized Bayes Inference," *Annals of Statistics* 1: 478–85.

de Finetti, B. (1937) "La prévision: Ses lois logiques, ses sources subjectives," *Annales de l'Institut Henri Poincaré*," 7: 1–68. Tr. as "Foresight: Its Logical Laws, Its Subjective Sources," in H. E. Kyburg, Jr. and H. Smokler (eds.), *Studies in Subjective Probability*. Huntington, NY: Krieger, 1980.

Dempster, A. P. (1967) "Upper and Lower Probabilities Induced by a Multivalued Mapping," *Annals of Mathematical Statistics* 38: 325–39.

——(1968) "A Generalization of Bayesian Inference," *Journal of the Royal Statistical Society, Series B* 30: 205–49.

Diaconis, P. and Freedman, D. A. (1985) "Partial Exchangeability and Sufficiency," in J. Gosh and J. Roy (eds.), pp. 205–36. *Statistics: Applications and New Directions*. Calcutta: Indian Statistical Institute.

Diaconis, P. and Zabell, S. (1982) "Updating Subjective Probability," *Journal of the American Statistical Association* 77: 822–30.

---

[22] Research partially supported by N.S.F. grant SES–8605122.

—— (1983) "Some Alternatives to Bayes' Rule," Technical Report 205, Dept. of Statistics, Stanford University.

Dias, P. M. C. and Shimony, A. (1981) "A Critique of Jaynes' Maximum Entropy Principle," *Advances in Applied Mathematics* 2: 172–11.

Domotor, Z. (1980) "Probability Kinematics and the Representation of Belief Change," *Philosophy of Science* 47: 384–403.

Dynkin, E. (1978) "Sufficient Statistics and Extreme Points," *Annals of Probability* 6: 705–30.

Freedman, D. A. (1962) "Invariants under Mixing which Generalize de Finetti's Theorem," *Annals of Mathematical Statistics* 33: 916–23.

Freedman, D. A. and Purves, R. A. (1969) "Bayes' method for bookies," *Annals of Mathematical Statistics* 40: 1177–86.

Frieden, B. R. (1972) "Restoring with Maximum Likelihood and Maximum Entropy," *Journal of the Optical Society of America* 62: 511–18.

Friedman, K. and Shimony, A. (1971) "Jaynes' Maximum Entropy Prescription and Probability Theory," *Journal of Statistical Physics* 3: 381–4.

Gaifman, H. (1988) "A Theory of Higher-Order Probabilities," in W. Harper and B. Skyrms (eds.), *Causation, Cause and Credence*. Dordrecht: D. Reidel.

Gibbard, A. (1981) "Two Recent Theories of Conditionals," in Harper et al. (eds.), *Ifs*, pp. 211–47. Dordrecht: D. Reidel.

Goldstein, M. (1983) "The Prevision of a Prevision," *Journal of the American Statistical Association* 78: 817–19.

Good, I. J. (1950) *Probability and the Weighing of Evidence*. New York: Hafner.

—— (1963) "Maximum Entropy or Hypothesis Formation, Especially for Multi-dimensional Contingency Tables," *Annals of Mathematical Statistics* 34: 911–34.

—— (1981) "The Weight of Evidence Provided by Uncertain Testimony or from an Uncertain Event," *Journal of Statistical Computation and Simulation* 13: 56–60.

Hacking, I. (1967) "Slightly More Realistic Personal Probability," *Philosophy of Science* 34: 311–25.

Heath, D. and Sudderth, W. (1972) "On a Theorem of de Finetti, Oddsmaking and Game Theory," *Annals of Mathematical Statistics* 43: 2072–7.

—— (1978) "On Finitely Additive Priors, Coherence, and Extended Admissibility," *Annals of Statistics* 6: 333–45.

Hipp, C. (1974) "Sufficient Statistics and Exponential Families," *Annals of Statistics* 2: 1283–92.

Hunter, D. (1986) "Uncertain Reasoning Using Maximum Entropy Inference," in L. K. Konol and J. F. Lemmaer (eds.), *Uncertainty in Artificial Intelligence*, pp. 24–7. Amsterdam: Elsevier.

Jaynes, E. T. (1957) "Information Theory and Statistical Mechanics," *Physical Review* 106: 620–30.

—— (1963) "Information Theory and Statistical Mechanics," in K. W. Ford (ed.), *Statistical Physics*, pp. 181–218. New York: Benjamin.

—— (1967) "Foundations of Probability Theory and Statistical Mechanics," in M. Bunge (ed.), *Delaware Seminar in the Foundations of Physics*, pp. 77–101. Berlin: Springer.

—— (1974) *Probability Theory with Applications in Science and Engineering.* St. Louis: Department of Physics Washington University.

—— (1980) "Where Do We Stand on Maximum Entropy," in R. D. Levine and M. Tribus (eds.), *The Maximum Entropy Formalism*, pp. 15–118. Cambridge, MA: MIT Press.

Jeffrey, R. (1965) *The Logic of Decision.* New York: McGraw Hill. Second edition, Chicago: University of Chicago Press, 1983.

—— (1968) "Probable knowledge," in I. Lakatos (ed.), *The Problem of Inductive Logic*, pp. 1666–80. Amsterdam: North-Holland.

Kemeny, J. (1955) "Fair Bets and Inductive Probabilities," *Journal of Symbolic Logic* 20: 263–73.

Koopman, B. O. (1936) "On Distributions Admitting a Sufficient Statistic," *Transactions of the American Mathematical Society* 39: 399–409.

Kullback, S. (1959) *Information Theory and Statistics.* New York: Wiley.

Kullback, S. and Liebler, R. (1951) "On Information and Sufficiency," *Annals of Mathematical Statistics* 23: 8–102.

Kupperman, M. (1958) "Probabilities of Hypotheses and Information-Statistics in Sampling from Exponential Class Populations," *Annals of Mathematical Statistics* 29: 571–4.

Lane, D. and Sudderth, W. (1983) "Coherent and Continuous Inference," *Annals of Statistics* 11: 114–20.

Lehman, R. (1955) "On Confirmation and Rational Betting," *Journal of Symbolic Logic* 20: 251–62.

Lewis, D. (1973) *Counterfactuals.* Oxford: Blackwell.

—— (1976) "Probabilities of Conditionals and Conditional Probabilities," *Philosophical Review* 85: 297–315.

May, S. and Harper, W. (1976) "Toward an Optimization Procedure for Applying Minimum Change Principles in Probability Kinematics," in W. Harper and C. Hooker (eds.), *Foundations of Probability Theory, Inductive Inference, and Statistical Theories of Science*, vol. 1, pp. 137–66. Dordrecht: D. Reidel.

Ramsey, F. P. (1931) "Truth and Probability," in R. B. Braithwaite (ed.), *The Foundations of Mathematics and Other Essays*, pp. 156–98. New York: Harcourt Brace; and in H. Kyburg and H. Smokler (eds.), *Studies in Subjective Probability*. Huntington, NY: Krieger, 1980.

Seidenfeld, T. (1986) "Entropy and Uncertainty," *Philosophy of Science* 53: 467–91.

Shafer, G. (1976) *A Mathematical Theory of Evidence*. Princeton, NJ: Princeton University Press.

——(1981) "Jeffrey's Rule of Conditioning," *Philosophy of Science* 48: 337–62.

Shimony, A. (1955) "Coherence and the Axioms of Confirmation," *Journal of Symbolic Logic* 20: 1–28.

——(1973) "Comment on the Interpretation of Inductive Probabilities," *Journal of Statistical Physics* 9: 187–91.

Shore, J. and Johnson, R. (1980) "Axiomatic Derivation of the Principle of Maximum Entropy and the Principle of Minimum Cross-Entropy," *IEEE Transactions in Information Theory It* 26(1): 26–37.

Skyrms, B. (1980a) *Causal Necessity*. New Haven, CT: Yale University Press, Appendix 2.

——(1980b) "Higher Order Degrees of Belief," in D. H. Mellor (ed.), *Prospects for Pragmatism*. Cambridge: Cambridge University Press.

——(1983) "Zeno's Paradox of Measure," in R. S. Cohen and L. Laudan (eds.), *Physics, Philosophy, and Psychoanalysis*, pp. 223–54. Dordrecht: D. Reidel.

——(1984) *Pragmatics and Empiricism*. New Haven, CT: Yale University Press.

——(1985) "Maximum Entropy Inference as a Special Case of Conditionalization," *Synthese* 63: 55–74.

——(1987a) "Dynamic Coherence and Probability Kinematics," in *Philosophy of Science* 54: 1–20.

——(1987b) "Dynamic Coherence." In I. B. MacNeill and G. Umphrey (eds.), *Advances in the Statistical Sciences VII Foundations of Statistical Inference*, pp. 233–43. Dordrecht: D. Reidel.

——(1987c) "Coherence." In N. Rescher (ed.), *Scientific Inquiry in Philosophical Perspective*, pp. 225–42. Pittsburgh, PA: University of Pittsburgh Press.

——(1990) "The Value of Knowledge." In C. Wade Savage (ed.), *Justification, Discovery, and Evolution of Scientific Theories*, pp. 245–66. Minneapolis, MN: University of Minnesota Press.

Stalnaker, R. C. (1968) "A Theory of Conditionals." In N. Rescher (ed.), *Studies in Logical Theory*, pp. 98–112. London: Blackwell.

Teller, P. (1973) "Conditionalization and Observation," *Synthese* 26: 218–58.

——(1976) "Conditionalization, Observation, and Change of Preference." In W. Harper and C. Hooker (eds.), *Foundations of Probability Theory, Statistical Inference, and Statistical Theories of Science*, pp. 205–53. Dordrecht: D. Reidel.

Tjur, T. (1974) "Conditional Probability Distributions," Lecture Notes 2, Institute of Mathematical Statistics, University of Copenhagen, sections 36, 37.

van Campenhout, J. and Cover, T. (1981) "Maximum Entropy and Conditional Probability," *IEEE Transactions on Information Theory IT* 27: 483–9.

van Fraassen, B. (1980) "Rational Belief and Probability Kinematics," *Philosophy of Science* 47: 165–87.

——(1981) "A Problem for Relative Information Minimizers in Probability Kinematics," *British Journal for the Philosophy of Science* 32: 375–9.

——(1984) "Belief and the Will," *Journal of Philosophy* 81: 235–56.

Williams, P. M. (1980) "Bayesian Conditionalization and the Principle of Minimum Information," *British Journal for the Philosophy of Science* 31: 131–44.

Zabell, S. (1974) "A limit theorem for conditional expectations with applications to probability theory and statistical mechanics," Ph.D. dissertation, Harvard University, Cambridge, MA.

# 9

# The Structure of Radical Probabilism

## 1. Introduction

Richard Jeffrey advocates a skeptical epistemology grounded in *radical probabilism*. The fundamental concept of epistemology is not to be taken as knowledge, but rather degree of belief. It is rarely plausible that degrees of belief should take the extreme form of certainty. In particular, learning does not proceed by conditioning on observation statements which are learned with certainty. All sorts of learning processes are deemed possible, some—but not all—falling under Jeffrey's well-known model of probability kinematics.

In avoiding oversimplifications and illicit assumptions, radical probabilism meets high epistemological standards. But does this degree of realism leave us with any interesting structure in the general framework? In this chapter I will review results about how dynamic coherence provides structure in the radical probabilist picture, and how some central features of a conditioning model carry over to the more general approach of radical probabilism.

## 2. Basic Dynamic Coherence Results

The foundation for dynamic coherence arguments is a well-known argument by de Finetti (1937) for the definition of conditional probability as $\Pr(q|p) = \Pr(p\&q)/\Pr(p)$ when $\Pr(p) > 0$. Conditional probabilities are used

---

This chapter was read at the Luino conference on Probability, Dynamics and Causality June, 1995. The discussion of convergence is largely drawn from Skyrms (1995b). I would like to thank Dick Jeffrey, Persi Diaconis, and Sandy Zabell for helpful comments.

to evaluate conditional bets. But de Finetti pointed out that one can achieve the effect of a bet on $q$ conditional on $p$ by making two unconditional bets, one on $p\&q$ and another against $p$, at stakes such that the net payoff is zero if the condition, $p$, is not realized. For the two routes of evaluation to agree the usual definition of conditional probability is required.

Ian Hacking (1967) argued that this result is totally static, that it deals only with the coherence of conditional and unconditional probabilities at a single time, and that it gives no support whatsoever for Bayes' Rule of updating by conditioning on the evidence. It takes only a small twist, however, to turn de Finetti's observation into a dynamic argument for Bayes' Rule. Among philosophers, this step was taken by David Lewis and communicated by Paul Teller (1973). In the statistical literature the argument is often taken to be implicit in de Finetti, although what de Finetti actually says does not make exegesis straightforward.[1]

Suppose that there is a finite set of evidence statements, each with positive prior probability, one of which is to be learned for certain. And suppose that the epistemic agent is considering potential rules for updating subjective probability on the basis of the evidence learned. Mathematically, such a rule is a function from the possible evidence $E = \{e_1, e_2 \ldots, e_n\}$ to revised probability measures. Such a rule is incoherent if a bettor knowing the rule and making a finite number of bets initially and a finite number of bets after the evidence is in, can achieve a sure net gain. Mathematically, a bettor's strategy is a pair of functions, the first mapping the agent's initial probability and rule onto a finite set of initial bets; the second mapping the initial probabilities, rule and evidence learned onto a finite set of bets. The result is that it is necessary and sufficient for coherence that the agent adopt Bayes' Rule of updating by conditioning on the evidence. The leading idea of the proof is that in this situation the bettor can make a bet on $p$ conditional on $e$ in one of two ways. The first is to make a conditional bet in the de Finetti way; the second is to adopt a strategy of waiting until the evidence is in and betting on $p$ just in case the evidence is $e$. If these two ways disagree, it is obvious that the way is open to a strategy which guarantees a sure win conditional on $e$, and since $e$ has positive initial probability a suitable initial sidebet against $e$ converts this to a strategy which unconditionally guarantees a sure win. One might have some reservations as to the applicability of the argument on account of the restrictions that the set of potential evidential statements be (i) finite and (ii) such that each has positive prior probability (Kyburg, 1978), but it turns out that these conditions are inessential. Lane and Sudderth (1985) show that the result holds quite generally.

What happens when we pass from the foregoing to the radical probabilist model? Here the epistemic agent starts with an initial probability, $pr_1$, passes through a 'black-box' learning situation, and comes out with a final probability, $pr_2$. We are not supposed to speculate on what goes on inside the black box. Nevertheless, there is a dynamic coherence result due to Goldstein (1983) and van Fraassen (1984) parallel to that for conditioning. Suppose that the agent's prior probability for his posterior probability of $p$ is concentrated on a finite number of values, $a_1 \ldots a_m$. Then coherence requires that:

$$(M) pr_1(p|pr_2(p) = a_1) = ai \, (\text{for } i = 1 \text{ to } m)$$

which has as a consequence that the prior probability is the expectation of posterior probability.[2]

The bets used to make the Dutch Book are the same as before, except that instead of bets conditional on a statement of evidence, $e$, we have bets conditional on a statement of final probability, $pr_2(p) = a$. Dynamic coherence forces the black-box learner to behave *as if* she were conditioning on the statement of final probability, as in Skyrms (1980).[3]

There has been some question as to whether the foregoing dynamic coherence arguments hold up in the context of game theory or sequential decision theory, the thought being that if an incoherent agent 'sees a Dutch Book coming' she will simply refuse to bet at all and thus avoid the sure loss. See Maher (1992), Earman (1992). Analysis of the argument, however, shows that such is not the case. (For details, see Skyrms, 1993. That discussion is framed in terms of the Lewis conditioning model, but the same analysis works for the radical probabilist black-box model.) The incoherent agent, subsequent to the black-box experience, will accept the

---

[2] As before, the basic argument carries over to more general settings. See Skyrms (1980: Appendix 2), Goldstein (1983), Gaifman (1988), Skyrms (1990: ch. 5).

[3] In this regard, it may be of interest to juxtapose the coherence argument of Lewis for conditioning with the second-order coherence argument of Uchii (1973). I take this to be the point of some of Colin Howson's remarks at this conference.

cunning bettor's offer as a way of cutting her losses, while regretting the initial bets she made prior to going into the black box. But initially, even knowing the bettor's strategy, she will accept his initial offers as a means of cutting her losses while ruing the decisions that she believes she will be disposed to make once she has gone through the black box. The analysis also has consequences for the discussion of the next section.

Between the transparency of the conditioning model of learning and the opacity of the 'black box', we have models of various degrees of translucency generated by *Jeffrey's Rule* of updating by probability kinematics on a partition. Jeffrey's basic model assumes a finite partition each of whose members has positive prior probability. A probability, $pr_2$, is said to come from another $pr_1$ by probability kinematics on this partition just in case the final probabilities conditional on members of the partition, where defined, remain the same as the initial probabilities conditional on members of the partition. Conditioning on a member of the partition is the special case of probability kinematics in which that member gets final probability of one. Jeffrey had in mind a model in which one could approximate certain evidence without being forced to regard learning as learning for certain.

More general forms of the rule are possible. To say that $pr_2$ comes from $pr_1$ by probability kinematics on the partition is to say that it is a *sufficient partition* for $\{pr_1, pr_2\}$. The natural generalization says that $pr_2$ comes from $pr_1$ by probability kinematics on a sub-sigma-algebra, if it is a *sufficient sub-sigma-algebra* for $\{pr_1, pr_2\}$ (Diaconis and Zabell, 1982). Here, however, we focus on the simplest case.

From the point of view of conditioning, Jeffrey's Rule relaxes structure; from the point of view of the black-box model, Jeffrey's Rule (with respect to some fixed partition) imposes structure. In what sense can dynamic coherence be brought to bear on probability kinematics?

Suppose that the agent about to go into the black box believes that the only information she will gain will be information about a partition of colors, although the information may not be certain. One way to express this is to introduce a later 'reference point' in which she will find out the true member of the color partition. If the black box only provided information about color, then going through the black box and then finding out the true color with certainty should result in the same probability, $pr_3$, as one would have gotten by bypassing the black box and going directly from $pr_1$ *via* certain learning to $pr_3$. Then by the Lewis–Lane–Sudderth argument, the probabilities conditional on members of the partition should be the same in $pr_3$ as in $pr_2$ and they also should be the same in $pr_3$ as in $pr_1$. Therefore $pr_2$ must come from $pr_1$ by probability kinematics on the partition.

This is the leading idea of a Dutch Book argument for probability kinematics in Skyrms (1987a) and for a somewhat different Dutch Book theorem for probability kinematics based on ideas of Armendt (1980) in Skyrms (1990). What these theorems show is that if the agent believes with probability one that the learning experience *only* gives information about the partition in question, then coherence requires that belief change proceed by probability kinematics on that partition.

## 3. The Value of Knowledge

The fundamental theorem of epistemology is that knowledge is good for you. That is to say that the expected utility of acquiring pure cost-free information[4] is non-negative, and indeed positive if there is any positive probability that the information will change your mind as to the optimal act to perform. The theorem is proved in the context of the classical conditioning model by Savage (1954) and Good (1967).

It is, in fact, anticipated in a manuscript of Frank Ramsey that I discovered in the Ramsey archives at the University of Pittsburgh. The note is on two pages which were separated by another on a quite different topic. There is some indication that Ramsey was interested in extending the theorem to something like Jeffrey's Rule, but this is a matter of interpretation. It is discussed in Skyrms (1990: 93–6). These notes of Ramsey were subsequently transcribed and published by Nils-Eric Sahlin and by Maria Carla Galavotti.

In 1989 Paul Graves showed how the value of knowledge theorem can be demonstrated in a model in which agents update by Jeffrey's Rule. In this model agents satisfy condition (M) of the previous section as well as a sufficiency condition for the partition used by Jeffrey's Rule. Subsequently it became clear to Graves and to myself that condition (M) alone is all that is required for the value of knowledge theorem (Skyrms, 1990: ch. 4). The

---

[4] We assume the act of acquiring the information—performing the experiment or making the observation—does not itself affect the probabilities or values of outcomes of the decision in question. For further discussion, see Maher (1990) and Skyrms (1990).

heart of the argument is very simple. Let $B(pr)$ be the expected utility of the Bayes act—the act that maximizes expected utility—according to the probability pr. Then, under the assumptions of the theorem which I discuss in the foregoing reference:

$$U(\text{Act now}) = B[E(pr_f)]$$

and

$$U(\text{Learn now, act later}) = E[B(pr_f)]$$

That the utility of learning now and acting later is greater than or equal to the utility of acting now is an immediate consequence of the convexity of $B$ by Jensen's inequality.

In this setting, condition (M) is sufficient for the value of knowledge theorem. Is it necessary? In other words, if condition (M) fails in the black-box situation can we find some decision problem such that with respect to it the expected utility of acting is greater than the expected utility of going through the black box and then acting? An affirmative answer follows immediately from the previous discussion of dynamic coherence. Suppose that the agent's beliefs about an impending black box violate condition (M) in the simplest case where the agent's prior probabilities are concentrated on a finite number of possible final probabilities. For example, suppose that $pr_i(Q|pr_f(Q) = 2/3) = 1/3$ and $pr_i(pr_f(Q) = 2/3) > 0$. The violation of condition (M) gives us conditional bets which look unattractive *ex ante* but which the agent believes will look attractive *ex post* if the condition is realized. For example consider an even money bet on $Q$ conditional on $pr_f(Q) = 2/3$. Now suppose that the decision problem is whether to accept or reject this bet. The decision maker will assign high expected utility to act now (and reject the bet) rather than going through the black box and acting later (and risking acceptance of the bet). I suggest elsewhere that failure of condition (M) be interpreted as reflecting the agent's belief that this black box is not properly thought of as a 'learning situation' but rather as some other kind of belief change.

Returning to the theme of this chapter, in the radical probabilist framework the fundamental theorem of epistemology holds just when we have dynamic coherence.

## 4. Convergence

But can radical probabilists prove anything about convergence in the long run? In *Bayes or Bust* John Earman is skeptical about the resources of skeptical philosophy:

> a Bayesianism that appeals to both Dutch Book and strict conditionalization is on a collision course with itself. The use of strict conditionalization leads to situations where $\Pr(A) = 1$ although $\not\models A$. As a result, something almost as bad as a Dutch Book befalls the conditionalizer; namely she is committed to betting on the contingent proposition A at maximal odds, which means that in no possible outcome can she have a positive gain and in some possible outcome she has a loss (a violation of what is called *strict coherence*). It is too facile to say in response that this is a good reason for abandoning strict conditionalization in favor of Jeffrey conditionalization or some other rule for belief change; for all the results about merger of opinion and convergence to certainty so highly touted in the Bayesian literature depend on strict conditionalization. (1992: 41)

There is, however, a general convergence theorem for radical probabilist learning with connections to a fuller treatment of dynamic coherence.

Contemplate, at the onset, the prospect of an infinite sequence of black-box learning situations. In each episode you go into the black box with a probability of proposition A and come out with a revised probability of proposition A. Here we make no assumptions about what goes on in the black box. We do not assume that you conditionalize on some evidential proposition delivered to you in the box. We do not assume anything else about the structure of your learning experience either. Now we can look for conditions which will get almost sure convergence. Let us look for a martingale.

Consider a probability space—here your degree-of-belief space—and let $x_1, x_2, \ldots$ be a sequence of random variables on that space and $F_1, F_2, \ldots$ be a sequence of subsigma fields. The sequence of random variables is a *martingale relative to the sequence of sigma-fields* if:

    (i)  The sequence of sigma-fields is non-decreasing
    (ii)  $x_n$ is measurable $F_n$
    (iii)  $E[|x_n|]$ is finite
    (iv)  with probability 1: $E[x_{n+1} \,||\, F_n] = x_n$

The sequence of random variables is a *martingale* if it is a martingale relative to some sequence of sigma-fields.

You are interested in whether you can have confidence that your sequence of revised probabilities will converge, so let us take the random variable $x_n$ to be the revised probability of proposition A after coming out of the nth black box. Since this is a probability, condition (iii) is automatically satisfied. We do not have any evidence statements given in our model to generate sigma-fields, so we might as well consider the sigma-fields generated by our random variables: $F_n = \sigma[x_1, \ldots, x_n]$. With these sigma-fields, (i) and (ii) are automatically satisfied and we are left as the requirement for a martingale:

$$(iv') E[x_{n+1} || x_1, \ldots, x_n] = x_n$$

If (iv') is not satisfied, you may very well think that your beliefs are likely to oscillate forever—for instance with revised probability of A being high after even black boxes and low after odd black boxes. But if (iv') is satisfied and if your degrees of belief are countably additive,[5] then by the martingale convergence theorem you believe with probability one that your sequence of revised probabilities of A will converge. Condition (iv') is a sufficient condition for almost sure convergence of opinion in a black-box learning situation, but does it have any special status for a radical probabilist?

## 5. Coherence Revisited

In this section we see the martingale condition (iv') is a necessary condition for dynamic coherence of degrees of belief in a setting where we have an infinite sequence of black-box learning situations. We will assume sigma coherence here, in order to ensure sigma additivity. That is to say a bettor can make a countable number of bets in his attempt to Dutch Book you, and you are sigma coherent if no Dutch Book can be made.

As a preliminary, consider the case of two black boxes. You now contemplate going through two black-box learning situations, coming out at time $t_1$ with a revised probability of A, $x_2$, and coming out at time $t_1$ with a further revised probability of A, $x_2$. Also at $t_1$ you will have a revised expectation of $x_2$ which we will call $y_1$. We assume that $y_1$ is measurable with respect to the sigma-field generated by $x_1$ and integrable. From your current standpoint at $t_0$, $y_1$ is also a random variable.

---

[5] I will not address here the question of countable additivity in radical probabilism, but I would like to point out that the Bolker representation for Jeffrey's system of personal probability yields countable additivity.

(Ca) Coherence requires that $y_1$ is a version of the conditional expectation:

$$E[x_2||x_1].$$

Let $G$ be a set in the $\sigma$-field generated by $x_1$. At $t_1$, a contract which pays off $x_2$ at $t_2$ has a fair price of $y_1$ to the agent. At $t_0$, a contract (CON1) with a fiducial agent to buy or sell such a contract at $t_1$ at its $t_1$ fair price, conditional on $G$ being the case at $t_1$, has a fair price of:

$$\int_G y_1 \, dp \text{ (CON1)}$$

At $t_0$, a contract, (CON2), conditional on $G$ which pays off at $x_2$ at $t_2$, has a fair price of:

$$\int_G x_2 \, dp \text{ (CON2)}$$

Since these contracts have the same consequences, coherence requires that they have equal value.

(Cb) Coherence requires that $y_1 = x_1$ almost everywhere.

If the agent were always coherent at $t_1$, then $y_1 = x_1$ by the Goldstein–van Fraassen argument. If the agent is incoherent at $t_1$ for a set, S, of positive measure in p, then the agent can be Dutch-Booked at $t_0$: bet at $t_0$ against S; if S is not true at $t_1$ collect; if S is true at $t_1$ pay off the original bet and proceed with the Dutch Book at stakes large enough to assure a net profit.

(C) Coherence requires that (for some version) $E[x_2||x_1] = x_1$.
From (Ca) and (Cb), $x_1$ is a version of $E[x_2||x_1]$.

The foregoing reasoning generalizes. You now contemplate an infinite sequence of black-box learning experiences together with the associated sequences of revised probabilities of $A$, $x_1$, $x_2$, $x_3$, ... Then the coherence argument for conditional expectation [as under (Ca)] gets us:

(CCa) Coherence requires that $y_{n+1}$ is a version of the conditional expectation:

$$E[x_{n+2}||x_1, \ldots, x_{n+1}].$$

and the coherence argument for future coherence [as under (Cb)] gets us:

(CCb) Coherence requires that $y_{n+1} = x_{n+1}$ almost everywhere. Putting these together we have:

(CC) Coherence requires the martingale condition, (iv′).

# 6. Another Martingale?

Let $I_A$ be the indicator function for $A$, $F_n = \sigma[x_1, \ldots, x_n]$ as before and F∞ be the sigma-field generated by the union of the $F_n$S. The random variables $E[I_A||\ F_n]$ form a martingale relative to the sigma-fields $F_n$. Because of the uniform integrability properties of conditional expectations we can not only say that this martingale converges with probability one, but we can also say something about the random variable to which it converges:

$$E[I_A||F_n] \rightarrow E(I_A||F_\infty)(\text{with probability} = 1)$$

We might gloss this by saying that with this martingale we have convergence to a maximally informed opinion.

Furthermore, we can say this without invoking any dynamic coherence arguments (although we presuppose static sigma-coherence). The reason is that our conclusion does not say anything about the temporal process of belief change, since there is nothing to link the conditional expectations, $E[I_A||F_n]$, to subsequent belief states.

Suppose, however, that we now assume dynamic coherence. Let $E_n(I_A)$ be the expectation of the indicator, $I_A$, that you have at $t_n$ according to your probabilities at $t_n$. By a coherence argument for conditional expectation like that given in section 3:

$$(CCC)\ E_n(I_A) = E[I_A||F_n]$$

and, by definition:

$$x_n = E_n(I_A)$$

Under the assumption of dynamic coherence, the martingale of this section is the same martingale as that of section 4:

$$\langle x_n, F_n \rangle = \langle E[I_A||F_n], F_n \rangle$$

So we have:

$$x_n \rightarrow E(I_A||F_\infty) = p(A||F_\infty)(\text{with probability} 1).$$

## 7. Convergence and Kinematics

What is the relation of probability kinematics to the martingale property? First, let us notice that the convergence results which we discussed for a single proposition, $A$, apply more widely. Consider a finite number of propositions, $A_1, \ldots, A_n$. Their probabilities are given by a vector, $\mathbf{x}$, in $[0, 1]^n$. The foregoing martingale convergence story continues to hold for the vector-valued random variables, $\mathbf{x}_1, \mathbf{x}_2, \ldots$ (see Neveu (1975) for vector-valued martingales).

Probability kinematics can be thought of as a technique for making the black box translucent. For example, suppose the black-box learning situations consist of repeatedly looking at a jellybean by candlelight. $R$ is the proposition that it is Red; $C$ is the proposition that it is cinnamon flavored, $\mathbf{x}_1, \mathbf{x}_2 \ldots$ are the probability vectors for these propositions at subsequent times, with the first coordinate being color and the second flavor: e.g. $\mathbf{x}_2$ [1] is the probability at time 2 that it is Red.

Suppose that you are certain that belief change will be by probability kinematics on $\{R, - R\}$; that probabilities conditional on $R$ and on $- R$ will remain unchanged. You do not automatically satisfy the martingale condition. You might believe that your probability for $R$ will be .99 at even numbered times and .01 at odd numbered times. In such a case you would expect your beliefs to oscillate forever, and you would be susceptible to a dynamic Dutch Book.

But if your beliefs do have the martingale property as well, then with probability one the vector-valued martingale, $\mathbf{x}_1, \mathbf{x}_2, \ldots$ converges to a vector-valued random variable $\mathbf{x}_\infty$. With probability one, the random variable $\mathbf{x}_\infty$ must take values which preserve the original probabilities of flavor conditional on $R$ and $-R$; that is to say the limiting beliefs come from the initial ones by probability kinematics on this partition.

If we consider sequences of belief change by probability kinematics where the kinematics does not take place with respect to a single fixed partition, the situation is much more complex. Some relevant results can be found in Rota (1962) and in Diaconis and Zabell (1982).

## 8. Conclusion

Radical Probabilism takes its structure from considerations of dynamic coherence. Where applicable, belief change by probability kinematics on a partition or a sigma-field adds more structure. But the structure imposed by coherence alone is sufficient for two very general theorems that are hallmarks of the Bayesian point of view: the convergence theorem and the theorem on the value of knowledge.

# Bibliography

Armendt, B. (1980) "Is There a Dutch Book Theorem for Probability Kinematics?," *Philosophy of Science* 47: 563–88.

de Finetti, B. (1937) "La Prévision: Ses lois logiques, ses sources subjectives," *Annales de l'Institut Henri Poincaré* 7: 1–68; tr. as "Foresight: Its Logical Laws, Its Subjective Sources," in H. E. Kyburg, Jr. and H. Smokler (eds.), *Studies in Subjective Probability*. Huntington, NY: Kreiger, 1980.

—— (1972) *Probability, Induction and Statistics*. New York: Wiley.

—— (1974) *Theory of Probability*, vol. 1. New York: Wiley.

—— (1975) *Theory of Probability*, vol. 2. New York: Wiley.

Diaconis, P. and Zabell, S. (1982) "Updating Subjective Probability," *Journal of the American Statistical Association* 77: 822–30.

Earman, J. (1992) *Bayes or Bust: A Critical Examination of Bayesian Confirmation Theory*. Cambridge, MA: MIT Press.

Freedman, D. and Purves, R. (1969) "Bayes Method for Bookies," *Annals of Mathematical Statistics* 40: 1177–86.

Gaifman, H. (1988) "A Theory of Higher Order Probabilities." In B. Skyrms and W. Harper (eds.), *Causation, Chance and Credence*. Dordrecht: D. Reidel.

Goldstein, M. (1983) "The Prevision of a Prevision," *Journal of the American Statistical Association* 78: 817–19.

Good, I. J. (1967) "On the Principle of Total Evidence," *British Journal for the Philosophy of Science* 17: 319–21.

Graves, P. (1989) "The Total Evidence Principle for Probability Kinematics," *Philosophy of Science* 56: 317–24.

Hacking, I. (1967) "Slightly More Realistic Personal Probability," *Philosophy of Science* 34: 311–25.

Heath, D. and Sudderth, W. (1972) "On a Theorem of de Finetti, Oddsmaking and Game Theory," *Annals of Mathematical Statistics* 43: 2071–7.

—— (1978) "On Finitely Additive Priors, Coherence and Extended Admissibility," *Annals of Statistics* 6: 333–45.

Hill, B. and Lane, D. (1985) "Conglomerability and Countable Additivity," in P. K. Goel and A. Zellner (eds.), *Bayesian Inference and Decision Techniques*. Amsterdam: North-Holland.

Jeffrey, R. (1965) *The Logic of Decision*. New York: McGraw-Hill. Second rev. ed. 1983, Chicago: University of Chicago Press.

—— (1968) "Probable Knowledge." In I. Lakatos (ed.), *The Problem of Inductive Logic*. Amsterdam: North-Holland.

—— (1970) "Review of 'A Paradox of Information' by David Miller," *Journal of Symbolic Logic* 35: 124–7.

—— (1974) "Preference among Preferences," *Journal of Philosophy* 71: 377–91.

—— (1988) "Conditioning, Kinematics and Exchangeability," in B. Skyrms and W. Harper (eds.), *Causation, Chance and Credence*. Dordrecht: Kluwer.

—— (1992) *Probability and the Art of Judgement*. Cambridge: Cambridge University Press.

Kyburg, H. (1978) "Subjective Probability: Criticisms, Reflections and Problems," *Journal of Philosophical Logic* 7: 157–80.

Lane, D. A. and Sudderth, W. D. (1983) "Coherent and Continuous Inference," *Annals of Statistics* 11: 114–20.

—— (1984) "Coherent Predictive Inference," *Sankhya* Series A, 46: 166–85.

—— (1985) "Coherent Predictions are Strategic," *Annals of Statistics* 13: 1244–8.

Maher, P. (1990) "Symptomatic Acts and the Value of Evidence in Causal Decision Theory," *Philosophy of Science* 57: 479–98.

—— (1992) "Diachronic Rationality," *Philosophy of Science* 59: 120–41.

Ramsey, F. P. [n.d.] "Weight or the value of knowledge," manuscript pages 006-20-01 and 005-20-03 in the Archives for Scientific Philosophy in the Twentieth Century at the Hillman Library of the University of Pittsburgh. Transcribed with introduction by N. E. Sahlin in *British Journal for the Philosophy of Science* 41 (1990): 1–3 and by M. C. Galavotti in Ramsey, F. P., *Notes on Philosophy Probability and Mathematics*. Naples: Bibliopolis, 1991.

Rota, G. (1962) "An 'Alternierende Verfahren' for General Positive Operators," *Bulletin of the American Mathematical Society* 68: 95–102.

Savage, L. J. (1954) *The Foundations of Statistics*. New York: Wiley.

Skyrms, B. (1980) *Causal Necessity*. New Haven, CT: Yale University Press.

—— (1984) *Pragmatics and Empiricism*. New Haven, CT: Yale University Press.

—— (1987a) "Dynamic Coherence and Probability Kinematics," *Philosophy of Science* 54: 1–20.

—— (1987b) "On the Principle of Total Evidence with and without Observation Sentences," in *Logic, Philosophy of Science and Epistemology* (Proceedings of the 11th International Wittgenstein Symposium), pp. 187–95. Vienna: Holder-Pichler-Tempsky.

—— (1990) *The Dynamics of Rational Deliberation*. Cambridge, MA: Harvard University Press.

—— (1993) "A Mistake in Dynamic Coherence Arguments?," *Philosophy of Science* 60: 320–8.

—— (1995a) "Strict Coherence, Sigma Coherence and the Metaphysics of Quantity," *Philosophical Studies* 77: 39–55.

—— (1995b) "Convergence in Radical Probabilism," in D. Hull, M. Forbes, and R. M. Burian (eds.), *PSA 1994*, pp. 349–53. East Lansing, MI: Philosophy of Science Association.

Teller, P. (1973) "Conditionalization and Observation," *Synthese* 26: 218–58.

Uchii, S. (1973) "Higher Order Probabilities and Coherence," *Philosophy of Science* 40: 373–81.

van Fraassen, B. (1984) "Belief and the Will," *Journal of Philosophy* 81: 235–56.

# 10

# Diachronic Coherence and Radical Probabilism

## 1. Introduction

Richard Jeffrey advocated a flexible theory of personal probability that is open to all sorts of learning situations. He opposed what he saw as the use of a conditioning model as an epistemological straitjacket in the work of Clarence Irving Lewis (1946). Lewis' cf. 81, 95 dictum "No probability without certainty" was based on the idea that probabilities must be updated by conditioning on the evidence. Jeffrey's *probability kinematics*— now also known as Jeffrey conditioning—provided an alternative (see Jeffrey, 1957, 1965, 1968).

It was not meant to be the only alternative. Jeffrey articulated a philosophy of *radical probabilism* that held the door open to modeling all sorts of epistemological situations. In this spirit, I will look at diachronic coherence from a point of view that embodies minimal epistemological assumptions and then add constraints little by little.

## 2. Arbitrage

There is a close connection between Bayesian coherence arguments and the theory of arbitrage (see Shin, 1992).

Suppose we have a market in which a finite number[1] of assets are bought and sold. Assets can be anything: stocks and bonds, pigs and chickens, apples and oranges. The market determines a unit price for each asset, and this information is encoded in a price vector $\mathbf{x} = \langle x_1, \ldots,$

---

[1] We keep things finite at this point because we want to focus on diachronic coherence and avoid the issues associated with the philosophy of the integral.

$x_n$. You may trade these assets today in any (finite) quantity. You are allowed to take a short position in an asset; that is to say, you sell it today for delivery tomorrow. Tomorrow, the assets may have different prices, $y_1, \ldots, y_m$. To keep things simple, we initially suppose that there are a finite number of possibilities for tomorrow's price vector. A *portfolio*, **p**, is a vector of real numbers that specifies the amount of each asset you hold. Negative numbers correspond to short positions. You would like to *arbitrage the market*, that is, to construct a portfolio today whose cost is negative (you can take out money) and such that tomorrow its value is nonnegative (you are left with no net loss), no matter which of the possible price vectors is realized.

According to the *fundamental theorem of asset pricing*, you can arbitrage the market if and only if the price vector today falls outside the convex cone spanned by the possible price vectors tomorrow.[2]

There is a short proof that is geometrically transparent. The value of a portfolio, **p**, according to a price vector, **y**, is the sum over the assets of quantity times price: the dot product of the two vectors. If the vectors are orthogonal, the value is zero. If they make an acute angle, the value is positive; if they make an obtuse angle, the value is negative. An arbitrage portfolio, **p**, is one such that **p** · **x** is negative and **p** · $y_i$ is nonnegative for each possible $y_i$; **p** makes an obtuse angle with today's price vector and is orthogonal or makes an acute angle with each of the possible price vectors tomorrow. If **p** is outside the convex cone spanned by the $y_i$'s, then there is a hyperplane that separates **p** from that cone. An arbitrage portfolio can be found as a vector normal to the hyperplane. It has zero value according to a price vector on the hyperplane, a negative value according to today's prices, and a nonnegative value according to each possible price tomorrow. On the other hand, if today's price vector is in the convex cone spanned by tomorrow's possible price vectors, then (by Farkas' lemma) no arbitrage portfolio is possible.

Suppose, for example, that the market deals in only two goods, apples and oranges. One possible price vector tomorrow is $1 for an apple, $1 for an orange. Another is that an apple will cost $2, while an orange is $1. These two possibilities generate a convex cone, as shown in Figure 1a. (We could add lots of intermediate possibilities, but that wouldn't make

---

[2] If we were to allow an infinite number of states tomorrow, we would have to substitute the *closed* convex cone generated by the possible future price vectors.

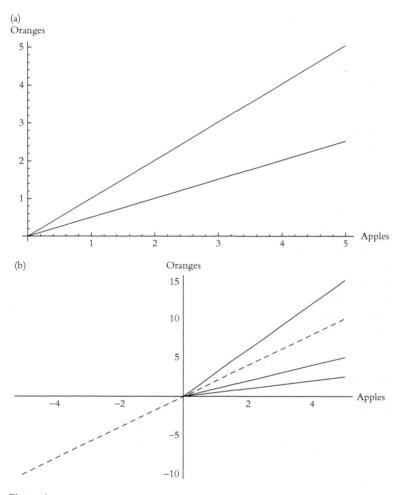

**Figure 1**

any difference to what follows.) Let's suppose that today's price vector lies outside the convex cone, say apples at $1, oranges at $3. Then it can be separated from the cone by a hyperplane (in two dimensions, a line), for example, the line oranges = 2 apples, as shown in Figure 1b. Normal to that hyperplane we find the vector ‹2 apples, −1 orange›, as in Figure 1c. This should be an arbitrage portfolio, so we sell one orange short and use

(c)

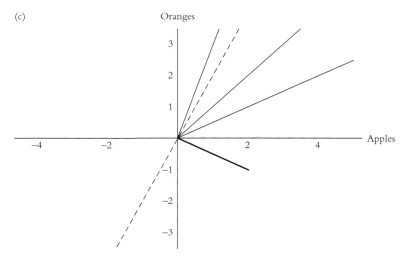

**Figure 1** (Cont.)

the proceeds to buy two apples. But at today's prices, an orange is worth $3; so we can pocket a dollar, or—if you prefer—buy three apples and eat one.

Tomorrow we have to deliver an orange. If tomorrow's prices were to fall exactly on the hyperplane, we would be covered. We could sell our two apples and use the proceeds to buy the orange. But in our example, things are even better. The worst that can happen tomorrow is that apples and oranges trade one to one, so we might as well eat another apple and use the remaining one to cover our obligation for an orange.

The whole business is straightforward: sell dear, buy cheap. Notice that at this point there is no probability at all in the picture.

## 3. Degrees of Belief

In the foregoing, assets could be anything. As a special case they could be tickets paying $1 if $p$, nothing otherwise, for various propositions, $p$. The price of such a ticket can be thought of as the market's collective *degree of belief* or *subjective probability* for $p$. We have not said anything about the market except that it will trade arbitrary quantities at the market price. The market might or might not be implemented by a single individual—the bookie of the familiar Bayesian metaphor.

Without yet any commitment to the nature of the propositions involved, the mathematical structure of degrees of belief, or the characteristics of belief revision, we can say that arbitrage-free degrees of belief today must fall within the convex cone spanned by the degrees of belief tomorrow. This is the fundamental diachronic coherence requirement. Convexity is the key to everything that follows.

# 4. Probability

Suppose, in addition, that the propositions involved are true or false and that tomorrow we learn the truth. We can also assume that we can neglect discounting the future. A guarantee of getting $1 tomorrow is as good as getting $1 today. Then tomorrow a ticket worth $1 if $p$, nothing otherwise, would be worth either $1 or $0 depending on whether we learn whether $p$ is true or not.

And suppose that we have three assets being traded that have a logical structure. There are tickets worth $1 if $p$, nothing otherwise; $1 if $q$, nothing otherwise; and $1 if $p$ or $q$, nothing otherwise. Furthermore, $p$ and $q$ are incompatible. This additional structure constrains the possible price vectors tomorrow, so that the convex cone becomes the two-dimensional object $z = x + y$ ($x$, $y$ nonnegative), as shown in Figure 2.

Arbitrage-free degrees of belief must be additive. *Additivity of subjective probability* comes from the *additivity of truth value* and the fact that *additivity is preserved under convex combination*. One can then complete the coherence argument for probability by noting that coherence requires a ticket that pays $1 if a tautology is true to have the value $1.

Notice that from this point of view, the synchronic Dutch Books are really special cases of diachronic arguments. You need the moment of truth for the synchronic argument to be complete. The assumption that there is such a time is a much stronger assumption than anything that preceded it in this development.

An intuitionist, for example, may have a conception of proposition and of the development of knowledge that does not guarantee the existence of such a time, even in principle. Within such a framework, coherent degrees of belief need not obey the classical laws of the probability calculus.

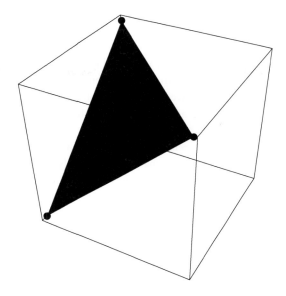

Figure 2

## 5. Probabilities of Probabilities

Today the market trades tickets that pay $1 if $p_i$, nothing otherwise, where the $p_i$'s are some 'first-order' propositions. All sorts of news come in, and tomorrow the price vector may realize a number of different possibilities. (We have not, at this point, imposed any model of belief change.) The price vector for these tickets tomorrow is itself a fact about the world, and there is no reason why we could not trade in tickets that pay off $1 if tomorrow's price vector is **p** or if tomorrow's price vector is in some set of possible price vectors, for the original set of propositions. The prices of these tickets represent subjective probabilities today about subjective probabilities tomorrow.

Some philosophers have been suspicious about such entities, but they arise quite naturally. And in fact, they may be less problematic than the first-order probabilities over which they are defined. The first-order propositions, $p_i$, could be such that their truth value might or might not ever be settled. But the question of tomorrow's price vector for unit wagers over them is settled tomorrow. Coherent probabilities of tomorrow's probabilities should be additive, no matter what.

## 6.  Diachronic Coherence Revisited

Let us restrict ourselves to the case in which we eventually do find out the truth about everything and all bets are settled (perhaps on Judgment Day), so degrees of belief today and tomorrow are genuine probabilities. We can now consider tickets that are worth $1 if the probability tomorrow of $p = a$ and $p$, nothing otherwise, as well as tickets that are worth $1 if the probability tomorrow of $p = a$.

These tickets are logically related. Projecting to the two dimensions that represent these tickets, we find that there are only two possible price vectors tomorrow. Either the probability tomorrow of $p$ is not equal to $a$, in which case both tickets are worth nothing tomorrow, or the probability tomorrow of $p$ is equal to $a$, in which case the former ticket has a price of $a$ and the latter has a price of $1. The cone spanned by these two vectors is just a ray as shown in Figure 3. So today, the ratio of these two probabilities (provided that they are well defined) is $a$. In other words, today the conditional probability of $p$, given that the probability tomorrow of $p = a$, is $a$. It then follows that to avoid a Dutch Book, the probability today must be the expectation of the probability tomorrow (see Goldstein, 1983; van Fraassen, 1984). Since convexity came on stage, it has been apparent that this expectation principle has been waiting in the wings. The introduction of probabilities of probabilities allows it to be made explicit.

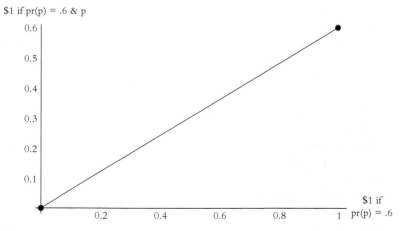

Figure 3

## 7. Coherence and Conditioning

In accord with Jeffrey's philosophy of radical probabilism, we have imposed no restrictive model of belief change. A conditioning situation is allowed, but not required. That is to say, there may be first-order propositions, $e_1, \ldots, e_n$, that map one-to-one to possible degrees of belief tomorrow, $q_1, \ldots, q_n$, such that, for our degrees of belief today, $p$, and for all propositions under consideration, $s$, $q_i(s) = p(s$ given $e_i)$, in which case we have a conditioning model. But there need not be such propositions, which is the case that radical probabilism urges us not to ignore. In this case, convexity still provides an applicable test of diachronic coherence.

On the other hand, with the introduction of second-order probabilities, coherence *requires* belief change by conditioning, that is to say, conditioning on propositions about what probabilities will be tomorrow (see Skyrms, 1980; Good, 1981). These are, of course, quite different from the first-order sense-data propositions that C. I. Lewis had in mind.

## 8. Probability Kinematics

Where does Richard Jeffrey's probability kinematics fit into this picture? Belief change by kinematics on some partition is not sufficient for diachronic coherence. The possible probability vectors tomorrow may have the same probabilities conditional on $p$ and on its negation as today's probability without today's probability of $p$ being the expectation of tomorrow's. Diachronic coherence constrains probability kinematics.

In a finite setting, belief change is always by probability kinematics on *some* partition, the partition whose members are the atoms of the space. But, as Jeffrey always emphasized, coherent belief change need not consist of probability kinematics on some non-trivial partition. That conclusion follows only from stronger assumptions that relate the partition in question to the learning situation.

Suppose that between today and tomorrow we have a learning experience that changes the probability of $p$, but not to zero or one. And suppose that then, by the day after tomorrow, we learn the truth about $p$. We can express the *assumption* that we have gotten information only *about* $p$ on the way through tomorrow to the day after tomorrow by saying that we move from now to then by conditioning on $p$ or on its negation. This is the assumption of *sufficiency* of the partition $\{p, -p\}$. Then one possible

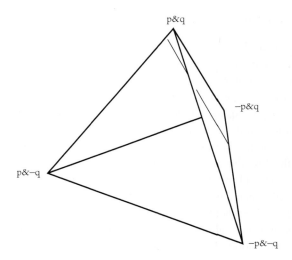

**Figure 4**

probability tomorrow has the probability of *P* as one and the probability of
*p* & *q* as equal to today's Pr(*q* given *p*) and the other possible probability
tomorrow has the probability of *P* as zero and the probability of −*p* & *q* as
equal to today's Pr(*q* given −*p*). This is shown in Figure 4 for Pr(*q* given *p*)
= .9 and Pr(*q* given −*p*) = .2. Diachronic coherence requires that tomorrow's probabilities must fall on the line connecting the two points representing possible probabilities the day after tomorrow and thus must come
from today's probabilities by kinematics on {*p*, -*p*}. This is the basic
diachronic coherence argument that in my earlier work (Skyrms, 1987,
1990) was cloaked in concerns about infinite spaces.

As Jeffrey always emphasized, without the assumption of sufficiency of
the partition, there is no coherence argument. But equally, if there is no
assumption that we learn just the truth of *p*, there is no argument for
conditioning on *p* in the case of certain evidence.

## 9. Tomorrow and Tomorrow and Tomorrow

Consider not two or three days, but an infinite succession of days. Assume
that degrees of belief are all probabilities (e.g., Judgment Day comes at
time *ω* + 1). The probability of *p* tomorrow, the probability of *p* the day

after tomorrow, the probability of $p$ the next day, and so forth are a sequence of random variables. Diachronic coherence requires that they form a *martingale* (see Skyrms, 1996; Zabell, 2002). Richer cases lead to vector-valued martingales.

## 10. Diachronic Coherence Generalized

Looking beyond the scope of this paper, suppose that you throw a point dart at a unit interval, and the market can trade in tickets that pay $1 if it falls in a certain subset, $0 otherwise. This is something of an idealization to say the least, and the question arises as to how coherence might be applied. One natural idea might be to idealize the betting situation so as to allow a countable number of bets, in which case coherence requires countable additivity, a restriction of contracts to measurable sets, and, in general, the orthodox approach to probability. Then the martingale convergence theorem applies: Coherence entails convergence.

An approach more faithful to the philosophy of de Finetti would allow a finite number of bets at each time. This leads to *strategic measure*, a notion weaker than countable additivity but stronger than simple finite additivity (see Lane and Sudderth, 1984, 1985). Orthodox martingale theory uses countable additivity, but there is a finitely additive martingale theory built on strategic measures (see Purves and Sudderth, 1976). A version of the 'coherence entails convergence' result can be recovered, even on this more conservative approach (see Zabell, 2002).

## Bibliography

Goldstein, Michael (1983) "The Prevision of a Prevision," *Journal of the American Statistical Association* 78: 817–19.

Good, Irving John (1981) "The Weight of Evidence Provided from an Uncertain Testimony or from an Uncertain Event," *Journal of Statistical Computation and Simulation* 13: 56–60.

Jeffrey, Richard (1957) "Contributions to the theory of inductive probability," Ph.D. dissertation, Princeton University.

——(1965) *The Logic of Decision.* New York: McGraw-Hill. Third rev. ed. Chicago: University of Chicago Press, 1983.

——(1968) "Probable Knowledge." In I. Lakatos (ed.), *The Problem of Inductive Logic.* Amsterdam: North-Holland.

Lane, David A. and William Sudderth (1984) "Coherent Predictive Inference," *Sankhya*, Series A, 46: 166–85.

——(1985) "Coherent Predictions Are Strategic," *Annals of Statistics* 13: 1244–8.

Lewis, Clarence Irving (1946) *An Analysis of Knowledge and Valuation*. LaSalle, IL: Open Court.

Purves, Roger and William Sudderth (1976) "Some Finitely Additive Probability," *Annals of Probability* 4: 259–76.

Shin, Hyun Song (1992) "Review of *The Dynamics of Rational Deliberation*," *Economics and Philosophy* 8: 176–83.

Skyrms, Brian (1980) "Higher Order Degrees of Belief." In D. H. Mellor (ed.), *Prospects for Pragmatism*, pp. 109–38. Cambridge: Cambridge University Press.

——(1987) "Dynamic Coherence and Probability Kinematics," *Philosophy of Science* 54: 1–20.

——(1990) *The Dynamics of Rational Deliberation*. Cambridge, MA: Harvard University Press.

——(1996) "The Structure of Radical Probabilism," *Erkenntnis* 45: 285–97.

van Fraassen, Bas (1984) "Belief and the Will," *Journal of Philosophy* 81: 235–56.

Zabell, Sandy (2002) "It All Adds Up: The Dynamic Coherence of Radical Probabilism," *Philosophy of Science* 69 (Proceedings): S98–103.

# PART III

# Induction

# Introduction

In the mid-twentieth century Rudolf Carnap pursued inductive logic following the tradition of Bayes–Laplace rules of succession. As his program evolved, it became more flexible and more inclusive. In his *Nachlass* he listed outstanding problems for the program—dealing with two kinds of analogy and with continuous magnitudes. These problems have been largely, if not completely, solved in Bayesian statistics. Chapter 11 "Carnapian Inductive Logic for Markov Chains" and Chapter 12 "Carnapian Inductive Logic and Bayesian Statistics" in Part III tell this story. Markov chains (in one dimension) and Markov random fields (in many) deal with order and periodicity. The relevant inductive logic comes from generalization of de Finetti's theorem by Diaconis and Freedman. This is Carnap's "analogy by proximity." His second kind of analogy, "analogy by similarity," can be dealt with by using mixtures of Carnapian inductive rules. I call them 'HyperCarnapian' methods. A treatment of continuous quantities along classical Carnapian lines is also available from Bayesian statistics: in particular the work of Ferguson, Blackwell, and MacQueen.

From a Bayesian standpoint, Carnap's program focused on a special, tractable corner of inductive inference. 'Bayesian Projectibility' is my version of a big picture (Chapter 13 in this Part). Generalizations of de Finetti's theorem are the key to a proper view of inductive logic. They go far beyond the original scope of coin flipping. Abstract ergodic theory provides a very general extension to degrees of belief exhibiting some symmetry. Symmetries provide an implicit definition of the repetition of an experiment with the same chance structure, a tie to relative frequency, and an account of induction. Inductive skepticism is seen in a new light.

# Bibliography

Carnap. R. 1980 "A Basic System of Inductive Logic, Part II." In R. C. Jeffrey (ed.), *Studies in Inductive Logic and Probability*, vol. 2. Berkeley and Los Angeles, CA: University of California Press.

# 11

# Carnapian Inductive Logic for Markov Chains

Then the criticism of the so-far-constructed "$c$-functions" is that they correspond to "learning machines" of very low power. They can extrapolate the simplest possible empirical generalizations, for example: "approximately nine-tenths of the balls are red," but they cannot extrapolate so simple a regularity as "every other ball is red."

Hilary Putnam, "Probability and Confirmation"

ABSTRACT. Carnap's inductive logic, like most philosophical discussions of induction, is designed for the case of independent trials. To take account of periodicities, and more generally of order, the account must be extended. From both a physical and a probabilistic point of view, the first and fundamental step is to extend Carnap's inductive logic to the case of finite Markov chains. Kuipers (1988) and Martin (1967) suggest a natural way in which this can be done. The probabilistic character of Carnapian inductive logic(s) for Markov chains and their relationship to Carnap's inductive logic(s) is discussed at various levels of Bayesian analysis.

## 1. Independence and Markov Dependence

Suppose that one is investigating a sequence of tosses of a coin with unknown bias, or a sequence of random drawings with replacement from an urn filled with balls of a finite number of different colors. Then Rudolf Carnap's inductive logic—his original inductive logic, $c^*$—will

I would like to thank Haim Gaifman, Richard Jeffrey, and John Kemeny for sharing recollections of the times when they assisted Carnap, and Persi Diaconis for comments on an earlier draft of this chapter. Research upon which this paper was based was partially supported by the National Science Foundation.

turn in a creditable performance. In the case of the biased coin, Carnap's advice is that before the first toss—in the absence of any prior know-ledge—you should consider heads and tails as equiprobable, and in gen-eral—on the evidence of $n$ heads in N tosses—you should take the probability of heads to depend on the relative frequency of heads and the number of tosses as follows:

$$\text{pr}(\text{Heads}) = \frac{n+1}{N+2}$$

In the case of the urn with balls of $k$ colors, Carnap uses the natural generalization from 2 to $k$ properties. In N trials in which color C comes up $n$ times we have:

$$\text{pr}(\text{C}) = \frac{n+1}{N+k}$$

If we take $\alpha = k/(N+k)$, then we can rewrite Carnap's Rule as a weighted average of the a priori probability and the relative frequency:

$$\alpha \frac{1}{k} + (1-\alpha)\frac{n}{N}$$

This rule gives reasonable results when the trials are—in fact—independ-ent,[1] and empirical investigation is like sampling from the great urn of nature.[2]

But nature serves up dependence as well as independence. Indeed, any investigation of causation—deterministic or probabilistic—must deal in dependence. Deterministic laws of periodicity are a special case, and Carnap's original system was vigorously criticized by Putnam (1963a, b) and Achinstein (1963) for its inability to confirm such laws.

The first, fundamental step in dealing with dependence is to consider Markov chains—in which the probability of the state of a system at a moment of time depends only on the state of the system at the preceding moment. Most of science deals with processes which—when properly described—exhibit this Markov property.

---

[1] That is, our degrees of belief make them independent conditional on the chance hypotheses. Unconditionally, our degrees of belief make them exchangeable.

[2] See Strong (1976) for an account of the historical life of this metaphor.

In the simplest case, we can replace the iconic example of the coin flip with that of the Markov thumb tack of Diaconis and Freedman (1980a). A thumb tack is repeatedly flicked as it lies. It can come to rest in either of two positions: point up or point down. The chance of the next state may well depend on the previous one. Thus there are unknown transition probabilities:

$$
\begin{array}{ccc}
 & \text{PU} & \text{PD} \\
\text{PU} & \Pr(\text{PU}|\text{PU}) & \Pr(\text{PD}|\text{PU}) \\
\text{PD} & \Pr(\text{PU}|\text{PD}) & \Pr(\text{PD}|\text{PD})
\end{array}
$$

which an adequate inductive logic should allow us to learn. Here are two extreme examples:

*Example 1, Independence*: Independent flips of a coin biased 9 to 1 in favor of heads.

$$
\begin{bmatrix}
.9 & .1 \\
.9 & .1
\end{bmatrix}
$$

*Example 2, Putnam*: This is an example of a strictly alternating sequence of the kind suggested in the epigraph to this chapter.

$$
\begin{bmatrix}
0 & 1 \\
1 & 0
\end{bmatrix}
$$

More generally, where the physical system has a finite number of states we can fix on the canonical urn model for a Markov chain (Feller, 1966). A Markov chain on a system with $k$-states is equivalent to an urn model with $k + 1$ urns. There are balls of $k$ different colors in the urns. A ball is drawn at random from the first urn to determine the first state of the system. The remaining $k$ urns are each labeled with a color. Depending on which of the $k$ colors is drawn at a given time, the next ball is drawn from the next urn to determine the next state of the system and then replaced.

# 2. Kuipers' Carnapian Inductive Logic for Markov Chains

How should one treat Markov chains in the spirit of Carnap's original inductive logic? Carnap never addressed this question in his published work. Taking into account both his publications and conversations and correspondence with his co-workers, I believe that the question would fall somewhere on Carnap's agenda for the future development of inductive logic but it was not one which he actively tried to answer.

However, there is a natural answer, which fits into Carnap's program much more neatly than some of the generalizations that he did consider. It is put forward by Theo Kuipers (1988). The leading idea is this: Carnap already has an inductive logic suitable for sampling from an urn with replacement. Just apply this inductive logic to the natural urn model of a Markov chain, under the assumption that transitions originating in one state give us no information about transitions originating in a different state. Parametric Bayesians, such as Martin (1967), operating in a somewhat different tradition, have followed the same path (see section 6).

Suppose that we have a Markov chain with unknown transition probabilities, and our inductive problem is to watch the system evolve and predict the transitions. Applying Kuipers' idea to Carnap's original logic, $c^\star$, for a two-state physical system gives the inductive rule:

$$\Pr(S_j|S_i) = \frac{1 + N[S_j, S_i]}{2 + N[S_j, S_i] + N[S_i, S_i]}$$

where $N[S_j, S_i]$ is the number of transitions from state $S_i$ to state $S_j$ observed.

More generally, for a physical system with states $S_1 \ldots S_k$, a Markov chain (with stationary transition probabilities) consists of a $k$-place probability vector for the initial state[3] together with a $k$-by-$k$ square matrix of transition probabilities. If a Carnapian is confronted with a totally new system which he wishes to treat as a Markov chain, he will assign equal probabilities for the initial state, and initially use transition probabilities which assign equal probabilities for every state given any state as predecessor, and update the transition probabilities using the transition counts in the style of $c^\star$:

$$\Pr(S_j|S_i) = \frac{1 + N[S_j, S_i]}{k + \sum_{m=1}^{k} N[S_m, S_i]}$$

---

[3] So to make the Markov thumbtack example into a full Markov chain we can imagine flipping a (possibly biased) coin to determine the initial position of the thumbtack.

(If it is possible to repeatedly restart a Markov chain or to observe many independent instantiations of it, then the probabilities for the initial state could be learned by Carnap's original inductive logic.)

Carnapian inductive logic for Markov chains is a natural generalization of Carnap's inductive logic for coin flipping. It learns properly in our two examples of independence and strict periodicity. It also can be shown to be the correct generalization at a deeper level.

## 3. Classical Bayesian Analysis

Carnap's inductive rule for coin flipping goes back to Bayes and Laplace. See Zabell (1989).

For a coin with known probability $p$ of heads, the probability of $n$ heads in N independent trials is:

$$\binom{N}{n} p^n (1-p)^{N-n}$$

Supposing unknown $p$, Bayes and Laplace put a uniform 'flat' prior *on* p. The probability of $n$ heads in N trials is gotten by mixing with respect to the prior: (N choose n)

$$\binom{N}{n} \int_0^1 p^n (1-p)^{N-n} \, dp$$

and the conditional probability of a head on the N + 1th trial given $n$ heads in N trials is then:

$$\frac{\int_0^1 p^{n+1} (1-p)^{N-n} \, dp}{\int_0^1 p^n (1-p)^{N-n} \, dp} = \frac{n+1}{N+2}$$

This is *Laplace's Rule of succession*.

Laplace also discussed the natural generalization from the binomial to the multinomial case of rolling a die or sampling from an urn with a finite number of colors. The full analysis is carried out in Lidstone (1920). Assuming a uniform prior and integrating gives us Carnap's inductive rule.

Suppose that we treat the case of the Markov thumbtack with unknown transition probabilities in the same spirit. For each state, the transition probabilities from that state to point up can range from 0 to 1. Any point in the unit square represents a possible combination of transition probabilities. An arbitrary subjective prior could be any probability distribution over the unit square. Some priors would make the rows in the Markov matrix dependent. That is, information about the true transition probabilities from state PU might be relevant to beliefs about the transition probabilities from state PD, or vice versa.

But let us, following classical intuitions of symmetry as before, take the uniform distribution over the unit square as the appropriate prior. This has the uniform distributions on the unit interval as marginals for transition probabilities from PU, $p1$, and from PD, $p2$. Moreover the distribution on the unit square is the product measure, $p = (p1)(p2)$; rows are independent. Let us suppose for the moment that we simply start the thumbtack point up. Consider an outcome sequence that has transition counts Tuu, Tud, Tdu, Tdd, and that ends with point up. The probability of a transition to PU on the next trial is:

$$\frac{\int_0^1 p_1^{Tuu+1}(1-p_1)^{Tud}dp_1}{\int_0^1 p_1^{Tuu}(1-P_1)^{Tud}dp_1} = \frac{Tuu+1}{Tuu+Tud+2}$$

This is Carnapian inductive logic for Markov chains.

Suppose we go to the more general case where we flip a biased coin to decide the initial position of the thumbtack. In this setting, the full specification of the Markov chain is a point in the unit cube, with one dimension for the probability of the initial state and the other two for the transition probabilities. Putting the uniform prior on the unit cube makes the probability of the initial state independent of the transition probabilities, so there is just one more term which cancels out in the calculation of the conditional probability, and the result is the same. Here again, independence is not an extra assumption but rather a consequence of the choice of the uniform prior as the appropriate quantization of ignorance.

If the physical system has some arbitrary finite number of states, the Bayesian analysis goes in much the same way. Each row in the Markov transition matrix can be thought of as sampling from an urn without replacement. Taking the uniform prior for a multinomial process gives us Carnap's inductive logic. Taking a uniform prior for Markov chains makes probability of the initial state and rows in the transition matrix independent and factors into uniform priors on each giving us the Carnapian inductive logic for Markov chains of section 2.

It is also desirable to consider physical systems whose state corresponds to the value of some continuous physical magnitude (or a vector of values of a number of physical magnitudes), and the associated Markov chains. But Carnap's inductive logic was not developed sufficiently to deal with such systems even when the trials are independent. The extension to continuous magnitudes was also on Carnap's agenda for inductive logic. Something can be done along these lines in the same spirit as the foregoing treatment.

# 4. Consistency

Suppose that we have a statistical model in which the chances are determined by a parameter whose value is unknown. An inductive rule is *consistent* (relative to the model) for a value of the parameter if when the parameter has that value, as more and more data are observed the inductive rule will (with chance equal to 1) yield degrees of belief which in the limit concentrate at a point mass on the true chance probability. The inductive rule is consistent for the model overall if it is consistent for every value of the parameter. See Diaconis and Freedman (1986).

Laplace's Rule of succession is consistent for coin tossing. By the strong law of large numbers, the limiting relative frequency coincides (almost surely in chance) with the single case chance probability. In the limit, application of Laplace's Rule leads to degrees of belief that correspond to relative frequencies. So we have consistency for all values of 'the chance of heads.' By the same reasoning, the Laplace–Lidstone–Carnap generalization to $n$-states is consistent for a multinomial process. It should be clear from the argument that we could formulate many consistent alternative rules as well.

We would like to investigate the question of consistency for Carnapian inductive logic for Markov chains. There are really a number of different questions depending on what is assumed known or unknown about the Markov chain, and how the data stream is generated. With regard to the last question, can we 'restart' a chain or observe arbitrarily many independent copies of it, or are we limited to observing one sequence of events?

To begin with, let us suppose that the initial state of the physical system is generated with probability 1 and known, but the (stationary) transition probabilities are unknown. The chain evolves and we observe just that one sequence of states, and update according to Carnapian inductive logic for

Markov chains. When do we have consistency? A simple example shows that we do not always have it. Suppose that there is a two-state system state in state 1 and that the transition matrix is of the following type:

$$\begin{bmatrix} 1 & 0 \\ x & (1-x) \end{bmatrix}$$

Then, with probability 1, the system will stay in state 1 and we will never get any data for transitions from state 2. Carnapian inductive logic is only consistent here for the case where $x = 1/2$ and our initial guess at the transition probabilities from state 2 happens to be right.

A state of a Markov chain is called *recurrent* if the probability that it is visited an infinite number of times is 1. The chain is recurrent if all its states are recurrent. Both the examples of section 1, started deterministically in any state, give recurrent Markov chains. In the Putnam example the states are periodic, while in the independence example they are ergodic.

*Carnapian inductive logic for Markov chains is consistent for recurrent Markov chains.* Here is a quick sketch of a proof. Suppose that the true state of nature is a recurrent Markov chain (with a finite number of states). Then the set of sample sequences in which some state does not recur has probability zero. Delete these sequences and restrict the chance measure to get a new probability space. In this space define the random variables $f[nij]$ as having the value 1 if the $n$th occurrence of state $i$ is followed by state $j$. The sequence $f[1ij], f[2ij], \ldots$ is an infinite sequence of independent and identically distributed random variables, so the strong law of large numbers applies. This means that the limiting transition relative frequencies from $i$ to $j$ equal the true transition probabilities with chance 1. Thus if the true state of nature is a recurrent Markov chain, then there are only a finite number of ways in which Carnapian inductive logic for Markov chains can fail to learn the true transition matrix, and each of these has a chance of zero.

What are we to think of the failure of consistency of the Carnapian method for some non-recurrent Markov chains? It hardly seems a failure of the inductive method where nature conspires not to provide the relevant data. And Carnapians can take some comfort from two considerations: (1) From the classical Bayesian standpoint the non-recurrent chains have probability zero and (2) if nature prefers not to visit some states it may not be so important to know the true transition probabilities from those states.

On the other hand, if we can observe many independent Markov chains with the same transition probabilities, more learning possibilities open up. If we can arbitrarily start a process in any state we please, as seems natural in the thumbtack example, and do it independently as many times as we please, then Carnapian inductive logic can obviously learn the true transition probabilities for even non-recurrent chains. If we want to learn the probability vector for the initial state—say that a biased coin is flipped to decide the initial position of the thumbtack—then by looking at independent trials of the starting mechanism the correct chances for the initial state can be learned by Carnap's inductive rule. These sorts of possibilities are not usually discussed in the literature on Markov chains because they have nothing to do with the Markov structure. But they are nevertheless quite relevant to the application of inductive logic. If this kind of learning is allowed consistency of Carnapian inductive logic for Markov chains is unrestricted. Again, however, we should emphasize that Carnapian inductive logic for Markov chains is not unique in having this virtue. Many other inductive rules can be formulated which share it, some of which will be examined later in this essay.

## 5. Coordinate Languages, Stochastic Processes, and Cellular Automata

Carnap worked in a framework where names were mere indices, meant to convey no substantive information about the things named. This lay behind his adoption of a postulate of *symmetry*, that probability should be invariant under finite permutations of names. If the indices are a set with a natural order the principle of symmetry says that order makes no difference with respect to probability. In such a language, if one wants to express temporal or spatial order which is to make a difference, one would need to introduce relational predicates to carry the information.

It is simpler to let the indices carry information about order as is routinely done in the theory of stochastic processes. Carnap believed, early and late,[4] that a mature inductive logic should have a formulation for such *coordinate languages*. This is the sort of framework that we have implicitly been using in the foregoing discussion of Markov chains. Let us

---

[4] See Carnap (1950: sec. 15B), (1963b: 226), (1971: 118–20), (1980: 69–70).

make the framework explicit. A stochastic process is a family $[X_i: i \in I]$ of random variables on a probability space (W, F, pr). The sort of Markov chains we considered are discrete, one-sided stochastic processes where the index set I consists of the positive integers. The indices are usually taken to represent discrete times and their order to represent temporal order. The possible states of the system are the same at every time, so the measurable space (W, F) is a product of the measurable spaces for a single trial. The values of the random variables represent the state of the system at the time of its index. In the case we considered the system has only a finite number of possible states, so the random variables need take on only a finite number of values. The Markov property can then be written:

$$\Pr(X_{n+1} = x | X_1 = x_1 \& \ldots \& X_n = x_n) = \Pr(X_{n+1} = x | X_n = x_n)$$

In linguistic terms, W is a set of possible worlds and F is a Boolean $\sigma$-algebra of propositions. The indices of the random variables are names of times, and that a random variable takes on a value corresponds to the proposition in F which is the inverse image of that value under that random variable.

Carnap was—of course—interested in coordinate languages with more than one dimension. There is no reason why the indices have to only be ordered in one dimension. All sorts of orderings or partial orderings of the index set are possibilities. For example, we could consider the case of a product space for a physical system with a finite number of states where we have three dimensions of finite discrete space, and one dimension of one-sided infinite time. The appropriate Markov property would be that the state of a spatial point at time $t + 1$ depends only on that of that point and its neighbors at time $t$. Possible instantiations would be Ising spin models of ferromagnets, lattice gases, or stochastic cellular automata. If a Carnapian started by observing all points at time 1 and then at each point in time observed all points again, how should she update her probabilities? I will briefly sketch an answer.

For each point in space, there is an associated transition matrix. If the physical system in question has $k$ possible states, then the matrix has $k$ columns. If the point has $m$ neighbors, the number of rows is $m_k + 1$, with each row specifying the state of that point and its neighbors at the preceding time. (The number of neighbors depends here on whether the spatial point is on a vertex, edge, face, or in the interior.) Thus the transition matrix determines an urn model where each row in the matrix corresponds to an urn containing balls of $k$ different colors. Applying Carnap's inductive logic to the urns gives us an answer. Initially, each entry in each transition matrix will be $1/k$. A Carnapian will update the transition matrix for a point using the transition counts, so that if the number of transitions from row $r$ to column $c$ is $Trc$ and the total number of transitions from row $r$ to any column is $Tr$, the updated probability in the cell of the transition matrix for that point is:

$$\frac{Trc + 1}{Tr + k}$$

Perhaps the true transition probabilities are assumed stationary in space as well as time. That is, every interior point must have the same true transition probabilities—and likewise for every point on a face, on an edge, at a vertex. Then updating at a time, a Carnapian can use for any point in the interior the total transition counts for all points in the interior—and likewise for the other spatial classes of points.

It would be of some interest to explore the Carnapian inductive logic of general coordinate languages. Here the proper setting—at least initially—is the theory of Markov random fields.[5] Another direction for generalization is to consider higher-order Markov chains—where the probability of a state depends on some finite number, $k$, of preceding states. For a system with a finite number, $n$, of states the transition matrix has $n^k$ rows and $n$ columns, each row corresponding to an urn for the transition matrix from the natural urn model as before. One sort of application with some physical motivation would be a cellular automaton that is Markov in time but only higher-order Markov in space.

# 6. Parametric Models, Conjugate Priors, and Continua of Inductive Methods

In 1952 Carnap generalized his original inductive logic to a continuum of inductive rules. The continuum of 1952 gives us an inductive method which depends on a parameter, $\lambda$. The inductive method of 1950 is a special case. In the posthumously published "Basic System" Carnap introduced another parameter, $\gamma$. The resulting $\lambda - \gamma$ continuum gives a

---

[5] See Preston (1976) and Georgii (1979).

treatment identical to the parametric Bayesian approach. The change in viewpoint is dramatic. Originally, inductive logic was to be for Carnap an a priori organon which evaluated the claims of all beliefs to support by empirical evidence. But what is the status of the parameters? Are they to be evaluated on the basis of empirical evidence and if so, how? Or can they be freely chosen, opening the doors to subjectivism and relativism? In his intellectual autobiography (1963b) Carnap appears to lean in the latter direction:

As far as we can judge the situation at the present time, it seems that an observer is free to choose any of the admissible values of $\lambda$ and thereby an inductive method. If we find that the person X chooses a greater value of $\lambda$ than a person Y, then we recognize that X is more cautious than Y, i.e. X waits for a larger class of observational data than Y before he is willing to deviate in his estimate of relative frequency by a certain amount from its a priori value. (75)

In part I of the "Basic System" (1971) he leaves the question open:[6]

There will presumably be future axioms, justified in the same way by considerations of rationality. We do not know today whether in this future development the number of admissible M-functions will always remain infinite or will become finite and possibly even be reduced to one. Therefore, at the present time I do not assert that there is only one rational $Cr_0$-function. (27)

The inductive methods in Carnap's (1952) $\lambda$-continuum generalize his (1950) rule by adding a parameter, $\lambda$ ($\lambda > 0$), which determines how much weight is put on the a priori probability. Instead of:

$$\mathrm{pr}(C) = \frac{n+1}{N+k}$$

---

[6]  As he does in Carnap (1980: 119):

Suppose that at some point in the context of a given problem, say, the choice of a parameter value, we find that we have a free choice within certain boundaries, and at the moment we cannot think of any additional rationality requirement which would constrict the boundaries. Then it would certainly be imprudent to assert that the present range of choice will always remain open. How could we deny the possibility that we shall find tomorrow an additional requirement? But it would also be unwise to regard it as certain that such an additional requirement will be found, or even to predict that by the discovery of further requirements the range will shrink to one point.

we have:

$$\text{pr}(C) = \frac{n + \lambda}{N + \lambda k}$$

If $\lambda$ is 1, we get the original rule. If $\lambda$ is smaller, the relative frequencies swamp the a priori probabilities more quickly; if $\lambda$ is smaller the relative frequencies exert their effect more slowly.

In his (1971) "Basic System of Inductive Logic," Carnap added another parameter, $\gamma$. The effect is to enlarge the $\lambda$-continuum so that the various outcomes need not be equiprobable a priori. If there are $m$ possible outcomes, let $\gamma_1 \ldots \gamma_m$ be positive numbers summing to 1. Then the rule of succession becomes:

$$\text{pr}(C_i) = \frac{n + \lambda \gamma_t}{N + \lambda k}$$

It should be clear from the discussion of section 4 that all of the inductive rules in this continuum are *consistent*.

The foregoing generalizations have a Bayesian interpretation in terms of *natural conjugate priors*.[7] As an example, consider once more flipping a coin with unknown bias and assume that the prior probability density for $x$ = chance of heads on [0, 1] is Beta (with parameters $\alpha$ and $\beta$):

$$f_{\alpha\beta}(x) = \frac{\Gamma(\alpha + \beta)}{\Gamma(\alpha) + \Gamma(\beta)} x^{\alpha-1}(1 - x)^{\beta-1}$$

The first term is simply a normalizing constant to make the integral on [0, 1] come out to 1. The (degree of belief) probability of heads is then just the expectation of chance:

$$\frac{\alpha}{\alpha + \beta}$$

Suppose that a coin is flipped N times giving $n$ heads. The probability of this result conditional on the chance of heads being $x$ is:

$$x^n (1 - x)^{N-n}$$

Then by Bayes' Theorem the posterior density for $x$ is again Beta with new parameters $\alpha' = \alpha + n$ and $\beta' = \beta + (N - n)$. The Beta is known as

---

[7] See Raiffa and Schlaifer (1961) for analyses using natural conjugate priors. Giving a satisfactory characterization of natural conjugate priors which is not vacuously satisfied is not unproblematic. See Diaconis and Ylvisaker (1979).

the *natural conjugate prior* for a Bernoulli process. Use of the Beta prior leads to a generalized rule of succession. On the evidence of a series of N trials with $n$ heads, the probability of heads is:

$$\frac{\alpha'}{\alpha' + \beta'} = \frac{\alpha + n}{\alpha + \beta + N}$$

When $\alpha = \beta = 1$ the Beta prior is flat and we have Laplace's Rule of succession.

For a multinomial model, such as sampling from an urn with replacement, the story is similar. Suppose that an run contains balls of $k$ different colors, and let the unknown chance of color 1 be $x_1, \ldots$, color $k$ be $x_k$. Then the prior density will be on the random vector $\mathbf{X} = \langle x_1, \ldots, x_k \rangle$. The natural conjugate prior on the appropriate simplex is the Dirichlet:

$$f_\alpha = \frac{\Gamma(\alpha_1 + \ldots + \alpha_k)}{\Gamma(\alpha_1) \ldots \Gamma(\alpha_k)} x_1^{\alpha_1 - 1} \ldots x_k^{\alpha_k - 1}$$

with parameter $\alpha = \langle \alpha_1, \ldots, \alpha_k \rangle$ (all $\alpha_i$ positive).

The a priori probability of color $i$ is the expectation of its chance:

$$E(x_i) = \frac{\alpha_i}{\sum_{j=1}^{k} \alpha_j}$$

Since the likelihood is proportional to the prior density, the posterior on the evidence of a sample of N balls, $n_1$ of color $1 \ldots n_k$ of color $k$, is again with parameter $\alpha' = \langle \alpha_1 + n_1, \ldots, \alpha_k + n_k \rangle$. This yields a generalized rule of succession. The posterior probability of color $i$ is:

$$\frac{\alpha_i + n_i}{\sum_{j=1}^{k} \alpha_j + n_j}$$

If we restrict ourselves to symmetric Dirichlet priors, this gives us Carnap's $\lambda$-continuum. If we allow arbitrary Dirichlet priors, we get the $\lambda - \gamma$ continuum of "Carnap's Basic System."

How can one get a reasonable conjugate prior analysis for Markov chains with unknown transition probabilities? The standard parametric Bayesian approach, as in Martin (1967), is to apply the foregoing analysis to the natural urn model for the transitions and take the product measure to get the appropriate prior. Here independence is simply assumed, rather than being derived from indifference as in the classical Bayesian approach of section 3. Martin calls this prior the "Matrix Beta" prior. This approach yields a Carnapian $\lambda - \gamma$ continuum of inductive methods for transition probabilities of Markov chains:

$$(\mathrm{PrS}_j | \mathrm{S}_i) = \frac{\lambda \gamma_{ij} + \mathrm{N}[\mathrm{S}_j, \mathrm{S}_i]}{\lambda k + \sum_{m=1}^{k} \mathrm{N}[\mathrm{S}_m, \mathrm{S}_i]}$$

The suggestion of Kuipers (1988) was, in fact, to use the part of this continuum which corresponds to Carnap's $\lambda$-continuum. All of these methods share the consistency properties of Carnapian Inductive Logic for Markov chains that were pointed out in section 4.

# 7. Subjective Bayesian Analysis

Subjective Bayesians do not believe in chances, and will not postulate a chance statistical model such as coin flipping or multinomial sampling or a Markov chain. The role that statistical models play for parametric Bayesians is, for them, taken over by *symmetries* in degrees of belief. The fundamental example is that of what de Finetti called *exchangeability*. Carnap defended a principle of symmetry that bears a superficial resemblance to exchangeability in his work on inductive logic, that is that the probability should be invariant under permutations of names. This was done in systems for finite languages, in which names were supposed to be mere identifying tags carrying no additional information as to order. Carnap was well aware that in the context of a temporal coordinate language the assumption of symmetry cannot have a priori status.[8] Here the indices carry information about temporal order, and the principle of symmetry tells us that temporal order makes no probabilistic difference. De Finetti may be thought of as working in a coordinate language where the $n$th integer names the $n$th trial. A degree of belief probability is *exchangeable* if it is invariant under finite permutations of trials. If we know that we are flipping a biased coin with the tosses independent in the true chance probabilities but are uncertain as to the bias so that we mix the possible Bernoulli processes, the result gives us degrees of belief probabilities which do not make the trials independent, but do make them exchangeable. De Finetti proved the converse. Exchangeable sequences

---

[8] See Carnap (1971: 118–20), (1980: 69–70).

have a unique representation as mixtures of independent ones. This is true not only for two valued random variables, but also for the random variables taking a finite number of values that we have discussed (and for much more general cases as well).[9] Thus a subjective Bayesian can take symmetry of degrees of belief here as a mark that one will act *as if* one were drawing balls from an urn of unknown composition. In other words, for all intents and purposes the symmetry in the degrees of belief here is tantamount to identifying a statistical model.

Exchangeability has an equivalent formulation that brings out an important connection with relative frequencies. Suppose that we have a physical system with a finite number of states, $S_1 \ldots S_m$, and are considering a sequence of trials on each of which the system takes one of these states. Sampling from an urn or rolling a die are examples. For a finite sequence of trials consider $C = \langle C_1, \ldots, C_n \rangle$, the vector of frequency counts of occurrences of the states $S_1, \ldots, S_n$, respectively. C will be said to be a *sufficient statistic* if any two finite sample sequences with the same value of C are equiprobable. A probability measure is exchangeable just in case it makes C a sufficient statistic. Thus we can say that if the vector of frequency counts is a sufficient statistic, relative to degrees of belief, then the beliefs are as if they came from a multinomial sampling model. The prior on the parameters is, however, so far undetermined.

A stronger sense of sufficiency gets stronger results. Suppose in addition to exchangeability that the probability of the outcome on the next trial given the sample size and relative frequency of the outcome in all previous trials is equal to the probability of that outcome on the next trial given the complete record of all previous trials. Suppose also that for any state the numerical dependence is the same: that is, that the probability of that state on the next trial given a frequency count for it and number of trials is the same as the probability of any other state given the same number of trials and the same frequency count for the latter state. That is, the probability of a state, $S_i$, on the next trial depends only on $C_i$ and $\Sigma_j C_j$. This is W. E. Johnson's (1932) "*sufficientness postulate*." See Zabell (1982). If the physical system has 3 or more states and if we have both exchangeability and Johnson's sufficiency postulate satisfied by degrees-of-belief, then they are as if we put a symmetric Dirichlet prior on a multinomial model. That is to say that we are operating within Carnap's $\lambda$-continuum of inductive methods.

---

[9] See Hewitt and Savage (1955).

If, for repeated trials with a finite number of outcomes, you have an initial probability which is exchangeable and which makes every relative frequency of outcomes equally likely for a fixed sample size (equiprobability of structure descriptions in Carnap's terms) then you get Carnap's (1950) $c^*$ inductive logic. This was demonstrated by W. E. Johnson (1924), before either Carnap or de Finetti.[10] Exchangeability was Johnson's "permutation postulate." Equiprobability of structure descriptions was Johnson's "combination postulate." The permutation postulate was tantamount to identifying a statistical model of multinomial sampling. The combination postulate in addition was tantamount to assuming a flat prior on the parameters of the model. Together they give the generalization of Laplace's Rule of succession that Carnap advocated in *Logical Foundations of Probability* (1950).

In dealing with Markov chains we do not have exchangeability, but perhaps a weaker kind of symmetry condition can play a role with respect to Markov processes analogous to that played by exchangeability with respect to Bernoulli processes. Such an analysis is developed in Freedman (1962), de Finetti (1974), Diaconis and Freedman (1980b). Let us return to the Markov thumbtack. Suppose we are sure that this was a Markov process but were unsure about the transition probabilities and probability of the initial state, and mixed over the possibilities. The result would be a stochastic process which would, in general, not be Markov, but which has the property that the vector of initial state and transition counts as a sufficient statistic for all finite sequences of given length, generated by the process. That is to say, that sequences of the same length, having the same transition counts and the same initial state, are equiprobable. When this is the case, say the process is *Markov exchangeable*.

Markov exchangeability, like ordinary exchangeability, can also be given an equivalent formulation in terms of invariance (Diaconis and Freedman, 1980). A primitive block-switch transformation of a sequence takes two disjoint blocks of the sequence with the same starting and ending states and switches them. A block-switch transformation is the composition of a finite number of primitive block-switch transformations. A probability is then Markov exchangeable just in case it is invariant under all block-switch transformations.

---

[10] See Zabell for details of both this and of Johnson's (1932) generalization.

Diaconis and Freedman (1980) show that *recurrent* stochastic processes of this type which are Markov exchangeable have a unique representation as a mixture of Markov chains. The leading idea of the proof involves looking at sequences of blocks. A 1-block of an infinite sequence is a finite string of states that begins with state 1 and proceeds until (but not including) the next occurrence of state 1. Consider the infinite sequence of 1-blooks, which is well defined with probability 1 because of recurrence. Permuting 1-blocks leave the transition counts in the original sequence unchanged. Then, as a consequence of Markov exchangeability, the sequence of 1-blocks is exchangeable. De Finetti's theorem is applied to this higher-order sequence of 1-blocks to get the desired conclusion. The resulting representation theorem for recurrent Markov-exchangeable stochastic processes gives us the foundation for a wholly subjective approach to the theory of Markov chains.

In this spirit, Carnapian inductive logic for Markov chains can be given a purely subjective development parallel to W. E. Johnson's pathbreaking analyses of generalized rules of succession. Suppose that in degrees of belief we have a recurrent, Markov exchangeable, stochastic process with a finite number of states. Then by the Diaconis and Freedman result, our degrees of belief are as if we had a Markov chain with unknown transition probabilities. Now suppose further that for all states, our degrees of belief for transitions from that state satisfy the appropriate form of W. E. Johnson's *sufficientness postulate*. That is that $Pr(S_j|S_i)$ depend only on $N[S_j, S_i]$ and $\Sigma_m N[S_m, S_i]$. Notice that this automatically gets us the independence that Martin and Kuipers assume. If our beliefs satisfy the postulate then transition counts from one state are not taken as giving any evidence about transitions from another state. Furthermore, our beliefs about transitions from a state must be as if we were sampling from an urn with unknown composition and symmetric Dirichlet prior, with the same prior for each state. In other words, we are in the Kuipers $\lambda$-continuum of Carnapian inductive methods for Markov chains:

$$Pr(S_j|S_i) = \frac{\lambda + N[S_j, S_i]}{\lambda k + \sum_{m=1}^{k} N[S_m, S_i]}$$

If the degrees of belief in addition satisfy the analogous form of Johnson's *combination postulate*, then they embody the Carnapian inductive logic for Markov chains of section 2. However, from a subjective point of view none of Johnson's postulates has any *logical* status; they merely serve to characterize cases in which degrees of belief have certain interesting and computationally tractable symmetries.

# 8. Order, Periodicity, and Inductive Logic

In the 1960s Carnap was challenged by Achinstein and Putnam to extend his inductive logic to make it sensitive to questions of order and periodicity. Achinstein (1961) looked towards a higher-order language as the proper framework to accomplish this task. Carnap (1963a) replies by trying to code the order information into first-order predicates:

Achinstein studies chiefly laws of periodicity...He believes that a solution will require a much stronger language containing predicates and quantified variables of higher order.

I do not share this belief. I will briefly indicate how I would approach the problem of a coordinate language in inductive logic. As an example, let us think of a family of five predicates for simple qualitative properties $P_1,\ldots,P_5$, say colors. An $m$-segment is a series of $m$ consecutive positions. I introduce $Q^m$- for the possible properties ('$m$-species') of $m$-segments. For example, I define:

$$(6) \qquad Q^3_{5,1,4}(n) =_{df} P_5(n).P_1(n+1).P_4(n+2)$$

Thus the sentence '$Q^3_{5,1,4}(8)$' ascribes to the 3-segment beginning with position 8 the 3-species consisting of $P_5$, $P_{1,4}$ in this order; but formally '$Q^3_{5,1,4}$' is a one-place predicate of positions.

These two approaches are perhaps not so far apart as Carnap seems to suppose. If we are not too particular about details we might say that the analysis in terms of blocks is consonant with the general spirit of Achinstein while the argument sketched in section 4 is closer to the general spirit of Carnap.

At this time Carnap was then already in his seventies, and he spent the time he had left pursuing other generalizations of his system. Order was to be dealt with properly within a framework of coordinate languages whose implementation was seen as far in the future. The natural place to start such an investigation is with the question of inductive logic for finite Markov chains. Far from being impossible—or even difficult—the adaptation of Carnapian methods here is smooth and natural. Generalization to higher-order Markov chains and to finite cellular automata is equally straightforward. In such a setting Carnapian inductive logic can learn the laws of chance that are responsible for the order in some very complicated phenomena.

The problem here for Carnap's original program is not that one cannot get a good inductive learning machine, but that there are so many ways in which one can do it. Any member of the full $\lambda$—$\gamma$ continuum of Carnapian inductive methods for Markov chains will do. All of them share the desirable consistency properties, but they are not the only methods that have such consistency properties. And there is even some reason to look outside this class of methods because in some applications the 'sufficiency' postulates may be inappropriate. Perhaps transitions from one state may be evidentially relevant to our beliefs about the transitions from another state. Suppose that there are 100 states, and there have been 100,000 trials. State 100 always has gone to state 1, state 1 to state 2 . . . state 98 to state 99. Might this evidence not raise slightly the transition probability that the system will go to state 100 given that it was previously in state 99? Such analogical reasoning should not be excluded a priori. Carnap had already met the problem of non-uniqueness in inductive logic for multinomial sampling. There he moved to more and more general continua of inductive methods. Consideration of wider domains of stochastic phenomena can only reinforce this tendency to move towards an all-embracing Bayesian methodology. Both Carnap (1959), (1971), (1980) and de Finetti (1938), (1972) discuss additional forms of dependence which are important for inductive reasoning. These discussions point to promising territory for further extension of inductive methods in the spirit of Carnap.

# References

Achinstein, P. (1963) "Confirmation Theory, Order and Periodicity," *Philosophy of Science* 30: 17–35.

Bayes, Thomas (1765) "An Essay Toward Solving a Problem in the Doctrine of Chances," *Philosophical Transactions of the Royal Society of London* 53: 370–418.

Burks, A. (1970) *Essays on Cellular Automata.* Urbana, IL: University of Illinois Press.

Carnap, R. (1950) *Logical Foundations of Probability.* Urbana, IL: University of Illinois Press. Second ed. 1962. Chicago: University of Chicago Press.

——(1952) *The Continuum of Inductive Methods.* Chicago: University of Chicago Press.

——(1963a) "Variety, Analogy and Periodicity in Inductive Logic," *Philosophy of Science* 30: 222–7.

——(1963b) "Replies and Systematic Expositions." In P. A. Schilpp (ed.), *The Philosophy of Rudolf Carnap*, pp. 711–37. LaSalle, IL: Open Court.

——(1971) "A Basic System of Inductive Logic, Part 1." In R. Carnap and R. C. Jeffrey (eds.), *Studies in Inductive Logic and Probability*, vol. 1. Berkeley, CA: University of California Press.

——(1980) "A Basic System of Inductive Logic, Part 2." In R. C. Jeffrey (ed.), *Studies in Inductive Logic and Probability*, vol. 2. Berkeley, CA: University of California Press.

Carnap, R. and Stegmüller, W. (1959) *Induktive Logik und Wahrscheinlichkeit*. Vienna: Springer.

De Finetti, B. (1937) "La Prévision: Ses lois logiques, ses sources subjectives," *Annales de l'Institut Henri Poincaré* 7: 1–68; tr. as "Foresight: Its Logical Laws, Its Subjective Sources," in H. E. Kyburg, Jr. and H. Smokler (eds.), *Studies in Subjective Probability*. Huntington, NY: Kreiger, 1980.

——(1938) "Sur la condition d'equivalence partielle," *Actualités scientifiques et industrielles*, No. 739. Paris: Hermann; translated by P. Benacerraf and R. Jeffrey as "On the Condition of Partial Exchangeability," in R. C. Jeffrey (ed.), *Studies in Inductive Logic and Probability*, vol. 2, pp. 193–205. Berkeley, CA: University of California Press.

——(1974) *Probability, Induction and Statistics*. New York: Wiley.

Diaconis, P. and Freedman, D. (1980) "De Finetti's Theorem for Markov Chains," *Annals of Probability* 8: 115–30.

——(1981) "Partial Exchangeability and Sufficiency," in *Statistics: Applications and New Directions* (Proceedings of the Indian Statistical Institute Golden Jubilee International Conference), pp. 205–36. Calcutta: Indian Statistical Institute.

——(1986) "On the Consistency of Bayes Estimates," *Annals of Statistics* 14: 1–26.

Diaconis, P. and Ylvisaker, D. (1979) "Conjugate Priors for Exponential Families," *Annals of Statistics* 7: 269–81.

Dynkin, E. (1978) "Sufficient Statistics and Extreme Points," *Annals of Probability* 6: 705–30.

Feller, W. (1966) *An Introduction to Probability Theory and its Applications*, vol. 1, 2nd ed. New York: Wiley.

Freedman, D. (1962) "Mixtures of Markov Processes," *Annals of Mathematical Statistics* 2: 615–29.

Georgii, H. O. (1979) *Canonical Gibbs Measures* (Lecture Notes in Mathematics 760). Berlin: Springer.

Good, I. J. (1965) *The Estimation of Probabilities: An Essay on Modern Bayesian Methods*. Cambridge, MA: MIT Press.

Hewitt, E. and Savage, L. J. (1955) "Symmetric Measures on Cartesian Products," *Transactions of the American Mathematical Society* 80: 470–501.

Johnson, W. E. (1924) *Logic, Part III: The Logical Foundations of Science*. Cambridge, MA: MIT Press.

—— (1932) "Probability: The Deductive and Inductive Problems," *Mind* 49: 409–23.

Kemeny, J. (1964) "Carnap on Probability and Induction." In P. A. Schilpp (ed.), *The Philosophy of Rudolf Carnap*, pp. 711–37. LaSalle, IL: Open Court.

Kuipers, T. A. F. (1988) "Inductive Analogy by Similarity and Proximity." In D. H. Helman (ed.), *Analogical Reasoning*. Dordrecht: Kluwer.

Lidstone, G. J. (1920) "Note on the General Case of the Bayes–Laplace Formula for Inductive or a posteriori Probabilities," *Transactions of the Faculty of Actuaries* 8: 182–92.

Martin, J. J. (1967) *Bayesian Decision Problems and Markov Chains*. New York: Wiley.

Preston, C. (1976) *Random Fields* (Springer Lecture Notes in Mathematics 534). Berlin: Springer.

Putnam, H. (1963a) "Degree of Confirmation and Inductive Logic." In P. A. Schilpp (ed.), *The Philosophy of Rudolf Carnap*, pp. 761–83. LaSalle, IL: Open Court. Reprinted in H. Putnam, *Mathematics, Matter and Method. Philosophical Papers*, vol. 1, pp. 270–92. Cambridge: Cambridge University Press, 1975.

—— (1963b) "Probability and Confirmation." In *The Voice of America, Forum Philosophy of Science* 10. U.S. Information Agency. Reprinted in H. Putnam, *Mathematics, Matter and Method. Philosophical Papers*, vol. 1, pp. 293–304. Cambridge: Cambridge University Press, 1975.

Raiffa, H. and Schlaiffer, R. (1961) *Applied Statistical Decision Theory*. Division of Research, Boston, Graduate School of Business Administration, Harvard University.

Strong, J. V. (1976) "The Infinite Ballot Box of Nature: De Morgan, Boole and Jevons on Probability and the Logic of Induction," *PSA*, vol. 1 (Proceedings of the Philosophy of Science Association). East Lansing, MI.

Zabell, S. L. (1982) "W. E. Johnson's 'Sufficientness' Postulate," *Annals of Statistics* 10: 1091–9.

—— (1988) "Symmetry and Its Discontents," in B. Skyrms and W. L. Harper (eds.), *Causation, Chance and Credence*, pp. 155–90. Dordrecht: Kluwer.

—— (1989) "The Rule of Succession," *Erkenntnis* 31: 283–321.

—— (2005) *Symmetry and Its Discontents*. Cambridge: Cambridge University Press. [Includes Zabell (1982), (1988), (1989) and much more.]

# 12

# Carnapian Inductive Logic and Bayesian Statistics

## 1. Introduction

In 1941, at the age of 50, Rudolf Carnap embarked on the project of developing inductive logic. In the early days of the Vienna Circle the logical positivists, heavily influenced by Hilbert, looked to deductive logic and the axiomatic method to analyze the scientific method. Over the years Carnap, Hempel, Reichenbach and others came to the conclusion that important aspects of scientific method were irreducibly inductive. The analysis of inductive inference thus became central to the development of scientific philosophy.

While Reichenbach focused on relative frequency and the consistency of statistical estimators, Carnap investigated probability as rational degree of belief. He started with Bayes and progressed to Laplace. By the end of his life, he had moved from a logical conception of probability inspired by Keynes and a unique inductive rule based on a flat prior for an IID process to a subjective conception of probability and a class of inductive rules corresponding to the Dirichlet priors.

Carnap hoped that after his death co-workers would carry forward the construction of inductive logic. In his last (posthumous) work (1980) he lists three major tasks for future research. One is the construction of confirmation functions for the case where the outcome can take on a continuum of possible values. The others have to do with the construction of confirmation functions sensitive to two kinds of analogy, which he calls "analogy by proximity" and "analogy by similarity."

I would like to thank Persi Diaconis, Haim Gaifman, Richard Jeffrey, John Kemeny, Jim MacQueen, and Sandy Zabell for valuable discussions.

Within three years of his death, Carnap's first problem had been completely solved in a way quite consonant with Carnapian techniques, by Ferguson (1973) and Blackwell and MacQueen (1973). Carnap's 'co-workers' have turned out, in large measure, to be Bayesian statisticians rather than philosophers. In addition to the solution to the problem of a value continuum, Bayesian statistics can throw some light on Carnap's two problems of analogy.

## 2. Carnap's Continua

Suppose that we have an exhaustive family of $k$ mutually exclusive categories, and a sample of size $N$ of which $n$ are of category $F$. Carnap (1950) originally proposed the following inductive rule, $C^\star$, to give the probability that a new sampled individual, $a$, would be in $F$ on the basis of the given sample evidence, $e$.

$$Pr(Fa|e) = \frac{1 + n}{k + N}$$

On the basis of no sample evidence, each category gets equal probability of $1/k$. As the sample grows larger, the effect of the initial equiprobable assignment shrinks and the probability attaching to a category approaches the empirical average in the sample, $n/N$. Soon Carnap (1952) shifted from this method to a class of inductive methods of which it is a member, the $\lambda$-continuum of inductive methods.

$$Pr(Fa|e) = \frac{\lambda + n}{\lambda k + N}$$

Here again, we have initial equiprobability of categories and predominance of the empirical average in the limit with the parameter, $\lambda(\lambda > 0)$, controlling the rate at which the sample evidence swamps the prior probabilities. In his posthumous (1980) paper, Carnap introduced the more general $\lambda - \gamma$ continuum:

$$Pr(F_i a|e) = \frac{\lambda \gamma_i + n}{\lambda + N}$$

The new parameters, $\gamma_i > 0$, allow unequal a priori probabilities for different categories. For Carnap these are intended to reflect different "logical widths" of the categories. The parameter, $\lambda$, again determines how quickly the empirical average swamps the prior probability of an outcome. One could equivalently formulate Carnap's $\lambda - \gamma$ rules as follows. Take any $k$ positive numbers, $b_1, \ldots, b_k$, and let the rule be:

$$pr(F_i a | e) = \frac{b_i + n}{\Sigma_j b_j + N}$$

where $\lambda = \sum_j b_j$ and $\gamma_i = b_i / \lambda$.

We can think about the problem addressed by Carnap's inductive rules in the following way. The experiment is represented by a discrete random variable, taking as possible numerical values the integers 1 through $k$, according to whether the experimental result is $F_1, \ldots, F_k$. This experimental result generates a measurable space, $S = \langle W, A \rangle$, where the points in $W$ are the $k$ possible outcomes and the propositions (measurable sets) in $A$ are gotten by closing the atoms under Boolean combination.

Induction takes place when the experiment is iterated and a general analysis does not place any finite upper bound on the number of possible iterations. Thus we are led to consider an infinite sequence of such random variables, indexed by the positive integers. The relevant measurable space is a product of an infinite number of copies of the one shot probability space, $S_1 \times S_2 \times S_3 \times \ldots$ The points in the infinite product space are infinite sequences, $w_1, w_2, \ldots$, of integers from 1 through $k$. In this setting we can give a fairly general definition of an inductive rule.

An *inductive rule*, R, takes as input any finite initial sequence of results, $\langle w_1, \ldots, w_j \rangle$ and any proposition about the experimental outcome the next time around, $a_{j+1}$ in $A_{j+1}$ and outputs a numerical prediction in $[0, 1]$ such that: (i) for any finite outcome sequence, $\langle w_1, \ldots, w_j \rangle$, the rule gives a probability, $R(\langle w_1, \ldots, w_j \rangle, \cdot)$ on the space for the next moment of time, $\langle W_{j+1}, A_{j+1} \rangle$ and (ii) for every proposition about the next outcome, $a_{j+1}$, $R(\cdot, a_{j+1})$ is measurable on the space of histories up until then, $S_1 \times \cdots \times S_j$.

Note on (i): This includes empty sequences, so the rule must specify a prior probability on $S_1$. Note on (ii): This technical regularity requirement is automatically satisfied in the finite case considered in this section, but is required for a definition which will generalize.

Then an *inductive rule* determines a unique probability on the infinite product space, $S_1 \times S_2 \times \cdots$, according to which the probabilities given by the inductive rules are conditional probabilities (Neveu, 1965: ch. V).

Thus, the properties of an inductive rule can be studied at either the 'operational' level of a predictive rule or at the 'metaphysical' level of a prior probability on an infinite product space.

The rules in Carnap's $\lambda - \gamma$ continuum are all inductive rules in the foregoing sense. For each of these rules the corresponding probability on the infinite product space is *exchangeable*: that is, invariant under finite permutations of outcomes. By de Finetti's theorem, any such probability has a unique representation as a mixture of probabilities which make the outcome random variables independent and identically distributed. That is to say that the Carnapian inductive logician behaves as if she were multinomial sampling. The examples of throwing a die with unknown bias or sampling with replacement from an urn of unknown composition are canonical.

# 3. The Classical Bayesian Parametric View of Carnap's $\lambda - \gamma$ Continuum

One way of thinking about Carnap's rules is to take this representation at face value. There is a fixed statistical model of the chance mechanism with subjective prior uncertainty as to the true values of the parameters of the model. There is a chance setup (the die and the throwing mechanism) generating a sequence of independent and identically distributed random variables, but the distribution of the random variables (the bias of the die) is initially unknown. Inductive inference depends on this prior uncertainty via Bayes' theorem. The goal of inductive inference is to learn the true bias of the coin. This is the parametric Bayesian conceptualization of the problem.

From this point of view, Carnap's postulate that inductive methods should satisfy the *Reichenbach Axiom*—that the probabilities given by the inductive rule converge to the empirical average as the number of trials goes to infinity—is well motivated. By the strong law of large numbers, this is just the requirement that with chance equal to one, the inductive rule learns in the limit true bias of the die, no matter what the true bias is. That is to say that Carnap's methods correspond to priors on the bias which are Bayesian consistent with respect to the multinomial statistical model.

Not every consistent prior for multinomial sampling generates an inductive rule which is a member of Carnap's $\lambda - \gamma$ continuum. Carnap's rules correspond to the class of natural conjugate priors for multinomial sampling: the Dirichlet priors. As the predictive rules which are generated by Dirichlet priors, Carnap's $\lambda - \gamma$ methods are well known to Bayesian statisticians, Good (1965), DeGroot (1970: ch. 5). Carnap's (1942) $\lambda$ continuum is generated by the symmetric Dirichlet priors and his (1950) confirmation function, $c^\star$, by the uniform prior.

## 4. The Subjective Bayesian View of Carnap's $\lambda - \gamma$ continuum

For pure subjective Bayesians to talk of objective chances is strictly meaningless and the multinomial statistical model discussed in the last section is only an artifact of the de Finetti representation. Exchangeability is consistent with degrees of belief which give rise to inductive rules outside Carnap's continuum. Is there any subjective characterization of the $\lambda - \gamma$ continuum?

There is. It is due to the Cambridge logician W. E. Johnson. Johnson introduced the concept of exchangeability or symmetry in 1924 (before de Finetti). We defined exchangeability in terms of the infinite product space induced by an inductive rule, as invariance under finite permutations of trials. There is an equivalent formulation in terms of the inductive rule itself. That is that the vector of frequency counts of the possible outcomes is sufficient to determine the probabilities for the next trial: $R(<w_1, \ldots, w_j>, \cdot) = R(<w'_1, \ldots, w'_j>, \cdot)$ if the outcome sequences $< w_1, \ldots, w_j >$ and $<w'_1, \ldots, w'_j>$ have the same frequency counts. For example, in rolling a die, the outcome sequences 1234561 and 1135264 would lead to the same probabilities for the eighth trial; order is presumed not to be relevant.

Johnson was led to postulate a stronger kind of sufficiency. That is that (i) The probability of an outcome on the next trial should only depend on the frequency that *it* has occurred in the preceding trials (for each fixed number of trials) and not on the relative frequencies of the other trials, and (ii) The dependence should be the same for all categories. In the example of the die, (i) says that the probability of a one on the eighth trial given initial outcome sequences 1213654 and 1155555 should be the same; (ii) adds that this probability should be equal to the probability of a 2 on the eighth trial given the initial sequence 1253266. Taken together (i) and (ii) are Johnson's *sufficientness postulate*.

If we have (1) exchangeability but not independence, (2) sufficientness in Johnson's sense, (3) the number of categories is at least three, and (4) the relevant conditional probabilities are all well defined, then we get Carnap's 1952 $\lambda$-continuum of inductive methods. If Johnson's (ii) is dropped from the foregoing, we get Carnap's $\lambda - \gamma$ continuum (Zabell, 1982). Thus, from a purely subjective point of view, Carnap's continua correspond to strong symmetries in a predictor's degrees of belief.

## 5. Blackwell–MacQueen Inductive Rules

Carnap was interested in developing inductive logic to the point where it could make contact with mathematical physics. He saw the first important step to be to generalize his methods so that they could deal with the case where the outcome of an experiment could take on a continuum of values. We will accordingly change our canonical example from that of a die to that of a wheel of fortune with unit circumference. Repeated spins of the wheel produce as (ideal) outcomes, real numbers in the interval [0, 1). We equip this outcome space with the metric corresponding to the shortest distance measured around the circumference of the circle. We will take as our problem the specification of an inductive rule in this setting. The techniques which solve this problem, however, will apply very generally.

One could approach this problem by thinking about how a Carnapian in possession only of Carnap's $\lambda - \gamma$ continuum for finite numbers of outcomes could approximate a solution. The natural thing to try might be to partition the unit interval into a finite number of subintervals, and apply a method from the $\lambda - \gamma$ continuum taking the elements of the partition as outcomes. Finer and finer partitions might be thought of as giving better and better approximations. Recall the reformulation of Carnap's $\lambda - \gamma$ continuum of section 2. Take any $k$ positive numbers, $b_1, \ldots, b_k$, and let the rule be:

$$pr(F_i a|e) = \frac{b_i + n}{\Sigma_j b_j + N}$$

where $\lambda = \sum_j b_j$ and $\gamma_i = b_i/\lambda$. Thus, for a partition into $k$ subintervals, we have a class of Carnapian inductive rules whose members are specified by $k$ parameters, $b_1, \ldots, b_k$.

In the case of a continuum of possible outcomes, the appropriate parameter will be a nonnegative bounded measure, $\alpha$, defined on the Borel algebra of the unit interval. As a generalization of Carnap's condition that the $b_i$s should be positive in the finite case, we will require that the measure, $\alpha$, be absolutely continuous with respect to Lebesgue measure on the unit interval. For any Borel set, $O$, in the unit interval and evidence, $e$, consisting of $n$ points in $O$ in $N$ trials, we will take the inductive rule with parameter, $\alpha$, to give the probability of an outcome in $O$ in the next trial as:

$$pr(O|e) = \frac{a(O) + n}{a([0,1)) + N}$$

We will call this the Blackwell–MacQueen inductive rule, since Blackwell and MacQueen used this formula in generalizing Polya urn models for what philosophers know as Carnap's $\lambda - \gamma$ inductive rules, to more general Polya urn models for non-parametric Bayesian inference.

It can be seen that the Blackwell–MacQueen rules are consistent with Carnap's $\lambda - \gamma$ continuum in the following sense: For a Blackwell–MacQueen rule and a 'coarse-graining' of outcomes according to which member of a finite partition they fall into, the induced inductive rule for the finite partition is a member of Carnap's $\lambda - \gamma$ continuum. For a simple illustration, let the parameter, $\alpha$, for the Blackwell–MacQueen rule just be Lebesgue measure. In particular, if $I$ is a subinterval of $[0,1)$, then $\alpha(I)$ is just the length of $I$. Partition the unit interval into $k$ equal subintervals. Then for some fixed one of these subintervals, $I$, let $n$ be the number of sample points in $I$ and $N$ be the total number of sample points. Then the Blackwell–MacQueen rule gives the probability that the next point will fall into $I$ as:

$$pr(I|e) = \frac{\frac{1}{k} + n}{1 + N}$$

which is a member of Carnap's $\lambda$-continuum. (Notice that as the partitions get finer the value of $\lambda$ gets proportionately smaller to preserve consistency with the Blackwell–MacQueen rule.) It should be clear that this class of inductive rules is the natural generalization of Carnapian rules to problems where the outcomes can be represented as real numbers in the unit interval.

Blackwell–MacQueen rules are *Inductive Rules* in the sense made precise in section 2. Thus they induce a probability measure on the infinite product space. This probability measure makes the random variables which represent the experimental outcomes exchangeable. By de Finetti's theorem, it can be represented as a mixture of probabilities which make the trials independent and identically distributed. From a classical Bayesian viewpoint, the mixing measure is the ignorance prior over the true chances governing the IID process. The IID probabilities correspond to a distribution on $[0, 1)$. The prior corresponds to a distribution on the distributions on $[0, 1)$.

# 6. The Classical Bayesian Non-Parametric View: Ferguson Distributions

One might try to generalize Carnap's inductive methods in a different way—by working at the level of the de Finetti priors rather than at the level of inductive rules. As noted in section 3, the members of Carnap's $\lambda - \gamma$ continuum are just those rules which arise from multinomial sampling with Dirichlet priors. The natural generalization of a Dirichlet prior is a Ferguson distribution (called by Ferguson, and also known as, the Dirichlet process). A *Ferguson distribution* with parameter $\alpha$ is a distribution which for every k member partition of the interval, $P_1, \ldots, P_k$, is distributed as Dirichlet with parameters, $\alpha(P_1), \ldots, \alpha(P_n)$. A Ferguson distribution is a distribution over random chance distributions for a random chance probability, $p$. The parameter, $\alpha$, of the Ferguson distribution can be any finite, non-null measure on $[0,1)$. Thus for any finite measurable partition, $\{P_1, \ldots, P_n\}$ of $[0,1)$, there is a corresponding vector of numbers, $< \alpha_1, \ldots, \alpha_n >$ where $\alpha_i = \alpha(P_i)$. The requirement is then that for any such partition, the random chance probability vector for members of the partition, $< p(P_1), \ldots, p(P_n) >$, has a Dirichlet distribution with parameter $< \alpha_1, \ldots, \alpha_n >$.

The good news for Carnap's program is that both roads lead to the same place. The de Finetti prior distribution corresponding to the probability on the infinite product space induced by a Blackwell–MacQueen inductive rule with parameter $\alpha$ is a Ferguson distribution with parameter $\alpha$. In fact,

the paper of Blackwell and MacQueen was written to give a simple proof
of the existence of Ferguson distributions.

Furthermore, just as the class of Dirichlet probabilities is closed under
multinomial sampling, the class of Ferguson distributions is closed under
IID sampling of points in [0,1). Consider a finite sample sequence consist-
ing of data points $x_1, \ldots, x_n$, and let $\delta_1, \ldots, \delta_n$ be probability measures
giving mass one to the points $x_1, \ldots, x_n$, respectively. Let the prior be
given by a Ferguson distribution with parameter $\alpha$. Then conditioning on
the data points takes one to a posterior which is a Ferguson distribution
with parameter $\alpha'$, where:

$$\alpha' = \alpha + \sum_{i=1}^{n} \delta_i$$

From the classical Bayesian viewpoint, Ferguson distributions are natural
conjugate priors for this non-parametric sampling problem in just the same
way that Dirichlet priors are natural conjugate priors for multinomial
sampling.

Blackwell–MacQueen Inductive Rules satisfy a version of *Reichenbach's
axiom*, Freedman (1963), Fabius (1964), Diaconis and Freedman (1986). As
evidence accumulates the probability for the next trial is a weighted
average of the a priori probability and the empirical relative frequency
probability, with all weight concentrating on the empirical relative frequency probability as the number of data points goes to infinity. Can we
say in the classical Bayesian setting that Blackwell–MacQueen inductive
rules will, with chance one, learn the true chances?

In this case "learning the true chances" is not just learning the values of a
finite number of parameters as in the multinomial case, but rather learning
the true chance probability on [0, 1). Thus we need a sense of convergence
for the space of all probability measures on [0, 1). A sequence of probabilities measures, $\mu_n$, converges weak* to measure $\mu$ iff for every bounded
continuous function of [0, 1), its expectation with respect to the measures
$\mu_n$ converges to its expectation with respect to $\mu$.

A prior (or alternatively the corresponding inductive rule) is Bayesian
consistent with respect to a chance probability $\mu$, if with probability one in
$\mu$, the posterior under IID (in $\mu$) sampling will converge weak* to $\mu$.
A prior is Bayesian consistent if it is Bayesian consistent for all possible
chance probabilities. In the multinomial case, all the rules of Carnap's

$\lambda - \gamma$ continuum (alternatively, the corresponding Dirichlet priors) are Bayesian consistent.

The Blackwell–MacQueen rules as defined in section 5 are also Bayesian consistent in this sense. It should be noted that this is a consequence of a restriction that I put on the parameter, $\alpha$, of those rules; that $\alpha$ be absolutely continuous with respect to Lebesgue measure on the unit interval. I take this to be a natural generalization of Carnap's requirement of regularity (or strict coherence) in the finite case. Likewise, Bayesian consistency is a natural generalization of Reichenbach's axiom.

# 7. Subjective Bayesian Analysis of Blackwell–MacQueen Inductive Rules

In this section we return to the subjective point of view. The notion of random variables which are independent and identically distributed according to the true unknown chances gives way to the subjective symmetry of exchangeability. In the case where the random variables take on a finite number of values, an additional symmetry assumption—W. E. Johnson's sufficientness postulate—(together with a few other technical assumptions) get us Carnap's $\lambda - \gamma$ continuum. In the case under consideration, where our random variables can take on a continuum of values in [0,1), we have the analogous result. That is—roughly speaking—that Exchangeability + Sufficientness gives the Blackwell–MacQueen inductive rules.

Let us first review the case of random variables taking a finite number of values discussed in section 4 in a little more detail. This is based on Zabell (1982). Suppose that we have an infinite sequence of random variables, $X_1$, $X_2, \ldots$, each taking values in a finite set $O = \{1, \ldots, k\}$. And suppose that the number of possible outcome values, $k$, is at least three. We consider a number of conditions on our probabilities: (1) *Exchangeability*: This guarantees by de Finetti's theorem that our (degree of belief) probability can be uniquely represented as a mixture of probabilities which make the outcomes independent and identically distributed. (2) *Non-Independence*: If our beliefs make the outcomes independent then we will not learn from experience. (3) *Strict Coherence*: The probability of any finite outcome sequence is non-zero. This is a kind of open-mindedness condition. It guarantees that all the conditional probabilities in the next condition are well defined. (4) *Generalized Sufficientness*: Let $n_i$ be the frequency count of outcomes in category $i$ in the trials $X_1, \ldots, X_n$. Then:

$$Pr(X_{N+1} = i | X_1, \ldots, X_N) = f_i(n_i)$$

That is, for each category, $i$, the probability of the next outcome being in that category is a function only of the frequency count for that category in the preceding sequence of observations. (Johnson assumed that these functions would be the same for all categories, but that is not assumed here.) Zabell shows that under assumptions 1–4, the predictive conditional probabilities:

$$Pr(X_{N+1} = i | X_1, \ldots, X_N)$$

are just those given by the inductive rules of Carnap's $\lambda - \gamma$ continuum.

Now consider the case of the wheel of fortune, where an infinite sequence of random variables takes on values in the interval $[0, 1)$. We assume (1) *Exchangeability* and (2) *Nonindependence* as before. As (3★) *Regularity* we assume that for any measurable set, $B$, which has non-zero Lebesgue measure and for any finite sequence of observations, $X_1, \ldots, X_n$:

$$Pr(X_{N+1} \in B_i | X_1, \ldots, X_N) > 0.$$

As (4★) *Generalized Sufficientness* we require that for any measurable set, $B_i$, and any finite sequence of observations, the probability that the next observation fall in $B_i$ is a function only of the count, $n_i$, of previous observations that have fallen in $B_i$:

$$Pr(X_{N+1} \in B_i | X_1, \ldots, X_N) = f_i(n_i)$$

If 1, 2, 3★, and 4★ are fulfilled, then our predictive conditional probabilities are Blackwell–MacQueen inductive rules.

This is almost immediate from the finite case. Here is a sketch of an argument. If 1, 2, 3★ and 4★ are fulfilled then for any finite partition of the unit interval whose members have non-zero Lebesgue measure, 1, 2, 3, 4 hold. Then for any such partition with three or more members, Zabell's version of W. E. Johnson's result holds. Thus the probabilities of falling in members of the partition update according to Carnap $\lambda - \gamma$ rules. This must also be the case for even partitions of only two members, which can be seen by subdividing them into partitions of four members. Then the de Finetti priors for all these partitions must be distributed as Dirichlet, and the de Finetti prior for $[0,1)$ must be a Ferguson distribution. Thus the inductive rules induced by the prior must be Blackwell–MacQueen inductive rules.

Carnap would not have thought that inductive logic for a value continuum ended with the class of Blackwell–MacQueen inductive rules but rather that it started there. These rules are just right for those settings which characterize them—where 1, 2, 3★ and 4★ hold. But in some contexts they will not all hold.

## 8. Analogy by Similarity

Ferguson (1974) considers 4★ as a drawback of the use of Dirichlet Processes (Ferguson distributions):

> One would like to have a prior distribution for $P$ with the property that if $X$ is a sample from $P$ and $X = x$, then the posterior guess at $P$ gives more weight to values close to $x$ than the prior guess at $P$ does. For the Dirichlet process prior, the posterior guess at $P$ gives more weight to the point $x$ itself, but it treats all other points equally. In particular, the posterior guess at $P$ actually gives less weight to points near $x$ but not equal to $x$. (Ferguson, 1974: 622). [Note that in Ferguson's characterization 3 on that page, T1, T2, and T3 are eliminated by my non-independence and regularity conditions.]

Carnap makes exactly the same point in his last writings on inductive logic under the heading of the problem of *analogy by similarity*. Carnap raises the question in the context of his current system where there are only a finite number of possible outcomes.

Where it is desirable that sample x gives more weight to values close to x, W. E. Johnson's Sufficientness postulate must be given up. Sufficientness is just the statement that we do not have analogy by similarity. Thus we must move outside Carnap's continuum of inductive methods. The most conservative move outside Carnap's $\lambda - \gamma$ continuum would be to consider finite mixtures of methods that are themselves in the $\lambda - \gamma$ continuum. One could think of this as putting a 'hyperprior' probability on a finite number of metahypotheses as to the values of the $\lambda$ and $\gamma_i$ hyperparameters. Conditional on each metahypothesis, one calculates the predictive probabilities according to the Carnapian method specified by that metahypothesis. The probabilities of the metahypotheses are updated using Bayes' theorem. We will call these *hyperCarnapian* Methods.

The hierarchical gloss, however, is inessential. The model just described is mathematically equivalent to using a prior on the multinomial parameters which is not Dirichlet but rather a finite mixture of Dirichlet priors. It is evident that if the number of Carnapian methods in the mixture is not too great, the computational tractability of Carnapian methods is not severely compromised. Furthermore, Bayesian consistency is retained. Finite mixtures of Dirichlet priors are consistent (Diaconis and Freedman, 1986).

Furthermore, they can exhibit the kind of analogy by similarity that Carnap wished to model (Skyrms, 1993a). We can illustrate this by means of a simple example: A wheel of fortune is divided into four quadrants: N, E, S, W. There are four 'metahypotheses' which are initially equiprobable. Each requires updating by a different Carnapian rule as indicated in the following table:

| | N | E | S | W |
|---|---|---|---|---|
| H1 : | $\dfrac{5+n}{10+N}$ | $\dfrac{2+n}{10+N}$ | $\dfrac{1+n}{10+N}$ | $\dfrac{2+n}{10+N}$ |
| H2 : | $\dfrac{2+n}{10+N}$ | $\dfrac{5+n}{10+N}$ | $\dfrac{2+n}{10+N}$ | $\dfrac{1+n}{10+N}$ |
| H3 : | $\dfrac{1+n}{10+N}$ | $\dfrac{2+n}{10+N}$ | $\dfrac{5+n}{10+N}$ | $\dfrac{2+n}{10+N}$ |
| H4 : | $\dfrac{2+n}{10+N}$ | $\dfrac{1+n}{10+N}$ | $\dfrac{2+n}{10+N}$ | $\dfrac{5+n}{10+N}$ |

where $n$ is the number of successes in $N$ trials.

Since the hypotheses are initially equiprobable, the possible outcomes, N, E, S, W, are also initially equiprobable. Suppose that we have one trial whose outcome is N. Then updating the probabilities of our hypotheses by Bayes' theorem, the probabilities of H1, H2, H3, H4 respectively become .5, .2, .1, .2. Applying the Carnapian rule of each hypothesis and mixing with the new weights gives probabilities:

$$pr\,(\mathrm{N}) = 44/110$$
$$pr\,(\mathrm{E}) = 24/110$$
$$pr\,(\mathrm{S}) = 18/110$$
$$pr\,(\mathrm{W}) = 24/110$$

The outcome, N, has affected the probabilities of the non-outcomes E, S, W differentially even though each Carnapian rule treats them the same. The outcome N has reduced the probability of the distant outcome, S, much more than that of the close outcomes, E and W, just as Carnap thought it should.

In a certain sense, this is the only solution to Carnap's problem. Carnap clearly was interested in sensitivity to analogy by similarity in the presence of exchangeability. For this problem we are, in effect, restricted to choosing a prior over IID processes. But every prior can be approximated arbitrarily well by finite mixtures of Dirichlet priors (Diaconis and Freedman, 1986). HyperCarnapian inductive methods are the general solution to Carnap's problem of analogy by similarity.

There is an investigation of hyperCarnapian inductive methods at the level of Blackwell–MacQueen rules in Antoniak (1974). Of course, analogy by similarity may also be important in other domains where exchangeability fails to hold.

## 9. Analogy by Proximity

Carnap also discussed a different kind of analogy which his methods could not represent as the problem of *analogy by proximity*. This is the problem of taking into account temporal patterns in the data, for instance in inference about Markov chains. How should one treat Markov chains in the spirit of Carnap's original inductive logic? Carnap never addressed this question in his published work. I believe that the question would fall somewhere on Carnap's agenda for the future development of inductive logic but it was not one which he actively tried to answer. In response to an inquiry, John Kemeny replied that Carnap never discussed Markov chains with him, and in fact that when he worked as Carnap's research assistant he had not yet heard of a Markov chain. Richard Jeffrey and Haim Gaifman, who also worked with Carnap, confirm that Carnap did not actively investigate this problem.

There is, however, a natural treatment of inductive logic for finite Markov chains, which fits neatly into Carnap's program. It is put forward by Theo Kuipers in Kuipers (1988). The leading idea is this: Carnap already has an inductive logic suitable for sampling from an urn with replacement. Just apply this inductive logic to the natural urn model of a Markov chain, under the assumption that transitions originating in one state give us no information about transitions originating in a different state. Parametric Bayesians, such as Martin (1967), operating in a somewhat different tradition, have followed the same path. We have a Markov chain with finite state space and known initial state, but unknown transition probabilities and we observe the successive states. Our inductive problem is to predict future states from history. The Carnapian solution is to apply Carnapian inductive rules to transition probabilities.

From a parametric Bayesian point of view, we can raise Reichenbach's question of *consistency*. A state of a Markov chain is called *recurrent* if the probability that it is visited an infinite number of times is one. The chain is recurrent if all its states are recurrent. Carnapian inductive logic for Markov chains is consistent for recurrent Markov chains. Here is a quick sketch of a proof. Suppose that the true state of nature is a recurrent Markov chain (with a finite number of states). Then the set of sample sequences in which some state does not recur has probability zero. Delete these sequences and restrict the chance measure to get a new probability space. In this space define the random variables $f[ni]$ as having the value $j$ if the $n$th occurrence of state $i$ is followed by state $j$. For each fixed $i$, the sequence $f(1i)$, $f(2i), \ldots$, is an infinite sequence of independent and identically distributed random variables so the strong law of large numbers applies. This means that the limiting transition relative frequencies from $i$ to $j$ equal the true transition probabilities with chance 1. Thus if the true state of nature is a recurrent Markov chain, then there are only a finite number of ways in which Carnapian inductive logic for Markov chains can fail to learn the true transition matrix, and each of these has a chance of zero.

From the subjective Bayesian point of view, the treatment is again parallel to that of Carnapian inductive methods, as long as we have a recurrent stochastic process. In dealing with Markov chains we do not have exchangeability, but rather a weaker kind of symmetry condition which can play a role with respect to Markov processes analogous to that played by exchangeability with respect to Bernoulli processes. The analysis is developed in Freedman (1962), de Finetti (1974), Diaconis and Freedman (1980). A stochastic process is *Markov exchangeable* if the vector of initial state and transition counts is a sufficient statistic for all finite sequences of given length generated by the process. That is to say, that sequences of the same length, having the same transition counts and the same initial state, are equiprobable. Markov exchangeability, like ordinary exchangeability, can also be given an equivalent formulation in terms of invariance (Diaconis and Freedman, 1980). A primitive block-switch transformation of a sequence takes two disjoint blocks of the sequence with the same starting and ending states and switches them. A block-switch transformation is the composition of a finite number of primitive block-switch transformations. A probability is then Markov exchangeable just in case it is invariant under all block-switch transformations. Diaconis and Freedman (1980) show that *recurrent* stochastic processes of this type which are Markov exchangeable have a unique representation as a mixture of Markov chains.

Zabell (1995) shows that the subjective condition which guarantees that the de Finetti prior for a recurrent Markov exchangeable stochastic process is of the type that induces Carnapian inductive logic for Markov chains is again a form of W. E. Johnson's sufficientness postulate that $Pr(S_j|S_i)$ depend only on $i$, $j$, $N[S_j, S_i]$ and $\sum_m N[S_m, S_i]$, where $N[S_j, S_i]$ is the transition count. Notice that this automatically gets us the independence that Martin and Kuipers assume. If our beliefs satisfy the postulate then transition counts from one state are not taken as giving any evidence about transitions from another state. Since a recurrent Markov exchangeable process is a mixture of recurrent Markov chains, for each $i$ the embedded process $f(1i), f(2i), \ldots$ discussed above is a mixture of IID processes and thus exchangeable. The sufficientness postulate for Markov chains gives the original sufficientness postulate for these embedded processes, and the application of the original sufficientness argument (Zabell, 1982) to them gives the desired result.

As before, W. E. Johnson's sufficientness postulate has no *logical* status. It merely serves to characterize cases in which degrees of belief have certain interesting and computationally tractable symmetries.

# 10. Conclusion

At the beginning of his investigations in inductive logic Carnap hoped that all of scientific inference could be based on one inductive rule. That rule would have a necessary status. The logical character of inductive logic would derive from the logical status of this rule and of the prior which led to it. He soon started down the road that leads from Keynes to de Finetti. Ever larger classes of inductive rules were seen as part of inductive logic. In the end he saw a need for further expansion, in particular to deal with the three problems discussed here, and in general to arrive at an adequate treatment of scientific inference.

In posthumous *Basic System* (1971), (1980), Carnap realizes somewhat reluctantly that he has become a subjective Bayesian. The logic in inductive logic is now the logic of coherence. From this point of view, it is not just that Bayesian statistics has useful things to contribute to inductive logic. From the most general convergence theorems, such as that of Blackwell and Dubins (1962), to the analysis of particular problems— Bayesian statistics *is* inductive logic.

# Bibliography

Antoniak, C. (1974) "Mixtures of Dirichlet Processes with Applications to Bayesian Nonparametric Problems," *Annals of Statistics* 2: 1152–74.

Blackwell, D. and Dubins, L. (1962) "Merging of Opinions with Increasing Information," *Annals of Mathematical Statistics* 33: 882–6.

Blackwell, D. and MacQueen, J. B. (1973) "Ferguson Distributions via Polya Urn Schemes," *Annals of Statistics* 1: 353–5.

Carnap, R. (1950) *Logical Foundations of Probability*. Chicago: University of Chicago Press (2nd ed., 1962).

—— (1952) *The Continuum of Inductive Methods*. Chicago: University of Chicago Press.

—— (1971) "A Basic System of Inductive Logic, Part 1." In R. Carnap and R. Jeffrey (eds.), *Studies in Inductive Logic and Probability*, vol. 1, pp. 35–165. Berkeley, CA: University of California Press.

—— (1980) "A Basic System of Inductive Logic, Part 2." In R. C. Jeffrey (ed.), *Studies in Inductive Logic and Probability*, vol. 2. Berkeley, CA: University of California Press.

Costantini, D. (1983) "Analogy by Similarity," *Erkenntnis* 20: 103–14.

De Finetti, B. (1974) *Probability, Induction and Statistics*. New York: Wiley.

DeGroot, M. (1970) *Optimal Statistical Decisions*. New York: McGraw-Hill.

Diaconis, P. and Freedman, D. (1980) "De Finetti's Theorem for Markov Chains," *Annals of Probability* 8: 115–30.

—— (1986) "On the Consistency of Bayes Estimates," *Annals of Statistics* 14: 1–26.

Fabius, J. (1964) "Asymptotic Behavior of Bayes Estimates," *Annals of Mathematical Statistics* 35: 846–56.

Ferguson, T. (1962) "Mixtures of Markov Processes," *Annals of Mathematical Statistics* 2: 615–29.

—— (1973) "A Bayesian Analysis of Some Non-Parametric Problems," *Annals of Statistics* 1: 209–30.

—— (1974) "Prior Distributions on Spaces of Probability Measures," *Annals of Statistics* 2: 615–29.

Freedman, D. (1963) "On the Asymptotic Behavior of Bayes' Estimates in the Discrete Case," *Annals of Mathematical Statistics* 24: 1386–403.

Good, I. J. (1965) *The Estimation of Probabilities: An Essay on Modern Bayesian Methods*. Cambridge, MA: MIT Press.

Johnson, W. E. (1924) *Logic, Part III: The Logical Foundations of Science*. Cambridge: Cambridge University Press.

—— (1932) "Probability: The Deductive and Inductive Problems," *Mind* 49: 409–23.

Kuipers, T. A. F. (1978) *Studies in Inductive Logic and Rational Expectation*. Dordrecht: D. Reidel.

—— (1984a) "Two Types of Inductive Analogy by Similarity," *Erkenntnis* 21: 63–87.

—— (1984b) "Inductive Analogy in the Carnapian Spirit." In P. D. Asquith and P. Kitcher (eds.), *PSA 1984*, ver. 1. East Lansing, MI: Philosophy of Science Association.

—— (1988) "Inductive Analogy by Similarity and Proximity." In D. H. Helman (ed.), *Analogical Reasoning*. Dordrecht: Kluwer.

Martin, J. J. (1967) *Bayesian Decision Problems and Markov Chains*. New York: Wiley.

Neveu, J. (1965) *Mathematical Foundations of the Theory of Probability*, tr. A. Feinstein. San Francisco, CA: Holden-Day.

Niiniluoto, I. (1981) "Analogy and Inductive Logic," *Erkenntnis* 16: 1–34.

—— (1988) "Analogy and Similarity in Scientific Reasoning." In D. H. Helman (ed.), *Analogical Reasoning*. Dordrecht: D. Reidel.

Putnam, H. (1963) "Degree of Confirmation and Inductive Logic." In P. A. Schilpp (ed.), *The Philosophy of Rudolf Carnap*, pp. 761–83. LaSalle, IL: Open Court. Reprinted in Putnam, H. *Mathematics, Matter and Method: Philosophical Papers*, vol. 1, pp. 270–92. Cambridge: Cambridge University Press, 1975.

Skyrms, B. (1991) "Carnapian Inductive Logic for Markov Chains," *Erkenntnis* 35: 439–60.

—— (1993a) "Analogy by Similarity in HyperCarnapian Inductive Logic." In Earman et al. (eds.), *Philosophical Problems of the Internal and External Worlds*. Pittsburgh, PA: University of Pittsburgh Press.

—— (1993b) "Carnapian Inductive Logic for a Value Continuum." In H. Wettstein (ed.), *The Philosophy of Science*. Midwest Studies in Philosophy, vol. 18, pp. 78–89. South Bend, IN: Indiana University of Notre Dame Press.

Spohn, W. (1981) "Analogy and Inductive Logic: A Note on Niiniluoto," *Erkenntnis* 16: 35–52.

Zabell, S. L. (1982) "W. E. Johnson's 'Sufficientness' Postulate," *Annals of Statistics* 10: 1091–9.

—— (1992) "Predicting the Unpredictable," *Synthese* 90: 205–32.

—— (1995) "Characterizing Markov Exchangeable Sequences," *Journal of Theoretical Probability* 8: 175–8.

# 13

# Bayesian Projectibility

Undoubtedly we do make predictions by projecting the patterns of the past into the future, but in selecting the patterns we project from among all those that the past exhibits, we use practical criteria that so far seem to have escaped discovery and formulation.

Nelson Goodman, "A Query on Confirmation" (1946)

## 1. Introduction

In 1946 Nelson Goodman raised the problem of the projectibility of hypotheses in a note addressing the confirmation theory of Rudolf Carnap. He later gave a sensational illustration: the hypothesis "All emeralds are grue," which came to be discussed as the Goodman Paradox. The predicate "grue" was so manifestly pathological many were led into thinking that the problem was to find some criterion which would exclude similar pathology from inductive reasoning.

Goodman sees clearly that the problem of projectibility is much more general, and that judgments of projectibility must be central to any adequate theory of confirmation. He believes that a theory of projectibility should be a pragmatic theory, and sketches the beginnings of such a theory in the last chapter of *Fact, Fiction and Forecast*.

I believe that the broad outlines of Goodman's approach to a theory of projectibility are just right. The theory will not attempt to tell one in a

This chapter grew out of two philosophical talks given in October 1991 to a conference entitled "Recent Developments of Exchangeable Random Processes" in Cortona, Italy, sponsored by the Instituto Nazionale di Alta Matematica. I would like to thank the organizers for inviting me, and the participants—especially Persi Diaconis and Colin Mallows—for helpful discussions. I would also like to thank Ermanno Bencivenga, Donald Davidson, Persi Diaconis, Ian Hacking, Richard Jeffrey, Hugh Mellor, Peter Woodruff, Jim Woodward, and Sandy Zabell for useful comments on earlier versions of this work.

vacuum which predicates are projectible. Rather it will explain how present judgments of projectibility should be based on past judgments of projectibility together with the results of past projections. The circularity involved in such a theory is not to be viewed as vicious. The theory can still inform our understanding of projectibility. And a theory with this sort of "virtuous circularity" is really the best that can be expected. However, the implementation of Goodman's program for a theory of projectibility does not seem very far advanced. There is, however, a preexisting pragmatic framework which offers precise tools for addressing the question: the theory of personal probability. How is projectibility represented within this framework? This question leads straight to central concepts of Bayesian statistics.

## 2. Goodman on Projectibility

Goodman sees the problem of projection as of a piece with the problem of counterfactual conditionals and the related problem of lawlikeness. Counterfactuals—at least the kind that underlie disposition terms in science—are supported by laws. Not every true generalization is a law. Goodman gives "All coins in my pocket on VE day were silver" as an example of an accidentally true generalization. One mark of its accidental nature is that it is not projectible: it would not be well confirmed *via* its instances unless all of them were surveyed. Goodman parses the problem as: (1) A law is a true lawlike statement. (2) "A statement is lawlike if its determination does not depend on any given instance."[1]

In *Fact, Fiction and Forecast* Goodman concocts the "grue" hypothesis to show both the ubiquity of the problem of projectibility, and the hopelessness of syntactical theories of confirmation. The predicate "grue" applies to all things examined before $t$ just in case they are green and to all other things just in case they are blue. At time $t$ our evidence is that all previously examined emeralds have been green. Then, provided we know what time it is, our evidence is also to the effect that all previously examined emeralds have been grue. We do not take the two hypotheses "All emeralds are green" and "All emeralds are grue" to be equally well

---

[1] Goodman (1955: 230).

confirmed on the evidence, but syntactically the relation between generalization and evidence seems to be the same.[2]

He concludes that by similar tricks a theory which uncritically assumes that any generalization is confirmed by its instances can be made to predict anything. This remark is amplified in a footnote:

For instance, we shall have equal confirmation, by our present definition, for the prediction that roses subsequently examined will be blue. Let "emerose" apply just to emeralds examined before time *t*, and to roses examined later. Then all emeroses so far examined are grue, and this confirms the hypothesis that all emeroses are grue and hence the prediction that roses subsequently examined will be blue. The problem raised by such antecedents has been little noticed, but is no easier to meet than that raised by similarly perverse consequents.[3]

Donald Davidson used the technique of gerrymandering predicates in both the antecedent and the consequent to show that the lawlikeness or projectibility of a hypothesis is not simply a function of the projectibility of its constituent predicates "taken one by one," but must take into account their relation to one another.[4] An *emerose* is something which is an emerald examined before *t* or a rose not examined before *t*. It is *gred* if green and examined before *t* or red and not examined before *t*. Davidson invites us to consider:

*H1*: All emeroses are gred

which he takes to be lawlike. Goodman replies that *H1* is not confirmed by its instances[5] in the proper way. Instances of *H1* observed before *t* do not increase the probability of instances of *H1* after *t*: green emeralds do not increase the probability of roses observed after *t* being red. This reply

---

[2] To Carnap's complaint that "grue" was positional—i.e., has an explicit time in its definition—Goodman replied that if grue and bleen were taken as primitive, then "green" and "blue" would be positional.

[3] This is footnote 9 to ch 3, "The New Riddle of Induction" (Goodman, 1955: 85–6).

[4] Davidson's example (originally "All emerires are grue") had circulated by word of mouth for years and was reported in Jeffrey (1966) and Wallace (1966) and addressed in Goodman's "Comments" (1966). Davidson's (1966) "Emeroses by Other Names" is his rejoinder to Goodman's "Comments."

[5] The concept of an instance is left somewhat ambiguous here and in much of the related literature. Properly, the instance of a universal generalization, "All *F*s are *G*s" is not the conjunction "This is an *F* and a *G*," but rather the material conditional "This is either no *F* or a *G*." But if we suppose that we are sampling *F*s, then this background knowledge collapses the potentially pernicious ambiguity.

derives from the conception of confirmation set forth in *Fact, Fiction and Forecast*: "Confirmation of a hypothesis occurs only when an instance imparts to the hypothesis some credibility which is conveyed to other instances."[6] Thus, despite the plausibility of Davidson's conclusion, his example does not make his point on Goodman's own terms.

This is not to say that Davidson is wrong, but rather that he is working with a different notion of confirmation than Goodman. If confirmation means *increase in probability of the hypothesis*, then Davidson is right. But, as we have seen, Goodman wants to build more into the notion of confirming a universal generalization. (This distinction will take on added significance in the light of the upcoming discussion in section 3.)

Goodman established the pervasiveness of the problem of projection by an elementary logical construction. He saw the problem of projection as the real problem of induction that has been neglected while philosophers have debated the empty schema of confirmation of a generalization by its instances. Thus, in "A Query on Confirmation":

Undoubtedly we do make predictions by projecting the patterns of the past into the future, but in selecting the patterns we project from among all those that the past exhibits, we use practical criteria that so far seem to have escaped discovery and formulation.

And in *Fact, Fiction and Forecast*:

To say that valid predictions are those based on past regularities, without being able to say *which* regularities, is quite pointless. Regularities are where you find them and you can find them anywhere. As we have seen, Hume's failure to recognize and deal with this problem has been shared by even his most recent successors.[7]

Goodman's remarks here are, I believe, quite accurate except, perhaps, for the parting shot. It seems to me that this is not quite fair to Hume. Hume's famous passage about eggs indicates that some resemblances seem *to be more projectible than others*: "Nothing is so alike as eggs; yet no one on account of this appearing similarity, expects the same taste and relish in all of them."

Furthermore, looking at the problem of projectibility in the most general terms, let us suppose that we do not have to construct hypotheses by elementary means, but rather take hypotheses in a free-swinging way as sets of possible world scenarios. Then the analogue of the grue problem is

---

[6] Goodman (1955: 69).     [7] Ibid., 82.

the multiplicity of incompatible hypotheses which are compatible with a given history up to now, and it is exactly true that confirmation by positive instances can be made to predict *anything*. But this most general formulation of the new riddle of induction is precisely the most general formulation of Hume's problem.[8]

On the other hand, Hume did not have such abstract general formulations in mind; they represent a more modern point of view. His general theory is that induction is based on habit, and this leaves open questions as to the possibility and plausibility of habits. Even if Hume did show some awareness of the problem, we must agree with Goodman that Hume does not make any real contribution to the development of the logic of projectibility.

As for "Hume's most recent successors," I suppose that here Goodman had in mind Carnap and Hempel. But there was another—more Humean—successor who did recognize the problem, and who made major advances in dealing with it. That was Bruno de Finetti.

## 3. Exchangeability

De Finetti is at least as radical as Goodman in questioning the basis of the received categories:

What are sometimes called repetitions or trials of the same event are for us so many distinct events. In general they will have common or symmetric characteristics which make it natural to attribute equal probabilities to them, but there is no a priori reason which prevents us in principle from attributing to the events $E_1 \ldots E_n$ distinct and absolutely arbitrary probabilities $p_1 \ldots p_n$. In principle there is no difference for us between this case and that of $n$ events which exhibit no similarities; the similarity which suggests the name "trials of the same event" (we would say "of the same phenomenon") is not intrinsic: at the very most, its importance lies in the influence it may have on our psychological judgement.[9]

Judgments of similarity are, for de Finetti, subjective and they are embodied in one's subjective probabilities. How?

Suppose that we have an infinite sequence of random variables which may or may not be thought of as trials "of the same phenomenon." For

---

[8] John Earman has discovered some unpublished correspondence in which Hempel makes just this point.

[9] (1938).

simplicity, we suppose them to be dichotomous—a sequence of yes or no answers to unspecified questions. (Perhaps it is a sequence of observation reports of the color of observed emeralds or emeroses; answers to the question "Is it green?" or "Is it grue?") Our prior degrees of belief over possible outcome sequences determine our inductive behavior as the data comes in and we condition on it.

According to de Finetti, we treat the trials as maximally analogous when our degrees of belief are *exchangeable*, that is, invariant under finite permutations of trials. Another way of saying this is to say that relative frequency is a sufficient statistic: that is, that all initial segments of the same length, with the same numbers of Yeses and Nos, are equally probable. De Finetti showed that such exchangeable probabilities have a unique representation as expectations of probabilities which make the trials independent and identically distributed. That means that if your beliefs are exchangeable here, your inductive behavior is the same as if you believed that the trials were generated by flipping a coin with unknown bias, you had a prior distribution over the possible biases, and you updated by using Bayes' theorem and conditioning.

Bayesian inductive behavior for the biased coin is well known. Suppose that the prior over the possible bias is *open-minded* in that for each possible value of the bias every open interval containing that point receives positive prior probability. Then with chance[10] equal to one, induction will converge to a probability of the next instance being heads equal to the limiting relative frequency of heads in the outcome sequence.[11] (Absolute inductive skepticism is not an option for this Bayesian observer.) Should nature serve up a sequence of all heads, the probability that the next trial will yield heads goes up as each piece of data comes in, just as Goodman says that it should in the case of projectibility, and converges to one.

This is not quite enough to guarantee inductive inference to the universal generalization that every trial is a head, however. For the stated conditions could hold when the prior probability of the sequence consisting of all heads was zero. And in that case it would remain zero on any finite data. One could, with Ramsey, Carnap, and many earlier probabilists, take the position that prediction of future instances is all we should

---

[10] With 'chance' replaced by 'degree of belief,' the statement is true without the assumption of open-mindedness.

[11] With degree-of-belief one this limiting relative frequency exists.

care about in confirming a generalization. But if it is desired that the universal generalization be well confirmed by positive instances as well, we might impose in addition to the foregoing *UG open-mindedness*:[12] that is that the two outcome sequences consisting of all heads and of all tails each receive positive prior probability. Then, indeed, the probability of 'All heads' goes up with each head, and converges to one if it is true that every trial gives heads; likewise for tails.

De Finetti showed that we can use this analysis without any assumptions about unknown chances. The exchangeability of our degrees-of-belief over outcome sequences gives us the de Finetti representation, and the open-mindedness conditions on priors on Bernoulli trials become conditions on virtual priors which are artifacts of the representation. The restriction to dichotomous variables was for purely expository reasons. If the exchangeable sequence of random variables take on a finite sequence of values, the de Finetti representation gives a mixture of multinomial probabilities and inductive behavior is like sampling from "the great urn of nature." The representation theorem has been generalized to exchangeable sequences of random variables taking values in more general spaces.[13]

Suppose a coin of unknown bias is about to be flipped, and you are to be presented with the results in an unusual way. For the first 100 trials there is a random variable that takes the value 1 if heads, 0 otherwise. For the subsequent trials there are random variables which take the value 0 if heads, 1 otherwise. If you have ordinary beliefs about coin flipping, this 'Goodmanized' sequence of random variables will not be exchangeable for you. It seems that much of the intuitive concept of projectibility is captured in a subjective Bayesian setting by *exchangeability*, or *open-minded exchangeability*, or *exchangeability that is both open-minded and UG open-minded*. With the latter condition a universal generalization is confirmed by an incomplete survey of its positive instances both in the sense that they raise its probability and in the sense that in the limit they raise it to one. And that confirmation transfers to unexamined instances in the way Goodman supposed in his interchange with Davidson.[14] This cannot,

[12] For some early history of UG-open-mindedness, see Zabell (1989) and the 1919 article of Jeffreys and Wrinch to which he refers. For later developments, from somewhat different points of view, see Shimony (1967) and Hintikka and Niiniluoto (1980).

[13] See, for example, Hewitt and Savage (1955).

[14] For further discussion of exchangeability and projectibility, see John Earman (1992).

however, be a complete account of projectibility in a probabilistic setting because it makes nonsense of the passage from Goodman that I have taken as epigraph to this chapter; exchangeable subjective probabilities do not project patterns[15] in the data.

## 4. Markov Exchangeability

The simplest sorts of pattern in the data stream that we might want to project are those in which the outcome of a trial tends to depend on that of the preceding trial. Exchangeable degrees of belief cannot project such patterns because exchangeability is essentially the property that order makes no difference. The probability of heads on the eleventh toss conditional on the first ten tosses being HTHTHTHTHT must be the same as that conditional on the first ten tosses being HHHTHTTTHTH since the relative frequencies are the same. In terms of the de Finetti representation, having exchangeable degrees of belief is tantamount to concentrating one's beliefs on the hypothesis that the true chances—whatever they are—make the trials independent, and thus on the hypothesis that nature does not follow a pattern in the phenomenon under consideration.

Already in 1938 de Finetti suggested that exchangeability needed to be extended to a more general notion of partial exchangeability. The idea was that where full exchangeability fails, we might still have some version of conditional exchangeability. With respect to the kind of pattern just considered, the relevant condition would consist of the outcome of the preceding trial. The notion desired here is that of *Markov exchangeability*. It did not receive precise formulation, and the appropriate forms of the de Finetti representation theorem were not proved until the work of Freedman (1962a) and Diaconis and Freedman (1980).

We are considering a loosening of the assumption of patternlessness in the data stream to one where the simplest types of patterns can occur; that is, those where the probability of an outcome can depend on the probability of the previous outcome. One way to say this is that we loosen the assumption that the true chances make the trials independent to the

---

[15] If 'pattern' is construed so broadly that any regularity or stable relative frequency qualifies as a pattern, then exchangeability can be said to be compatible with patterns. But, as will be shown in the following discussion, this leaves out many important cases where there are patterns of probabilistic dependency.

assumption that the true chances make the trials *Markov dependent*. Here we can replace the iconic example of the coin flip with that of the Markov thumbtack of Diaconis and Freedman (1980). A thumb tack is repeatedly flicked as it lies. It can come to rest in either of two positions: point up or point down. The chance of the next state may well depend on the previous one. Thus there are unknown transition probabilities:

|     | PU          | PD          |
| --- | ----------- | ----------- |
| PU  | Pr(PU\|PU)  | Pr(PD\|PU)  |
| PD  | Pr(PU\|PD)  | Pr(PD\|PD)  |

which an adequate inductive logic should allow us to learn. More generally, for a physical system with states $S_1 \ldots S_k$, a Markov chain (with stationary transition probabilities) consists of a $k$-place probability vector for the initial state[16] together with a $k$-by-$k$ square matrix of transition probabilities.

The formulation of exchangeability that generalizes most smoothly to this case is the one based on sufficient statistics. A stochastic process is *Markov exchangeable* if the vector of initial state and transition counts is a sufficient statistic for all finite sequences of given length generated by the process. That is to say that sequences of the same length, having the same transition counts and the same initial state, are equiprobable.[17] A state of such a stochastic process is called *recurrent* if the probability that it is visited an infinite number of times is 1. Freedman (1962a) showed that any stationary Markov-exchangeable process is representable as a mixture of stationary Markov chains. Diaconis and Freedman (1980) show that *recurrent* Markov-exchangeable stochastic processes have a unique representation as a mixture of Markov chains. These are two forms of de Finetti's theorem for Markov chains. In this setting, we could investigate *recurrent Markov-exchangeable beliefs with various forms of open-mindedness* as further varieties of projectibility.[18]

---

[16] So to make the Markov thumbtack example into a full Markov chain we can imagine flipping a (possibly biased) coin to determine the initial position of the thumbtack.

[17] Markov exchangeability, like ordinary exchangeability, can also be given an equivalent formulation in terms of invariance (see Diaconis and Freedman, 1980). A primitive block-switch transformation of a sequence takes two disjoint blocks of the sequence with the same starting and ending states and switches them. A block-switch transformation is the composition of a finite number of primitive block-switch transformations. A probability is then Markov exchangeable just in case it is invariant under all block-switch transformations.

[18] Open-mindedness is related to Bayesian consistency. See Diaconis and Freedman (1986), for a discussion of Bayesian consistency.

It is of some interest to note here that the sorts of sequence of 0's and 1's gotten by 'Goodmanization' in the last section can arise naturally in the mathematics of representation theorems for Markov-exchangeable stochastic processes. Consider the class of 0–1-valued stochastic processes which are Markov exchangeable. This is a convex set, any member of which has a representation as a mixture of its extreme points. But the extreme points now contain more than Markov chains. The extreme points now consist of:

(1)  The recurrent Markov chains starting at 0.
(2)  The recurrent Markov chains starting at 1.
(3)  The 'Goodman 0, $k$' processes starting deterministically with $k$ zeros and then continuing with all ones.
(4)  The 'Goodman 1, $k$' processes starting deterministically with $k$ ones and then continuing with all zeros.

These 'Goodman processes' are Markov exchangeable in a rather degenerate way. Thus the process that puts probability one on the sample path 001111 . . . is Markov exchangeable because this is the unique sample path having this initial point and transition counts. Agents who put degree of belief one on the 'Goodman processes' have both inductive and counterinductive aspects to their beliefs, and are worthy of some philosophical attention.[19] 'Goodman processes' are neither stationary not recurrent, and so do not appear in the representation for stationary or recurrent Markovexchangeable beliefs. (End of digression: for more details, see Diaconis and Freedman (1980: sect. 3.))

It should be clear that the sort of analysis that I have sketched here can be applied to higher-order Markov chains, where the probability of an outcome depends on 2, 3, or $N$ previous outcomes. And there is no reason why the random variables with which we are concerned have to only be ordered in one dimension. All sorts of orderings or partial orderings are possibilities. For example, we could consider the case of ordering in three or more dimensions. Possible instantiations would be Ising spin models of ferromagnets, lattice gases, or stochastic cellular automata.

---

[19] For example, suppose someone puts a prior probability of .9 on HTTT . . . , .09 on HHTTT . . . , .009 on HHHTTT . . . , etc., gets an outcome sequence consisting of all heads, and updates by conditioning. Such an agent is coherent but her prior is not Bayesian consistent in the sense of fn. 18.

Some extensions of de Finetti's theorem to such domains exist in the literature[20] and provide the framework for extension of the foregoing analysis of projectibility. Investigation of the logic of the projectibility of patterns is a rich and flourishing enterprise.

## 5. Partial Exchangeability and Sufficient Statistics

De Finetti (1938) also had other sorts of cases of partial exchangeability in mind. He conceptualizes the question of partial exchangeability in general as modeling degree of *analogy* between events:

> But the case of exchangeability can only be considered as a limiting case: the case in which this "analogy" is, in a certain sense, *absolute* for all the events under consideration... To get from the case of exchangeability to other cases which are more general but still tractable, we must take up the case where we still encounter "analogies" among the events under consideration, but without attaining the limiting case of exchangeability.[21]

For his simplest example, he takes the case in which two odd-looking coins are flipped. If the coins look exactly alike, we may take a sequence consisting of tosses of both to be exchangeable. If they look quite different, we may take the trials of one to be subjectively independent of trials of the other. If they look almost alike, we will want an appropriate form of partial exchangeability where a toss of coin A may give us some information about coin B, but not as much as we would get from a toss of coin B. Later, he discusses a more interesting, but essentially similar, case in which animal trials of a new drug are partially exchangeable with human trials.

Here, the trials of coin one are exchangeable as are those of coin two, but they are not exchangeable with each other. One way to say this is to say that for a mixed sequence of trials of both coins, initial segments of the same length that have both the same number of heads on coin one and the same number of heads on coin two are equiprobable. In other words, the vector $\langle f1, f2 \rangle$ whose components are respectively those frequency counts is a sufficient statistic.

This case, that of Markov exchangeability, and many others can be brought under a general theory of partial exchangeability in which the concept of a sufficient statistic plays a key role. For simple coin tossing the statistic is the frequency of heads; for tossing several coins it is the vector of frequencies of heads of the respective coins; for the Markov case it is the vector of initial state and transition counts. In each case, under appropriate conditions we have (1) *a de Finetti type representation* of degrees of belief as mixtures of the extreme points of the convex set of probabilities for which that is a sufficient statistic and (2) *a projectibility result* to the effect that learning from experience will almost surely converge to one of these extreme points. For some more detail on this theory see Diaconis and Freedman (1980), (1981) and Dynkin (1978).

## 6. Invariance and Projectibility

Projectibility can also be studied from a different (though related) math-ematical viewpoint: that of ergodic theory.[22] From this perspective, the key concept for understanding projectibility is that of an *invariant measure*. If an agent has degrees of belief that are invariant with respect to a transformation, then that agent—in a sense to be made precise—believes in induction with respect to the notion of repetition of an experiment given by that transformation. But two agents whose degrees of belief are invariant with respect to different transformations differ in their judgments of projectibility. The philosophical analysis of inductive skepticism, there-fore, should focus on questions of the existence and nature of invariant degrees of belief. It is regrettable that this central concept is so little discussed in the philosophical literature on induction.

In order to set the foregoing remarks in context, I will give a thumbnail sketch of the early evolution of ergodic theory. Ergodic theory had its origin in statistical mechanics. Consider the dynamics of an idealized system of gas as it evolves in continuous time. We assume here that time is infinite in both directions. The state of the gas at any moment of time is given by a point in phase space. The laws of classical mechanics specify the time evolution of the system. Thus for a time interval—for example, 2—the dynamical laws specify for each point in phase space what point it would evolve into in two units of time. This gives a transformation of

---

[22]  See von Plato (1982) and Skyrms (1984). Also see Jeffrey's remarks on stationarity as a generalization of exchangeability in Jeffrey (1971).

phase space into itself, $T_2$. Likewise for any other real number, $r$, there is an associated transformation. By the law of conservation of energy, the system will always be in the same region of phase space with the same energy; this region is called a constant energy (hyper)surface.

Boltzmann wanted to prove the equality of time averages and phase space averages for such a system; that is to say that for some reasonable quantity[23] on the constant energy surface, and for any point on the surface, the limiting time average of the quantity as the system evolves from that point onwards is equal to the phase space average of that quantity over the surface where the weighting of the average is taken with respect to the natural measure on the surface.[24] As a basis for this program he advanced the ergodic[25] *hypothesis* approximately to the effect that for every point on the surface, its trajectory through phase space passes through every point on the surface. Notice that this hypothesis can be reformulated as saying that there is no proper subset of the surface such that the trajectory of every point in the subset remains within it. That is, there is no proper subset that is strictly invariant in that the dynamics maps it into itself. Viewed this way, we can call Boltzmann's ergodic hypothesis a hypothesis of *strict dynamic transitivity*. It soon became apparent to Boltzmann himself and others that, stated strictly, the ergodic hypothesis could not be satisfied. Boltzmann knew that the "approximately" in the foregoing statement of the ergodic hypothesis must somehow be taken seriously and made precise, but he did not know how to do it.[26] Despite considerable discussion of this problem, no satisfactory solution was put forward until the ergodic theorems of von Neumann and Birkhoff.

Von Neumann replaced Boltzmann's ergodic hypothesis with the hypothesis of *metric transitivity*. This uses the natural measure on the constant energy hypersurface to relax the assumption of strict dynamic transitivity. Metric transitivity says that there is no measurable invariant subset of the surface other than one of measure zero or one whose complement is of measure zero. A measure zero subset is negligible from a measure theoretic point of view, and a subset whose complement is of measure zero is hardly

---

[23] Bounded continuous real-valued function.

[24] The Liouville measure.

[25] Boltzmann's coinage from *ergon* = work for the constant energy hypersurface and *odos* = path for the trajectory of a point.

[26] The development of Boltzmann's thought in this area is a complex story. For a sympathetic discussion of Boltzmann's ideas, see von Plato (1994).

proper from a measure theoretic point of view. This weakening turns out to be just the right reformulation of Boltzmann's ergodic hypothesis, and 'ergodicity' in current usage just means metrical transitivity in the sense of von Neumann.

Metrical transitivity was a strong enough property to allow von Neumann and Birkhoff to prove equality of time averages and phase averages almost everywhere. And it is weak enough so that the physical systems under consideration might conceivably have it. But there was no proof that boxes of gas, or anything like them, are ergodic. It was known, however, that the natural measure is invariant under the transformations given by the dynamics.[27] Von Neumann showed that an invariant measure has a (unique) representation as a mixture of ergodic measures—measures such that if one of them is used in the formulation of metrical transitivity, metrical transitivity obtains. This is called the *ergodic decomposition of invariant measures*.[28]

Von Neumann established a convergence result,[29] which really gave what was required for Boltzmann's purposes, but Birkhoff proved convergence in an even stronger sense. Birkhoff showed that except for a set of points of measure zero in the invariant measure, the limiting time average over the orbit of a point exists and coincides with the phase space average according to one of the ergodic measures. This is the *Birkhoff pointwise ergodic theorem*. If the natural invariant phase space measure is ergodic, then we have equality of time and phase space average almost everywhere.

But the immediate importance of Birkhoff's ergodic theorem was not so much for physics—where the ergodicity of the natural physical measure proved remarkably difficult to demonstrate for any physical system of any complexity[30]—but rather for probability theory—and for the theory of induction. The connection with the theory of stationary stochastic

---

[27] Liouville's theorem.

[28] Other versions of this result are proved by Kryloff and Bogoliouboff (1937) and Oxtoby (1952). All the results require some regularity conditions. More will be said in this regard in the last section of this chapter.

[29] Von Neumann proved convergence in the $L^2$ norm.

[30] Birkhoff put forward the "Hypothesis of Metrical Transitivity" according to which it is generally true for Hamiltonian systems that the Liouville measure restricted to a constant energy hypersurface is ergodic. In the 1950s, Kolmogoroff, Arnold, and Moser showed that this hypothesis fails. Ergodicity is not generic for Hamiltonian systems, although there are some important special cases for which ergodicity has been established.

processes was explicitly made three years after Birkhoff's proof [31] by Doob, Hopf, and Kintchine. The pointwise ergodic theorem and the theorem on the ergodic decomposition of stationary measures hold for dynamical systems with discrete time. Consider a stochastic process as a sequence of random variables (for example, coin flips) infinite in both directions. Define the shift transformation as that which maps an infinite outcome sequence to one shifted forward one unit of discrete time. Then the stochastic process is *stationary* just in case the probability measure on the underlying space is *invariant with respect to the shift transformation*. The ergodic decomposition still applies. The invariant measure has an essentially unique representation as a mixture of ergodic measures. *If the invariant measure is ergodic, then Birkhoff's pointwise ergodic theorem gives a generalization of the strong law of large numbers from independent and identically distributed random variables to ergodic stationary stochastic processes.*

To recover the strong law of large numbers for coin flipping, consider a stationary stochastic process with independent, identically distributed 0–1-valued random variables. The shift transformation is ergodic with respect to the product measure on the product space. Then application of the Birkhoff ergodic theorem gives the strong law of large numbers for Bernoulli sequences.

Suppose an invariant measure is not ergodic. Then, as Freedman (1962b), (1963) shows, the ergodic decomposition of invariant measures gives a far-reaching generalization of the de Finetti representation theorem. In this case, the Birkhoff ergodic theorem still says that time averages exist almost everywhere, but they will not in general be equal to the phase space averages corresponding to the invariant measure. Rather, for almost all points, the time average corresponding to it will be equal to the phase space average of one or another of the ergodic measures of which the invariant measure is a mixture according to the ergodic decomposition of invariant measures. For example, consider again a stationary stochastic process with 0–1-valued random variables, but instead of independence assume invariance under finite permutations of trials. The ergodic measures in this class are the independent ones, so the ergodic decomposition gives the de Finetti representation of exchangeable measures as mixtures of independent and identically distributed ones. The Birkhoff ergodic

---

[31] 1934.

theorem then says that for almost every point, the time average along its orbit is equal to one of the independent and identically distributed ones. Freedman uses the ergodic representation to establish a general result that stationary stochastic processes characterized by a kind of sufficient statistic are mixtures of ergodic measures characterized by that statistic. He applies this to show, in particular, that stationary Markov-exchangeable stochastic processes are mixtures of stationary Markov chains.

It should be borne in mind that the ergodic theory is even more general than the foregoing application. The ergodic decomposition and convergence results do not depend on taking the points in our probability space to be sequences and the relevant transformation to be the shift transformation. For example, consider again a space whose outcome sequences are generated by sequences of coin flips, but suppose that up to and including time 0, 'Heads' is coded by a 1 and 'Tails' by a 0 while after time 0 the coding is reversed with 'Tails' being coded by a 1 and 'Heads' by a 0. Then if your degrees of belief would be invariant with respect to the shift transformation on the space of sequences of heads and tails, they will not be invariant with respect to the shift transformation on this 'Goodmanized' space. Rather they will be invariant under a more complicated transformation, $T^\star$, which is most intuitively described as (1) decode the Goodmanized sequence as the equivalent outcome sequence in the space of sequences of H and T, (2) do the shift transformation on the space of sequences of H and T, and (3) code the result into the space of Goodmanized sequences. Consider two agents, one sane and the other crazy, who have degrees of belief over the Goodmanized space of outcome sequences: the sane agent has degrees of belief that are invariant under $T^\star$; the crazy agent has degrees of belief that are invariant under the shift transformation. In a sense both will believe in induction: the sane agent with respect to $T^\star$ and the crazy agent with respect to the shift transformation. Although they both believe in the form of inductive reasoning, they differ in their application of it.

What is the significance of ergodic theory for the philosophy of induction? We can see it as providing the mathematical backing for a very general implementation of de Finetti's point of view. The invariant probability measure can be interpreted as degree-of-belief of a scientist. The transformation under which it is invariant can be taken, as Billingsley (1965) suggests, as defining a subjective notion of repetition of the same chance experiment—as providing a subjective individuation of the chance setup. The ergodic decomposition gives a representation in the form of an expectation of chance, with the ergodic measures being subjective surrogates for objective chances. The Birkhoff ergodic theorem shows that the scientist must expect—with degree-of-belief 1—that repetition of the experiment will converge to the true chances. Thus, in a certain sense, inductive skepticism is impossible for a scientist having invariant degrees-of-belief.

In this framework one can *settle* precise forms of various questions regarding inductive skepticism. For instance, we know that an agent with invariant degrees of belief cannot be an absolute inductive skeptic. Thus we may be led to ask whether it is true that for *any* transformation someone could have beliefs which would be invariant under that transformation. This question has been studied under various conditions. Here—under some topological regularity conditions—is an affirmative answer, due to Krylov and Bogoliubov:

> THEOREM: Suppose that the probability space on which your degrees-of-belief are to be defined is a compact topological space and the transformation with respect to which invariance is to be evaluated is continuous. Then an invariant degree-of-belief measure exists.[32]

This theorem establishes one precise version of Goodman's dictum:[33]

*Regularities are where you find them, and you can find them anywhere.*


## 7. Symmetry

All the foregoing varieties of projectibility are, in various ways, manifestations of probabilistic symmetries. Van Fraassen (1989) has argued persuasively that symmetries play a fundamental role in guiding the development of scientific theory. He believes that symmetry—rather than the old metaphysical notion of law—should be taken as basic in the analysis of science.[34] As van Fraassen points out, this perspective on laws seems natural to many scientists (for example, Wigner (1967)), but seems to have been somewhat neglected by philosophers.

---

[32] See Sinai (1976: 12–13).
[33] Goodman (1955: 82).
[34] See van Fraassen (1989: III).

I have advocated a closely related Humean view of the supposed natural necessity of laws. In a nutshell the position is that the apparent nomic force of statements taken as laws of nature derives not from any metaphysical necessity but rather from invariances—sometimes approximate invariances—in our scientifically informed degrees-of-belief. This is discussed in terms of the concept of *resiliency* in Skyrms (1980), (1984), (1991b). These invariances are symmetries in degrees-of-belief. We have seen in the foregoing discussion that symmetries in the probabilities on which induction is based are the fundamental determinants of varieties of projectibility. One of Goodman's fundamental insights—the association between projectibility and lawlikeness[35]—closes the circle. Another of Goodman's basic insights connects statements treated as laws and associated counterfactual conditionals. In a pragmatic Bayesian theory of subjunctive conditionals, symmetries of degrees-of-belief again play a key role (see Skyrms, 1984).

With these ideas in mind, it may be useful to set the foregoing in a general theory of probabilistic symmetry. I will begin in this section with a brief introduction to our most general notion of symmetry and then proceed to its application to probability.

Consider the symmetry of the equilateral triangle pictured in Figure 1. One symmetry is indicated by the fact that if we rotate each point 120 degrees about the midpoint of the triangle, we get the same figure. Another is that if we reflect each point on the triangle about the dotted midline shown, we get the same figure. Each of these operations can be viewed as a one-to-one transformation of the plane into itself which preserves the structure of the triangle. (Think of the points on the original triangle as black and the other points on the plane as white. That the transformation preserves the same structure means that black points get mapped to black and white points to white.) Obviously if we compose symmetry transformations, we get another.[36] Thus if we first rotate through 120 degrees and then reflect, we again get the same figure. Or if we rotate through 120 degrees and then do it again (giving a total rotation through 240 degrees), we preserve the figure. If we rotate

---

[35] This is not to endorse the exact form of the association proposed by Goodman—that lawlike sentences are just those which can be confirmed by an incomplete survey of their instances.

[36] For the transitivity of "same structure."

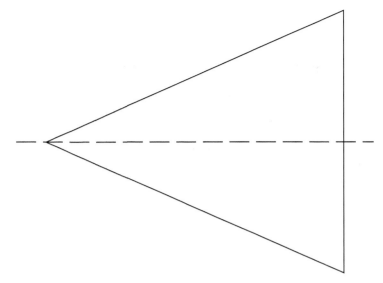

**Figure 1**

through 240 degrees and then rotate through 120 degrees, we map each point onto itself. This is the identity transformation, *I*, which obviously preserves structure. Notice that the 360-degree rotation can be described equally well as "First two 120 degree rotations, then another" or as "First one 120 degree rotation, then two others." Note also that since our transformations preserve structure, we can run them backwards (the inverse transformation) and still preserve structure. If rotation through 120 degrees gives the same structure then rotation through −120 degrees (= rotation through 240 degrees) also preserves structure. Of course running a transformation forwards and then running it backwards, or running it backwards and then running it forwards, gives no net change—i.e., the composition of a transformation with its inverse gives the identity transformation.

What has been illustrated in the last paragraph is that if we have a notion of same structure, then the symmetry transformations—those that preserve structure—form a group under composition. This can be taken as a characterization of symmetry in the abstract—*symmetry is invariance under a group of transformations which preserve structure.* A more detailed exposition of this point of view is contained in Weyl's classic book, *Symmetry* (1952).

For our purposes, the structure to be preserved is probabilistic structure. This makes it clear why exchangeability is a symmetry: it is invariance of probability under the group of finite permutations of trials. We can also see how the partial exchangeability with respect to a statistic discussed in the last section is a symmetry. Just consider the group of transformations of the probability space into itself which leave the sufficient statistic unchanged. And in the discussion of invariance in the last section, we have already been dealing with groups of transformations of the probability space. In the examples of stochastic processes with discrete time we iterate the shift transformation, so we have $T(w)$, $T2(w) = T(T(w))$. We are dealing with an infinite set of transformations: ... $T-2$, $T-1$, $T0$, $T1$, $T2$ ... which inherits the group structure of the integers under addition. Likewise, the continuous time dynamical systems deal with a group of transformations which inherit the group structure of the real line under addition. There is no reason why attention should be limited to these particular groups.[37]

## 8. Probability–Symmetry Structures

**Definition 1:** A *probability–symmetry structure* is an ordered quadruple, $<W,F, m,G>$ where $W$ is set, $F$ is the sigma-field of subsets of $W$, $m$ is a countably additive probability measure on $F$, and $G$ is a group of invertible, measurable, measure-preserving transformations on $<W,F,m>$. (Thus, by definition, the measure, m, is invariant with respect to every transformation, $T$, in $G$, that is for all $A$ in $F$ and all $T$ in $G$, $m(A) = m(T^{-1}(A))$.)

**Definition 2:** A measurable set, $A$, in $F$, is *an invariant set with respect to $G$* if it is invariant with respect to every member of $G$, that is, if for all $T$ in $G$, $A = T^1(A)$. (Since complements and countable unions and intersections of invariant sets are invariant, the invariant sets form a Boolean $\sigma$-algebra.)

**Definition 3:** A measure, $m$, of a probability–symmetry structure is *ergodic* if for every invariant set, $A$, $m(a) = 0$ or $m(A) = 1$.

Under mild topological regularity conditions, an analogue of the de Finetti representation theorem holds for probability–symmetry structures. Suppose that W is a standard Borel space (a complete separable metric space) and $F$ is its Borel $\delta$-field. Assume further that $G$ is countable. *Then*

---

[37] For instance, physicists have studied what are essentially stochastic processes in three-dimensional time. See Preston (1976) and Georgii (1979).

m *has a unique representation as a mixture of measures on <W,F> which are ergodic with respect to G*. Furthermore, the ergodic measures are the regular conditional probabilities with respect to the $\sigma$-field of sets invariant with respect to $G$.[38]

There are relevant generalizations of the Birkhoff ergodic theorem as well, although the picture here is less complete. For example, suppose that instead of a one-dimensional temporal sequence of coin flips, we have a three-dimensional array of coin flips, indexed by the set of triples of integers. The points in the associated probability space are infinite three-dimensional outcome arrays of zeros and ones. The natural generalization of stationarity to this case is invariance under the $n$-dimensional shift group of transformations. Suppose that we have a probability measure, $m$, that is invariant in this sense—i.e., our probabilities are spatially homogeneous. We want to think of the limiting relative frequencies of heads starting at a point in space, as gotten by taking the relative frequencies over bigger and bigger cubes centered at that point—that is, we are interested in the limit as n goes to infinity of (# of heads)/($n^3 + 1$) over cubes centered at our initial point. What guarantee is there that this limit exists? In the one-dimensional case the Birkhoff ergodic theorem guarantees its existence for almost every (with respect to m) point. The $n$-dimensional ergodic theorem which establishes the analogous result for $n$-dimensional space was proved by Norbert Wiener in 1939.[39] There are applications in the theory of the thermodynamic limit for lattice gases.[40]

From our philosophical point of view, the $n$-dimensional ergodic theorems show that in a certain sense, spatial homogeneity of our degrees-of-belief is incompatible with general inductive skepticism. General inductive skepticism, in the sense of Reichenbach, is giving weight to the possibility that limiting relative frequencies might not exist. If our weights (= degrees-of-belief) are spatially homogeneous in the foregoing sense, and the relative frequencies are to be taken in the foregoing way, then we simply cannot be general inductive skeptics.

The foregoing analysis generalizes. Exactly how far it generalizes is a matter of ongoing mathematical research. The sequence of cubes in the

---

[38] See Farrell (1962). This holds even if G is only a semigroup (Th. 5). It can be extended to separable locally compact groups (Cor. 4), and continuous groups (Th. 6).

[39] Cubes and spheres also work for continuous $n$-dimensional space.

[40] In this respect, see Mackey (1974).

random field example above is called a *universal averaging sequence*. The notion has been extended to more general probability–symmetry structures and in many cases such universal averaging sequences have been found.[41] These provide refutations of general inductive skepticism in very general contexts. However, it should also be emphasized that the refutations are not universal. There are always some regularity assumptions involved on the topology of the space of possibilities and on the symmetry group. Some potential inductive skeptics might be skeptical about these assumptions; others might not.

We see that—at increasingly general levels of abstraction—projectibility is a reflection of probabilistic symmetries. The logic of projectibility[42] is probability logic. At the most abstract and general level, it is the mathematics of probability–symmetry structures. Much of this logic is known as the result of the efforts of statisticians, mathematicians, and physicists. The scandal of philosophy is not that the logic of induction does not exist, but rather that philosophy has paid so little attention to it.

# Bibliography

Billingsley, P. (1965) *Ergodic Theory and Information*. New York: Wiley.

Davidson, D. (1966) "Emeroses by Other Names," *Journal of Philosophy* 64: 1778–90.

de Finetti, B. (1937) "La Prévision: Ses lois logiques, ses sources subjectives," *Annales de l'Institut Henri Poincaré* 7:1–68. Translated as "Foresight: Its Logical Laws, Its Subjective Sources." In H. E. Kyburg, Jr. and H. Smokler (eds.), *Studies in Subjective Probability*. Huntington, NY: Kreiger, 1980.

——(1938) "Sur la condition d'équivalence partielle," *Actualités scientifiques et industrielles*, No. 739. Paris: Hermann; translated by P. Benacerraf and R. Jeffrey as "On the Condition of Partial Exchangeability," in R. C. Jeffrey

---

[41] See Tempel'man (1972) and Krengel (1985), especially ch. 5.

[42] Ermanno Bencivanga and Hugh Mellor have complained that this chapter neglects the 'external' question of the justification of induction in favor of 'internal' questions connected with the logic of projectibility. This is not because I think that nothing at all sensible can be said about 'external' questions of reliability, but rather because the subject of this chapter is Bayesian projectibility. I approach the 'external' questions in terms of Bayesian consistency, where something precise can be said about reliability—but only relative to assumptions about the operative chance model. From this perspective internal questions are not irrelevant to external ones. See footnotes 18 and 19 and Skyrms (1991a), (1993a), (1993b). For his approach to external justification, see Mellor (1988).

(ed.), *Studies in Inductive Logic and Probability*, vol. 2, pp. 193–205. Berkeley, CA: University of California Press.

Diaconis, P. and Freedman, D. (1980) "de Finetti's Theorem for Markov Chains," *Annals of Probability* 8: 115–30.

——(1980) "de Finetti's Generalizations of Exchangeability." In R. Jeffrey (ed.), *Studies in Inductive Logic and Probability*, vol. 2. Berkeley, CA: University of California Press.

——(1981) "Partial Exchangeability and Sufficiency." In *Statistics: Applications and New Directions* (Proceedings of the Indian Statistical Institute Golden Jubilee International Conference), pp. 205–36. Calcutta: Indian Statistical Institute.

——(1986) "On the Consistency of Bayes Estimates," *Annals of Statistics* 14: 1–26.

Dynkin, E. (1978) "Sufficient Statistics and Extreme Points," *Annals of Probability* 6: 705–30.

Earman, J. (1992) *Bayes or Bust?*. Cambridge, MA: MIT Press. [Sec. 4.7, "Goodman's New Problem of Induction."]

Farrell, R. H. (1962) "Representation of Invariant Measures," *Illinois Journal of Mathematics* 6: 447–67.

Freedman, D. (1962a) "Mixtures of Markov Processes," *Annals of Mathematical Statistics* 33: 114–18.

——(1962b) "Invariants under Mixing which Generalize de Finetti's Theorem," *Annals of Mathematical Statistics* 33: 916–33.

——(1963) "Invariants under Mixing which Generalize de Finetti's theorem: Continuous Time Parameter," *Annals of Mathematical Statistics* 34: 1194–216.

Georgii, H. O. (1979) *Canonical Gibbs Measures* (Lecture Notes in Mathematics 760). Berlin: Springer.

Goodman, N. (1946) "A Query on Confirmation," *Journal of Philosophy* 43: 383–5.

——(1955) *Fact, Fiction and Forecast*. Cambridge, MA: Harvard University Press.

——(1966) "Comment," *Journal of Philosophy* 63: 328–31.

Hewitt, E. and Savage, L. J. (1955) "Symmetric Measures on Cartesian Products," *Transactions of the American Mathematical Society* 80: 470–501.

Hintikka, J. and Niiniluoto, I. (1980) "An Axiomatic Foundation for the Logic of Inductive Generalization." In R. Jeffrey (ed.), *Studies in Inductive Logic and Probability*, vol. 2, pp. 157–81. Berkeley, CA: University of California Press.

Jeffrey, R. (1966) "Goodman's Query," *Journal of Philosophy* 63: 281–8.

——(1971) "Probability Measures and Integrals." In R. Carnap and R. Jeffrey (eds.), *Studies in Inductive Logic and Probability*, vol. 1, pp. 169, 221. Berkeley, CA: University of California Press.

Krengel, U. (1985) *Ergodic Theorems*. Berlin: Walter de Gruyter.

Kryloff, N. and Bogoliouboff, N. (1937) "La théorie générale de la mesure dans son application à l'étude des systèmes de la mécanique non linéaire," *Annals of Mathematics* 38: 65–113.

Mackey, G. W. (1974) "Ergodic Theory and its Significance for Statistical Mechanics and Probability Theory," *Advances in Mathematics* 12: 178–268.

Mellor, D. H. (1988) *The Warrant of Induction: An Inaugural Lecture.* Cambridge: Cambridge University Press.

Oxtoby, J. C. (1952) "Ergodic Sets," *Bulletin of the American Mathematical Society* 58: 116–36.

Preston, C. (1976) *Random Fields* (Springer Lecture Notes in Mathematics 534). Berlin: Springer.

Shimony, A. (1967) "Amplifying Personal Probability," *Philosophy of Science* 34: 326–32.

Sinai, Y. (1976) *Introduction to Ergodic Theory.* Princeton, NJ: Princeton University Press.

——(1989) *Dynamical Systems II.* Berlin: Springer.

Skyrms, B. (1980) *Causal Necessity.* New Haven, CT: Yale University Press.

——(1984) *Pragmatics and Empiricism.* New Haven, CT: Yale University Press. [Ch. 3 "Learning from Experience."]

——(1991a) "Carnapian Inductive Logic for Markov Chains," *Erkenntnis* 35: 439–60.

——(1991b) "Stability and Chance." In *Existence and Explanation: Essays Presented in Honor of Karel Lambert*, pp. 149–63. Dordrecht: Kluwer.

——(1993a) "Analogy by Similarity in HyperCarnapian Inductive Logic." In J. Earman et al. (eds.), *Philosophical Problems of the Internal and External Worlds*, pp. 273–82. Pittsburgh, PA: University of Pittsburgh Press.

——(1993b) "Carnapian Inductive Logic for a Value Continuum." In H. Wettstein (ed.), *The Philosophy of Science.* Midwest Studies in Philosophy, vol. 18, pp. 78–89. South Bend, IN: University of Notre Dame Press.

Tempel'man, A. A. (1972) "Ergodic Theorems for General Dynamical Systems," *Transactions of the Moscow Mathematical Society* 26: 94–132.

van Fraassen, B. (1989) *Laws and Symmetry.* Oxford: Clarendon.

von Plato, J. (1982) "The Significance of the Ergodic Decomposition of Stationary Measures for the Interpretation of Probability," *Synthese* 53: 419–32.

——(1994) *Creating Modern Probability.* Cambridge: Cambridge University Press.

Wallace, J. (1966) "Goodman, Logic and Induction," *Journal of Philosophy* 63: 328–31.

Weyl, H. (1952) *Symmetry.* Princeton, NJ: Princeton University Press.

Wiener, N. (1939) "The Ergodic Theorem," *Duke Mathematical Journal* 5: 1–18.

Wigner, E. (1967) *Symmetries and Reflections*, ed. W. Moore and M. Scriven (Bloomington, IN: Indiana University Press).

Zabell, S. L. (1988) "Symmetry and Its Discontents." In W. Harper and B. Skyrms (eds.), *Causation, Chance and Credence*, pp. 155–90. Dordrecht: Kluwer.

——(1989) "The Rule of Succession," *Erkenntnis* 31: 283–321.

# Index